"All preachers, pastors, and other followers of Jesus who seek to understand the mysterious Letter to the Hebrews will find a source of God's loving and life-giving Word for today in this wise and insightful commentary. With reverent attention to the Jewish roots of Christian faith (and keen awareness of the damaging effects of Christian supersessionism), Debra J. Bucher and Estella Boggs Horning stay close to human experiences and struggles as they help us search for what it means to live faithfully and simply in today's multilayered and complex world."
—*Dawn Ottoni-Wilhelm, Brightbill Professor of Preaching and Worship at Bethany Theological Seminary and senior editor of the journal* Homiletic

"The rich theology of Hebrews comes to life in this well-written and accessible treatment by Debra J. Bucher and Estella Boggs Horning. They frame the main point of the book as an argument for understanding the work of Jesus in salvation and what faithful followers in the midst of struggle should do in response. To do so, this commentary on Hebrews draws heavily on texts from the Hebrew Bible, especially those from the Psalms, Jeremiah 31, and Leviticus. In addition to these primary texts, Bucher and Horning discuss links across the Hebrew Bible as well as other New Testament books and a wide range of material from the Second Temple period and the Greco-Roman world to illuminate the message of Hebrews within its first-century context, and also make helpful applications to contemporary concerns."
—*Steven Schweitzer, academic dean and professor at Bethany Theological Seminary*

"The Letter to the Hebrews provides a welcome addition to the Believers Church Bible series as it brings a believers church perspective to one of the most venerated and least understood epistles in the New Testament. The Greek of the epistle is more elegant but also more difficult, as it is different from much of the Greek elsewhere in the New Testament. Debra J. Bucher and Estella Boggs Horning bring Church of the Brethren tradition and cross-cultural and international experience that informs their reading of the epistle. This is a Believers Church treat."
—*Stephen Breck Reid, professor of Christian Scriptures at George W. Truett Theological Seminary and vice ~~~~~ ~ ~ ~ ~ ~ ~ belonging at Baylor University*

T0390634

"Debra J. Bucher and Estella Boggs Horning offer a timely gift as they read this beautiful and difficult New Testament book. Their essays on atonement and on anti-Jewish interpretations of Hebrews, by themselves, are worth the price of the volume. Beyond that, those with Anabaptist heritage and all Christians who pick up this commentary can grasp the through line of our call to be 'the people of God living in exile as resident aliens.'"
—*Nancy Heisey, professor emerita of biblical studies at Eastern Mennonite University*

"This study of Hebrews is the result of the best of the believers church traditions—the product of multiple persons gathered around the Scriptures. Debra J. Bucher and Estella Boggs Horning offer a rich resource not just for exploring the Letter to the Hebrews as a text, but as a companion for contemporary Christian discipleship. They have composed much more than a commentary in the classic sense of the genre and offer important essays to engage the questions that arise in contemporary readings of the letter. The product is a resource that should be found in the libraries of pastors and scholars, seminaries, and congregations."
—*Joshua Brockway, director of spiritual formation for the Church of the Brethren*

"In a clear and understandable style, Debra J. Bucher and Estella Boggs Horning chart an illuminating path through the famously difficult epistle to the Hebrews, providing an interpretation that deftly points toward Jesus as the best way to not lose our footing as we traverse territory that is at once familiar and strange to us as contemporary readers. I particularly appreciated their respectful treatment of Judaism throughout. Their attention to the history of interpretation of difficult passages is an effective way to show that there is never only one way to understand a particular text. The focus on perseverance and fidelity—alongside hope and love—in their reading of the epistle is very encouraging to those of us who are engaged with others, both past and present, in following Jesus today."
—*Nancy Elizabeth Bedford, Georgia Harkness Professor of Theology at Garrett-Evangelical Theological Seminary and author of* Who Was Jesus and What Does It Mean to Follow Him?

"Hebrews is one of the most complicated books in the New Testament, a theologically dense homily whose interpretation requires special sensitivity to its Jewish milieu. Debra J. Bucher and Estella Boggs Horning have written a commentary on Hebrews that judiciously balances attention to historical detail, the best of modern scholarship, and accessibility to a wide audience. Throughout the commentary, they display a particular sensitivity to the history of anti-Jewish interpretations of Hebrews, rejecting a 'Christian triumphalist' reading in favor of a reading of Hebrews 'within Judaism.' In doing so, they challenge the church's interpretive missteps while inviting a reading of Hebrews that is meaningful for the life of the church today."
—*Timothy Reardon, assistant professor of New Testament at Eastern Mennonite University*

"Hebrews richly rewards readers who listen well to its poetic preaching about the supreme but mysterious revelation that God has given us in Christ. Estella Boggs Horning and Debra J. Bucher skillfully lead readers through the linguistic and theological challenges of Hebrews into wise discussions of its implications for faith-filled living today. This thirty-seventh volume of the Believers Church Bible Commentary series is definitely worth the wait."
—*Daniel Ulrich, Wieand Professor of New Testament Studies at Bethany Theological Seminary*

"As a preacher, I was content to limit my sermons from Hebrews to the hoped-for substance of faith, that cloud of witnesses, and the intriguing possibility of entertaining angels unawares. That's why I am most pleased that Estella Boggs Horning (whose class in Hebrews I took many years ago) and Debra J. Bucher peel away my blinders to seemingly arcane topics like priests, temples, and cutting-edge covenants new and old, as well as sacrifice, which formerly seemed irrelevant to my Anabaptist attitudes. Thanks to their work, this homily proves to be infused with applicability, inspiration, and a serene beauty."
—*Frank Ramirez, Church of the Brethren pastor and writer*

Believers Church Bible Commentary

Douglas B. Miller and Loren L. Johns, Editors

BELIEVERS CHURCH BIBLE COMMENTARY

Old Testament

Genesis, by Eugene F. Roop, 1987
Exodus, by Waldemar Janzen, 2000
Leviticus, by Perry B. Yoder, 2017
Numbers, by Jackie Wyse-Rhodes, *forthcoming*
Deuteronomy, by Gerald Gerbrandt, 2015
Joshua, by Gordon H. Matties, 2012
Judges, by Terry L. Brensinger, 1999
Ruth, Jonah, Esther, by Eugene F. Roop, 2002
1-2 Samuel, by David Baker, *forthcoming*
1-2 Kings, by Lynn Jost, 2021
1-2 Chronicles, by August Konkel, 2016
Ezra-Nehemiah, forthcoming
Job, by Paul Keim, *forthcoming*
Psalms, by James H. Waltner, 2006
Proverbs, by John W. Miller, 2004
Ecclesiastes, by Douglas B. Miller, 2010
Isaiah, by Ivan D. Friesen, 2009
Jeremiah, by Elmer A. Martens, 1986
Lamentations, Song of Songs, by Wilma Ann Bailey and Christina A. Bucher, 2015
Ezekiel, by Millard C. Lind, 1996
Daniel, by Paul M. Lederach, 1994
Hosea, Amos, by Allen R. Guenther, 1998
Joel, Obadiah, Micah, by Daniel Epp-Tiessen, 2022
Nahum, Habakkuk, Zephaniah, by W. Derek Suderman, *forthcoming*
Haggai, Zechariah, Malachi, forthcoming

New Testament

Matthew, by Richard B. Gardner, 1991
Mark, by Timothy J. Geddert, 2001
Luke, by Mary H. Schertz, 2023
John, by Willard M. Swartley, 2013
Acts, by Chalmer E. Faw, 1993
Romans, by John E. Toews, 2004
1 Corinthians, by Dan Nighswander, 2017
2 Corinthians, by V. George Shillington, 1998
Galatians, by George R. Brunk III, 2015
Ephesians, by Thomas R. Yoder Neufeld, 2002
Philippians, by Gordon Zerbe, 2016
Colossians, Philemon, by Ernest D. Martin, 1993
1-2 Thessalonians, by Jacob W. Elias, 1995
1-2 Timothy, Titus, by Paul M. Zehr, 2010
Hebrews, by Debra J. Bucher and Estella Boggs Horning, 2024
James, by Sheila Klassen-Wiebe, *forthcoming*
1-2 Peter, Jude, by Erland Waltner and J. Daryl Charles, 1999
1, 2, 3 John, by Jay McDermond, 2011
Revelation, by John R. Yeatts, 2003

Old Testament Editors
Elmer A. Martens, Mennonite Brethren Biblical Seminary, Fresno, California
Douglas B. Miller, Tabor College, Hillsboro, Kansas

New Testament Editors
Howard Charles, Anabaptist Mennonite Biblical Seminary, Elkhart, Indiana
Willard M. Swartley, Anabaptist Mennonite Biblical Seminary, Elkhart, Indiana
Gordon Zerbe, Canadian Mennonite University, Winnipeg, Manitoba
Loren L. Johns, Anabaptist Mennonite Biblical Seminary, Elkhart, Indiana

Editorial Council
David W. Baker, Brethren Church
W. Derek Suderman, Mennonite Church Canada
Christina A. Bucher, Church of the Brethren
John R. Yeatts, Brethren in Christ Church
Gordon H. Matties (chair), Mennonite Brethren Church
Jo-Ann A. Brant, Mennonite Church USA

Believers Church Bible Commentary

Hebrews

Debra J. Bucher and
Estella Boggs Horning

HERALD PRESS
Harrisonburg, Virginia

Herald Press
PO Box 866, Harrisonburg, VA 22803
www.HeraldPress.com

Library of Congress Cataloging-in-Publication Data
Names: Bucher, Debra J., author. | Horning, Estella B. (Estella Boggs), 1929- author.
Title: Hebrews / Debra J. Bucher and Estella Horning.
Description: Harrisonburg, Virginia : Herald Press, [2024] | Series: Believers church Bible commentary ; vol 37 | Includes bibliographical references and index.
Identifiers: LCCN 2023043376 (print) | LCCN 2023043377 (ebook) | ISBN 9781513805979 (paperback) | ISBN 9781513805986 (ebook)
Subjects: LCSH: Bible. Hebrews—Criticism, interpretation, etc. | Jesus Christ—Royal office. | Jesus Christ—Influence. | BISAC: RELIGION / Biblical Commentary / New Testament / General | RELIGION / Biblical Commentary / General
Classification: LCC BS2775.52 .B83 2024 (print) | LCC BS2775.52 (ebook) | DDC 227/.87077—dc23/eng/20231214
LC record available at https://lccn.loc.gov/2023043376
LC ebook record available at https://lccn.loc.gov/2023043377

Except as otherwise indicated, the text of Hebrews and other Scripture quotations is from the *New Revised Standard Version Bible*, copyright © 1989 by the Division of Christian Education of the National Council of the Churches of Christ in the USA. Used by permission. All rights reserved worldwide (some emphases added). Scripture quotations marked (NRSVue) are from the *New Revised Standard Version* Updated Edition. Copyright © 2021 National Council of Churches of Christ in the United States of America. Used by permission. All rights reserved worldwide. Scripture quotations marked (ESV) are from the *ESV® Bible* (*The Holy Bible, English Standard Version®*), Copyright © 2001 by Crossway, a publishing ministry of Good News Publishers. Used by permission. All rights reserved.

BELIEVERS CHURCH BIBLE COMMENTARY: HEBREWS
© 2024 by Herald Press, Harrisonburg, VA 22803. 800-245-7894.
  All rights reserved.
Library of Congress Control Number: 2023043376
International Standard Book Number: 978-1-5138-0597-9 (paperback); 978-1-5138-0598-6 (ebook)
Printed in the United States of America
Cover by Merrill Miller
Interior design by Merrill Miller and Alice Shetler

All rights reserved. This publication may not be reproduced, stored in a retrieval system, or transmitted in whole or in part, in any form, by any means, electronic, mechanical, photocopying, recording, or otherwise without prior permission of the copyright owners.

28 27 26 25 24   10 9 8 7 6 5 4 3 2 1

To the memory of
Calvin Harvey Boggs and L. Gene Bucher,
both fathers who loved their families and pastors
who loved the Scriptures

ABBREVIATIONS AND SIGLA

*	*see* TBC
+	*see* TLC
#	number
/	or
//	is parallel to
[. . ., *p. 000*]	italic brackets for cross-reference to an essay
A . . . A′ . . . A″	parallel lines or phrases
AT	authors' translation/paraphrase
BCBC	Believers Church Bible Commentary
BCE	before the Common Era
c.	century, centuries
ca.	circa, approximately
CE	Common Era
cf.	*confer*, compare
ch(s).	chapter(s)
ed(s).	editor(s); edition
e.g.	*exempli gratia*, for example
emph.	emphasis
esp.	especially
ESV	English Standard Version, 2001
Heb.	Hebrew
Gk.	Greek
i.e.	*id est*, that is
KJV	King James Version, 1611
Lat.	Latin
lit.	literally
LXX	Septuagint (the Greek OT, cited with NRSV chapter and verse numbers)
mg.	marginal
MT	Masoretic Text (of the Hebrew Bible)
n(n).	note(s), footnote(s)
NETS	*see* Pietersma and Wright, in the Bibliography
NJPS	*Tanakh: The Holy Scriptures: The New JPS Translation according to the Traditional Hebrew Text*, 1985
NRSV	New Revised Standard Version
NRSVue	New Revised Standard Version Updated Edition
NT	New Testament
OT	Old Testament
𝔓	symbol for an ancient papyrus, such as $\mathfrak{P}^{46}$
pl.	plural
4QFlor	Florilegium, or Midrash on Eschatology, a Qumran scroll
11Q13	11QMelch = 11QMelchizedek, a Qumran scroll
TBC	The Text in Biblical Context
TDNT	*see* Kittel, Bromiley, and Friedrich, in the Bibliography
TLC	The Text in the Life of the Church
trans.	translator(s)

Contents

Abbreviations and Sigla 12
Series Foreword 17
Authors' Preface 19

Introduction to Hebrews 21
Purpose... 21
Brief Outline 22
Recurring Themes 23
Names, Categories, and Definitions 24
Important Biblical Passages 27
Literary Form or Genre 28
Authorship.. 29
The Intended Audience... 31
Dating and Location of Intended Audience 32
Broader Cultural Context 35
Is Hebrews Anti-Jewish?... 38
The Method of This Commentary................................... 40
The Essays 41
Using the Commentary: An Invitation............................. 42

**Prologue: Prophecy about the Son and His Place
Next to God, 1:1-4** 43
    * Wisdom, Kingship, and Priesthood in Scriptural
        Traditions 50
    + The Politics of Jesus as Son and Heir..................... 51
    + The Prologue in the Revised Common Lectionary 52

Part 1: Listen to What Is Said about Jesus and Follow His Example! 1:5–4:13 55
The Son Is Greater than the Angels, 1:5–2:4 .57
    * Hearing 64
    * Warnings 65
    * Angels. 66
    + Methods of Interpreting the Scriptures 68
Jesus the Son Is a Human Being, like Us in All Things, 2:5-18. 70
    * Understanding Texts through Shared Scriptures 79
    * Understanding Texts through Shared Themes 80
    + The Nature of Jesus 81
    + Perfection through Suffering 83
The Faithful Are to Enter into Rest, 3:1–4:13 84
    * The Word. 94
    * The Wilderness. 95
    * Jesus and Moses 96
    * The Sabbath Rest 97
    + Hold On!. 98

Part 2: Jesus' High Priesthood, 4:14–7:28 101
Jesus: Son and Great High Priest, 4:14–5:10 103
    * A Great High Priest Who Has Passed through the
        Heavens. 109
    * The High Priesthood. 110
    + Suffering in the Revised Common Lectionary 110
Grow Up! (A Message on Group Identity), 5:11–6:20. 112
    * Agricultural Motifs 119
    * Abraham 120
    + Baptisms and Laying On of Hands .121
    + Repentance of Apostates 121
Jesus the Son Is Foreshadowed by the Priest-King
        Melchizedek, 7:1-28 123
    * Melchizedek 131
    * Priests in the Jewish Scriptures 133
    * Priests during the Second Temple Period and in the
        New Testament 134
    * Priests in the Greco-Roman World. .136
    + Priesthood in the Christian Church. 136
    + Hebrews 7 in Anabaptist Thought 137
    + As Read in the Revised Common Lectionary 138
    + Melchizedek as Other 138

Part 3: Jesus' Priestly Ministry in a New Covenant, 8:1–10:18 139
Christ Is High Priest and Minister of a New Covenant, 8:1-13 . . .142
    * Covenants 148
    * Earthly and Heavenly Sanctuaries 150
    + Hebrews in the Revised Common Lectionary 151
    + The New Covenant and Supersessionist Readings
        of Scripture. 152
    + The Term "New Testament" in the Early Church 154
The Two Covenants, 9:1–10:18. 156
    * The Tabernacle/Temple 165
    * Sacrifice. 167
    + Responding to Jesus' Once-for-All Sacrifice 170

Part 4: A Call to Perseverance, Endurance, Faithfulness, 10:19–12:2. 171
Perseverance Is Essential, 10:19-31. 173
    * Apostasy in the Bible 178
    + Apostasy as a Breaking of Fellowship 179
    + Mutual Encouragement 180
What Faithfulness Looks Like, 10:32–12:2 181
    * Exhortations throughout the Bible .193
    * Summaries of Faithful People 194
    + The Faith of Our Fathers and Mothers. 198

Part 5: A Call to Service, 12:3–13:19 201
Recapitulation of Argument, 12:3-29 204
    * Esau, the Notorious Bad Boy 210
    * Earthquakes in Biblical Literature 211
    * God as Fire. 212
    + Trials as Divine Discipline? 213
    + A Willingness to Come with Reverence and Awe 213
Exhortation for Service Pleasing to God, 13:1-19 215
    * Outside the Gate: Aliens and Exiles .220
    + Community and Hospitality. 221
    + Prison Ministries 221
    + Redefinition of Sacrifice. 222

Epilogue: Benediction and Greetings, 13:20-25 224
    * Jesus as the Great Shepherd 226
    * Epistolary Conclusions 226
    + A Word of Hope 226

Outline of Hebrews 228
Essays.. 231
    Atonement.. 231
    Christology in Hebrews 235
    Diaspora 237
    Gnosticism 237
    Jewish Literature in Antiquity 238
    Logos 242
    The Parting of the Ways 243
    Perfection in Greco-Roman and Jewish Thought.......... 244
    Philo, Neoplatonism, and Hebrews 245
    Priscilla as Author..................................... 245
    Rhetorical Habits of the Author........................ 249
    The Role and Use of the Jewish Scriptures by
        Early Christians 251
    The Septuagint in Hebrews............................ 252
    Supersessionist and Anti-Jewish Interpretations
        of Hebrews 257
    Textual Variants 260
Map of the New Testament World 261
Bibliography 262
    Commentaries.. 262
    Primary Sources 263
    Other Books and Articles.............................. 263
Selected Resources... 272
    Bibles... 272
    Commentaries.. 273
    Other Books and Articles.............................. 273
Index of Ancient Sources..................................... 274
The Authors... 285

Series Foreword

The Believers Church Bible Commentary series makes available a new tool for basic Bible study. It is published for all who seek more fully to understand the original message of Scripture and its meaning for today—Sunday school teachers, members of Bible study groups, students, pastors, and others. The series is based on the conviction that God is still speaking to all who will listen, and that the Holy Spirit makes the Word a living and authoritative guide for all who want to know and do God's will.

The desire to help as wide a range of readers as possible has determined the approach of the writers. Since no blocks of biblical text are provided, readers may continue to use the translation with which they are most familiar. The writers of the series use the New Revised Standard Version and the New International Version on a comparative basis. They indicate which text they follow most closely and where they make their own translations. The writers have not worked alone, but in consultation with select counselors, the series' editors, and the Editorial Council.

Every volume illuminates the Scriptures; provides necessary theological, sociological, and ethical meanings; and in general makes "the rough places plain." Critical issues are not avoided, but neither are they moved into the foreground as debates among scholars. Each section offers "Explanatory Notes," followed by focused articles, "The Text in Biblical Context" and "The Text in the Life of the Church." This commentary aids the interpretive process but does not try to supersede the authority of the Word and Spirit as discerned in the gathered church.

The term *believers church* emerged in the mid-twentieth century to define Christian groups with direct or indirect connections to the

Radical Reformation, a distinctive faith expression that arose in Europe during the sixteenth century. These believers were concerned that the church be voluntary and not aligned with political government. *Believers church* has come to represent an identifiable tradition of beliefs and practices that includes believers (adult) baptism; a voluntary fellowship that practices church discipline, mutual aid, and service; belief in the power of love in all relationships; and a willingness to follow Christ by embracing his cross as a way of life. In recent decades the term has sometimes been applied to church communities informed by Anabaptism, evangelicalism, or pietism, such as Brethren Church, Brethren in Christ, Church of the Brethren, Mennonite Brethren, and Mennonites, as well as similar groups. The writers chosen for the series speak from within this tradition.

Believers church people have always been known for their emphasis on obedience to the simple meaning of Scripture. Because of this, they do not have a long history of deep historical-critical biblical scholarship. This series attempts to be faithful to the Scriptures while also taking archaeology and current biblical studies seriously. Doing this means that at many points the writers will not differ greatly from interpretations that can be found in many other good commentaries. Yet these writers share basic convictions about Christ, the church and its mission, God and history, human nature, the Christian life, and other doctrines. These presuppositions do shape a writer's interpretation of Scripture. Thus this series, like all other commentaries, stands within a specific historical church tradition.

Many in this stream of the church have expressed a need for help in Bible study. This is justification enough to produce the Believers Church Bible Commentary. Nevertheless, the Holy Spirit is not bound to any tradition. May this series be an instrument in breaking down walls between Christians in North America and around the world, bringing new joy in obedience through a fuller understanding of the Word.

—*The Editorial Council*

Authors' Preface

This commentary was written over a span of several decades, begun by Estella in the 1990s and finished by Deb in 2023. It was a collaborative process that neither one of us had ever imagined embarking upon. We could make analogies between our experience and that of Moses handing leadership to Joshua or runners in a relay race passing the baton to one another, but perhaps the best approach might be to use the language of Hebrews itself and honor the *cloud of witnesses*, both those living and those passed, who have been with us on this journey.

We want to give credit to the BCBC Editorial Council for entrusting us with this task. The Letter to the Hebrews is both enigmatic and straightforward. The text we work through in this volume is a difficult text in many ways. We thank the council for giving us the opportunity to learn from the extensive commentary and scholarly literature about Hebrews and to share it and our own insights with you. We are humbled and grateful to have had this amazing experience.

We are grateful for the countless scholars who have written extensively about Hebrews and whose ideas permeate the pages of this commentary. We especially want to lift up *The Jewish Annotated New Testament*, a commentary with essays written by and primarily for Jews that center Jewish life, literature, religion, and culture in the first century CE. Christians have a lot to learn from this collection of essays and commentaries. Pamela Eisenbaum's (2017) introduction to the Letter to the Hebrews was a guiding light as we worked through this challenging text.

We honor Loren Johns, David Garber, and Sara Versluis, whose editorial hands have shaped this commentary and smoothed out the rough edges. Loren's patience with a slow writing process, necessitated by Deb's work commitments, has been greatly appreciated. He has asked many thought-provoking questions and spurred further inquiry that has found its way into helpful insights throughout the commentary. Likewise, David Garber has asked many probing questions, which has further contributed to a text that is both interesting and easy to read. Both these editors have contributed greatly, though Estella and Deb take responsibility for any remaining errors.

We could not have completed this task without the support of our families. Deb thanks her husband, Mark Colvson, who has patiently listened to countless monologues about Hebrews, and who has always encouraged more questions. Our church families have also been a source of sustenance. Deb is grateful to the First Congregational Church/United Church of Christ in Poughkeepsie, New York, for moral and spiritual support, which has modeled a radical welcome so that she was able to *run with perseverance the race that is set before us* (Heb 12:1).

Finally, the process of writing this commentary has been a bit like walking through the wilderness for forty years. Where is it leading? How will we make it through? Why is this so difficult? When will it be over? As the author of Hebrews reminds us, if we hold fast, keep our faith, and encourage one another, we will get to the finish line and join the cloud of witnesses waiting for us. That cloud of witnesses includes Estella's husband, John, who died before the completion of this project, and Deb's father, Gene, who died before she became involved in it. But we know that they would be proud of and happy about our accomplishment.

Introduction to Hebrews

Imagine that you are part of a fledgling grassroots community somewhere in the ancient Mediterranean world. You identify with Jews and Judaism and have a deep love for the biblical message brought to you every week in a gathering place. You and your fellow worshipers also follow the teachings of Jesus, a carpenter from the Galilee region in Palestine who preached the coming of God's kingdom. Jesus was God's anointed one, the person who would help God usher in the new kingdom.

But the world is a hostile place; members of the congregation have been publicly abused, imprisoned, or robbed. The world is beginning to feel foreign. Now the faith of some members is faltering, and the beleaguered people are asking, Why go on?

The author of the Letter to the Hebrews responds to this question, reminding the congregation that Jesus—the Son, the pioneer, the high priest, the once-for-all sacrifice—is now sitting at the right hand of God, waiting for them to enter their final rest. Through his sacrifice, Jesus the Christ now mediates the new covenant; through his example, the recipients of the message discover what true faith looks like and how they, surrounded by the great cloud of faithful witnesses, can live faithful lives as well.

Purpose

At its most basic level, Hebrews considers what constitutes a faithful life and pleads with its audience to continue faithful living to find the "rest" that Christ offers. It begins with a poetic reflection on the one who lived the most faithful of lives—Jesus—and ends with words of exhortation to go and do likewise. In between, the author reformulates sacrifice and covenant based on the saving work of Jesus

22 — Introduction to Hebrews

and exhorts readers to live as individuals and as a community led by Jesus, the pioneer and high priest.

It can be hard to tease all this out of Hebrews, one of the most complex books of the New Testament. No one can say for sure who the author is, where it was written, who these "Hebrews" were, or where they lived. The text is informed by wider Greco-Roman philosophical traditions but is also firmly grounded in biblical (Jewish) texts and practices, putting Jesus in the context of Jewish salvific institutions such as the priesthood, temple sacrifice, the Day of Atonement, and the promises to Abraham, Moses, and the prophets.

Brief Outline

There are numerous detailed structural analyses of Hebrews. Here are two examples:

	C. Koester, *Hebrews* (Anchor Bible), 2001: 84–85	Thompson, *Hebrews* (Paideia), 2008: 19
Prologue	1:1–2:9—How God spoke in the past and how God is speaking in the present through the Son	1:1-4—God's word
Part 1	2:10–6:20—Jesus received glory through faithful suffering	1:5–4:13—Listening to God's word
Part 2	7:1–10:39—The suffering and sacrifice of Jesus enables others to approach the throne of God	4:14–10:31—Jesus as the example to follow
Part 3	11:1–12:27—The people also persevere through suffering	10:32–13:25—How to follow the lead of Jesus
Conclusions	12:28–13:25	

We have a slightly different outline:

Prologue	1:1-4	Prophecy about the Son and His Place Next to God
Part 1	1:5–4:13	Listen to What Is Said about Jesus and Follow His Example!
Part 2	4:14–7:28	Jesus' High Priesthood
Part 3	8:1–10:18	Jesus' Priestly Ministry in a New Covenant
Part 4	10:19–12:2	A Call to Perseverance, Endurance, Faithfulness
Part 5	12:3–13:19	A Call to Service
Epilogue	13:20-25	Benediction and Greetings

Introduction to Hebrews

This is a basic description and outline of a complex text. A more detailed outline appears throughout and at the end of the commentary.

Recurring Themes

Hebrews presents a sustained argument about the role of Jesus in salvation and what the response of his followers should be. Using biblical interpretation, exhortations, warnings, and a variety of rhetorical strategies [Rhetorical Habits of the Author, p. 249], the homilist lays out how Jesus' once-for-all saving act replaces the sacrificial system in Leviticus: Jesus' act requires his followers to consider the faithful actions of doing good and sharing what they have as their own sacrifices. The text first establishes Jesus' credentials for the saving act (Prologue and Parts 1–2). It then describes how Jesus' once-for-all salvation is part of the new covenant, replacing the old system of sacrifice (Part 3). After establishing the new system of salvation, the homilist expects the audience to rise to the occasion through faithfulness and service (Parts 4–5). The closing consists of prayers and an epistolary ending (Epilogue).

Names, Categories, and Definitions

Before we begin in earnest, we must define a few terms that describe the groups of people and texts we are studying. What do we mean by the terms Christian/Christianity and Jew/Judaism? Should they be used to describe people living in the first century CE? Likewise, how should we refer to their sacred texts? Why does all this matter?

Almost all scholars agree that using the term "Christian" to describe the first-century CE followers of Jesus, or "Christianity" to describe the beliefs and practices of those followers, is anachronistic. Use of these terms in the first century was rare, where it likely meant Christian Jews (Acts 11:26; see next paragraph). That is, the followers of Jesus would not have used these words to describe themselves as part of a religion separate from Judaism. Likewise, "Judaism" is also an anachronistic term for the first century (see esp. the articles by Cohen and Boyarin [2007] in the Bibliography). The Judaism of today is based on a rabbinic system developed after the Jerusalem temple was destroyed in 70 CE. In the first century CE, religious practice of Jews, at least those living in the land of Israel, centered on the sacrificial system of the temple. Jews of the first century would be completely unfamiliar with modern Judaism. In other words, "Christianity" and "Judaism" are modern terms that modern people have imposed on specific individuals, groups, and texts from the first and second centuries. At the time, affiliations related to religious practice and belief were complicated and in transition.

Within first-century Judaism, sometimes called Second Temple Judaism because it refers to the Judaism practiced during the Second Temple period (516 BCE–70 CE), was a wide variety of practice. Robert Kraft has written about "multiform Judaism" at the turn of the eras (1975). And Jacob Neusner expands on this to talk of "Judaisms," not merely one Judaism (27–36). More recently, historians have focused on the variety of experiences during the Second Temple period, none of which clearly mirrors modern Jewish experiences. Modern Judaism stands within the tradition of Rabbinic Judaism, which developed slowly, after the destruction of the temple in 70 CE through to the Middle Ages (see the same sources listed earlier). The "Judaism" of first-century Palestine included separatist movements like the Essenes, traditionalists like the Sadducees, reformers such as the Pharisees, and revolutionaries like the Sicarii. These were only a few of the groups located in Judea and Galilee in Palestine.

Other Jews, like Paul, lived in places like Alexandria in Egypt, Rome, Greece, and Asia Minor. Their experience of Judaism was quite different from those who lived in Jerusalem, Judea, or Galilee. We know of these Jews from a wide variety of sources, including literary texts written by Philo, a philosopher who lived in Alexandria; "histories" written by Josephus, who was born and raised in Jerusalem, was sent as a general to Galilee, fought in the First Jewish Revolt against Rome, then saved his life by switching sides and becoming an advisor to the Roman emperor Titus; and inscriptions from tombs in the catacombs of Rome. The principle that unified all these groups was the centrality of the Torah in their lives.

Out of this complex mix came a small messianic group that followed Jesus of Nazareth. These first followers of Jesus practiced the customs of Second Temple Judaism and probably spoke Aramaic and perhaps some Greek.

The earliest known writer of New Testament texts, Paul, identifies himself as a "member of the people of Israel, . . . a Hebrew born of Hebrews" (Phil 3:4-6). He wrote about his experience of the Christ event from that context, taking his message to the synagogues of the Diaspora and then, as the "apostle to the Gentiles" (Rom 11:13), to non-Jews. He wrote to audiences that were both Gentiles and Jews. The gospel writers also wrote as Jews, probably to a mix of Jews and Gentiles.

Introduction to Hebrews 25

From Paul's letters, the book of Acts, and the variety of approaches to Jesus within the New Testament itself, we know of factions among early Jesus followers. The word "Christian" appears only three times in the New Testament (Acts 11:26; 26:28; 1 Pet 4:16), and it is difficult to know what this term meant in the original contexts. In all three passages, the Greek has a passive verb, "were called," meaning that others (rather than they themselves) called them this name. From New Testament sources we know that followers of Jesus referred to themselves as "believers" (Acts 5:14; 10:45; Rom 1:16; 1 Tim 6:2), "brothers" (Acts 6:3; James 2:15), and "saints" (Acts 9:13; 1 Cor 1:2). Paul's statement in Galatians 3:28 that there is "no longer Jew or Greek" complicates the matter further. He did not say "no longer Jew or Christian." The term "Greek" is not for a religious group, but an ethnic designation based on a geographical location (and perhaps language). Therefore, the term "Jew" (Gk. *Ioudaios*) would have a similar connotation in this context. In fact, *Ioudaios* often referred to people living in the place called Judea and did not even clearly indicate a religious affiliation (Cohen: 211), though it is safe to say that most Judeans probably adhered to practices that we would put under the umbrella of "Judaism."

The question then becomes, If Paul and other early Jewish Christians didn't use the term "Christian," why should we? Are we assuming something about their religious experience that we should not? If so, how does that affect our reading of Hebrews (and other NT material) when we use terms anachronistically? Part of the aim of this commentary is to complicate and interrogate understandings of the Letter to the Hebrews that owe more to our modern understandings of Christianity than they do to the understandings of Christianity in the author's world. Some modern scholars are deliberate in their terminology. For example, Mark Kinzer refers to Jesus as Yeshua (Jesus is the Greek form of the Hebrew name Yeshua, or Joshua), and to Jesus believers as "Yeshua believers" in order to concretize the group's origination within Judaism (22). Others discuss the semantic difficulties, caution their readers about the assumptions they bring into the terms, but go ahead and use them as shorthand. It is challenging for authors to use awkward words and phrases consistently throughout a text.

What we most want to avoid is the assumption that the author of Hebrews was a Christian *or* a Jew such as we might meet in a pew today. We must let the author speak for himself or herself [*Priscilla as Author, p. 245*] and to the unique Hebrews audience. Only then can we appreciate the full flavor of the text. We can still read the text as

Christians without imposing our modern understanding of what we now call Christianity onto an author and audience that had no understanding of Christianity. So, throughout this commentary, we sometimes use terms such as "Christian" or "Jewish" or "Christianity" or "Judaism," knowing that each of these terms is problematic. Those who considered themselves Christ followers in the first century were quite different from today's Christians, and the variety of first-century "Judaisms" was certainly different from the various strands of present-day Judaism. Our modern terminology is necessarily imprecise, a mere shorthand, in our effort to communicate a complex set of ideas with their own historical situations.

This is related to another extremely complicated historical discussion concerning when Christianity became distinguishable from Judaism as a distinct religious tradition [*The Parting of the Ways, p. 243*].

No less complicated is the language that we use for Sacred Scriptures. It goes without saying that our concept of the Christian Bible as a complete text from Genesis to Revelation, divided into two sections called "Old Testament" and "New Testament," was unknown. The one-volume Bible as Christians use it today is a medieval invention. Prior to that, with some important exceptions, biblical texts circulated in small groups of texts (like the Gospels, or the Pauline letters). In the first century, Jews thought of their sacred writings in groupings: the Pentateuch (the first five books of the Bible), the Prophets, the Writings. But they did not circulate them together in any way that would be familiar to us, because Jews in the first century used scrolls, not codices (bound books as we know them today), and the scroll technology did not allow for groups of texts to be combined together. That could explain why, in the New Testament, they are referred to by the "author" of the text, such as "Moses," or "David." Sometimes Paul uses the phrase "as it is written" to signify a sacred text. But New Testament writers never call these writings "the Bible."

Finally, many Jews, like Paul and the other writers of the New Testament, used a Greek translation of the biblical texts, what we now call the Septuagint [*The Septuagint in Hebrews, p. 252*]. When Alexander the Great conquered much of the Mediterranean world in the fourth century BCE, the world changed. Greek became the lingua franca, and generations of Jews living outside the land of Israel since at least the Babylonian exile came to be Greek speakers. As a result, sometime in the fourth to third centuries BCE, the Sacred Scriptures were translated into Greek, probably in Alexandria. This translation

Introduction to Hebrews

came to be known as the Septuagint, or LXX, for the seventy (or seventy-two) Jewish elders who allegedly translated it. Jews living in the Diaspora used only this translation *[Diaspora, p. 237]*. A case in point is Philo, living in Alexandra, who did not know Hebrew and used the Greek translation exclusively. The New Testament authors, including the author of Hebrews, use this version at great length, displaying in-depth knowledge of the Psalms, portions of the Pentateuch, and the Prophets. Since the biblical text as we know it in the Septuagint is so important to Hebrews, we refer to it regularly throughout the commentary.

If Jews in the first century did not call their sacred writings "Bible," and some used a Greek version and not the original Hebrew, how should we refer to these writings in our discussion of the Letter to the Hebrews? We will sometimes call them "Jewish Scriptures." Other times we may say "Scriptures" or "biblical material." In all cases, these terms refer to the set of materials written by Jews (for Jews) and only much later used by Christians. We will refrain from using the term "Old Testament" unless there is some specific reason to do so, or even the term "Hebrew Bible," since so many Jews in the first century did not use the Hebrew texts, but the Greek translation of them. We use the term "New Testament" more frequently because it is a quick way to describe an entire set of texts written and compiled by people we now identify as Christians.

Important Biblical Passages

It is an understatement to say that Hebrews "uses" the Jewish Scriptures. They are so integral to the text that, without them, there would be nearly no text. We are referring to the number of biblical references (over twenty-five direct references, with many other allusions) as well as to the way our homilist is directly connected to them. They have shaped the worldview of the homilist. These Scriptures are not something the homilist just picked up, read, and decided to preach about. Instead, the homilist is intimately familiar with them and uses them to develop new ways to think about sacrifice based on the homilist's experience of Jesus.

Two specific Scripture passages and one entire book are central to the argument of Hebrews: Psalm 110, Jeremiah 31:31-34, and Leviticus. (For help, see Yoder's *Leviticus* in the BCBC series.) We strongly encourage people not already familiar with these texts to read them before embarking on Hebrews. References to Psalm 110—which begins with "The LORD says to my lord, 'Sit at my right hand until I make your enemies your footstool'"—run throughout

28   Introduction to Hebrews

Hebrews. Some modern commentators even consider Hebrews to be a commentary on it. This may be an overstatement, but without Psalm 110, Hebrews would be a very different text.

In some ways, Jeremiah 31:31-34 is the centerpiece of Hebrews. It speaks of the Lord's making "a new covenant with the house of Israel and the house of Judah" and writing it "on their hearts." This theme derives from a complicated prophetic tradition. Jeremiah 31 was written just before or at the start of the exile, the period between 597 and 539 BCE when some residents of Judah were banished from their homeland and forced to live in Babylon. This traumatic period for the people of Israel had a lasting influence. Even centuries afterward, the author of Hebrews identifies with the themes of displacement and exile expressed in Jeremiah. It is not coincidental that Jeremiah 31 has such a prominent place in Hebrews and that the text is used at such a pivotal moment. Exile and displacement demand new thinking and a new covenant. The homilist of Hebrews uses a previous moment in the history of Israel as the starting place to make a magnificent statement about the new covenant that Jesus mediates (Heb 8:6).

Literary Form or Genre

For almost two thousand years, a lively discussion has been underway about the genre of the Letter to the Hebrews. Is it a letter? Is it a sermon? Or something else? Its title certainly calls it a letter. The primary reason for that, however, is because it occurs in a very early manuscript collection of Paul's letters, a papyrus codex (book) compiled around 200 CE. This collection, designated as 𝔓⁴⁶ (𝔓 for papyrus), includes all the Pauline letters from the longest (Romans) to the shortest. Hebrews appears near the front of the codex, after Romans, because of its length. The titles of all the letters in the codex are constructed similarly (e.g., "To the Romans," "To the Galatians"). Even though today the prevailing wisdom is that Paul did *not* write Hebrews (see the next section and the essay *Priscilla as Author, p. 245*), it is easy to understand why, for most of its history, Hebrews was considered not just a "letter," but a Pauline letter. Its title, "To the Hebrews" (*pros Hebraious*), looks just like all the other titles in 𝔓⁴⁶ that we attribute to Paul with a high degree of certainty.

But a quick comparison between the Pauline letters and Hebrews reveals important differences: Hebrews does not have the requisite opening features, such as a traditional greeting and a word of thanksgiving. This book does not appear to be written in response to a question or specific situation in the congregation. The writer

Introduction to Hebrews

never self-identifies. In fact, Hebrews describes itself as a *word of exhortation* (13:22). This expression is also used for Paul's synagogue sermon in Acts 13:13-41. Lawrence Wills has analyzed both these texts along with others from early Christian and Jewish material and has discovered a pattern in all of them (279). Paul's sermon in Acts has three sections:

1. exempla (displaying scriptural texts and discussing them)

2. conclusion (the importance of these texts for the intended audience)

3. exhortation (call to action, often with "Let us . . . "; Acts 13:39; Heb 4:1 [twelve times in Hebrews])

Hebrews displays similar features but is much more complex. It repeats the pattern of exempla-conclusion-exhortation several times. Hebrews 3:1–4:16 and 8:1–10:25 are good examples, with a lengthy interlude between them (Wills: 282).

To complicate matters further, the closing lines of Hebrews are in the form of a letter. The author greets the Hebrews, gives news about mutual friends, and finishes with a blessing. This is the way Paul typically closes his letters. Perhaps Hebrews was originally a sermon but was changed into letter format so that it could circulate to other churches in a recognizable format within the context of $\mathfrak{P}^{46}$. Unless additional manuscripts of Hebrews are discovered, we will probably never know. Still, the genre of Hebrews differs from that of a letter such as 1 Corinthians, and the text probably did not originate in the context of correspondence.

This distinction may seem superfluous to the overall understanding of the text; yet understanding its origin and genre helps us understand the original situation of this text and better imagine how it might have been received by its audience.

For this commentary, we generally refer to Hebrews as a sermon, or homily, and identify the author variously as the author, the homilist, or the pastor, since we want to honor the distinctions between it and such other New Testament texts as letters and gospels. We also want to emphasize the oral aspects of this text. Imagine the dinner conversations after this homily was delivered!

Authorship

We do not know who wrote Hebrews. Since antiquity, people who have studied Hebrews have speculated on its authorship with varying degrees of uncertainty. We have already noted that the earliest manuscript evidence for the text is in a compilation of the letters of Paul. But several early Christian commentators expressed doubt about Pauline authorship. The most famous example is Origen, a third-century theologian from Alexandria, who said "God only knows" in response to the issue of authorship (reported by Eusebius, *History of the Church* 6.24.11–14). Origen and others noticed significant stylistic differences between texts like Romans or 1 Corinthians and Hebrews, which raised doubt in their minds. Throughout Christian history, this speculation continued. (For a more detailed account of the history of speculation on the subject and modern approaches to the topic, see the essay *Priscilla as Author, p. 245*.)

This does not mean we can say nothing about the author. We can use internal evidence from the text to say several important things:

- The author was well educated. The quality of the Greek is closer to classic literary Greek than any other text in the New Testament (all the NT texts, including Hebrews, were written in what is generally called Koine Greek, a later, less literary Greek). In addition, the author is knowledgeable about classical rhetorical forms and techniques; the argument of the sermon is carefully organized and anticipates themes for fuller development later *[Rhetorical Habits of the Author, p. 249]*.

- The homilist makes no apostolic claims, no claim to have been around during the time of Jesus, no allegation to write in the name of an early follower. Instead, the homilist claims a status as a second-generation believer (2:3), having heard the gospel from others, not from the Lord. This contrasts with the apostle Paul, who claims to have heard the gospel from the risen Christ himself (1 Cor 1:17; Gal 1:12).

- The author writes from a pastoral perspective. The message expresses long-term experience with and deep concern for the readers. This pastor expresses deep compassion not only for the past suffering of the readers and the threatening situation in which they now find themselves (6:9-12; 10:32-36), but also for the suffering of Christ in his time of testing (5:7-10).

- The author knows the importance of community, especially in situations where the minority community is undergoing stress from outside, majority forces. The many examples (esp. in ch. 11) of people of God who not just endured but also sought out moments for expressing their faithfulness through positive acts suggest that the author is working hard to build up the community through reminding hearers of the *cloud of witnesses* (12:1).

Introduction to Hebrews 31

- The writer is deeply steeped in and invested in the Jewish Scriptures in their Greek translation (LXX).

In summary, what we know about the author is what we can infer from the text and the manuscript itself: the earliest physical (manuscript) evidence associates it with the letters of Paul, but the text itself does not claim authorship by Paul nor divulge any clear information about the identity of the author.

The Intended Audience

Much the same can be said about the original audience. We know the writer has some connection with Italy, probably Rome (13:24). But we do not know the nature of that connection. Based on the title, "To the Hebrews," in the earliest manuscript ($\mathfrak{P}^{46}$), ancient and modern commentators have thought that the audience comprised Christ-following Jews. There is much to support that contention since the author's reliance on the Jewish Scriptures is so great. It assumes a detailed knowledge of the Scriptures and the priestly, sacrificial system.

The themes prevalent in the text—exile and exodus, faithfulness in the face of extreme difficulties, a new sacrificial system, and a new covenant with Jesus as the high priest—suggest a surprising context. Eisenbaum postulates that the presence of these themes may indicate that both the author and the recipients of the "letter" are reeling from the destruction of the temple in 70 CE and that the text was written in response to that event (2005). If this supposition is accurate, the audience is a mix of people who identify as Jesus-following Jews, Gentiles attracted to Judaism or the message about Jesus, or people who identify as both. A variant on this idea is that the audience is people living outside the land of Israel who have little knowledge of or wherewithal to go to the temple (if it is still standing) to make sacrifices. In this case, the ideas are developed to teach people how to live a life of sacrifice without the external system set up in Scripture. It may be that the author's tabernacle theology (with regard to both the earthly tabernacle and the heavenly one) was an attempt to craft a post-temple theology by reclaiming and reinterpreting an earlier pretemple tabernacle theology, with Jesus serving as the linchpin of that theology as high priest.

We do know that the author has a community in view. We learn that the audience

- depends on the testimony of eyewitnesses about Jesus (2:2),

- represents at least second-generation believers,

32 Introduction to Hebrews

- may be using a statement of confession (3:1; 10:23),
- has received basic instruction (6:1-2),
- has been baptized with the laying on of hands,
- believes in the resurrection and eternal judgment,
- has experienced the gifts and power of the Holy Spirit, and
- has tasted God's goodness and the powers of the age to come (6:4-5; 10:22).

The group has also gone through some hardships. At an earlier time, they have experienced some form of harassment or persecution that included loss of property, public ridicule and abuse, and prison—all of which they *cheerfully accepted* (10:34). Perhaps as a result, though, they are tempted to *drift away* (2:1); some may have already *fallen away* (6:6) and *spurned the Son of God* (10:29). Some no longer maintain regular attendance at worship (10:25). They are encouraged *not [to] abandon [their] confidence* (10:35) or *shrink back* (10:39).

In summary, even though we cannot say where the audience lived and what their precise background was, we can say that they were a group of people who shared a set of Scriptures, who understood Jesus to be the Son of God, and who had a common background of experiences as followers of Jesus. Their primary language was Greek.

Dating and Location of Intended Audience

Since the author is unknown, it is difficult to know where the intended audience was situated and who they were. Some suggest Rome, since 1 Clement, a letter written from Rome to Christians in Corinth between 90 and 120 CE, uses Hebrews. Others have suggested Jerusalem because of the title "To the Hebrews." However, Jerusalem seems unlikely since the text only concerns *the tent* (tabernacle) of Leviticus, not the Jerusalem temple, and the elegant Greek makes it unlikely that Jerusalemites were the intended audience (C. Koester 2001: 49).

First Clement is key in the effort to date Hebrews. Since 1 Clement uses Hebrews, then Hebrews cannot have been written after 1 Clement. Although 1 Clement was traditionally dated to the 90s, scholars today give it a wider range of dates (90–120 CE). This means that Hebrews could have been written as late as 100 or 110 CE. The destruction of the Jerusalem temple in 70 CE is another moment used in attempts to date Hebrews. Since so much of the text

Introduction to Hebrews

concerns the sacrifice of Jesus as the replacement for the sacrificial system that took place in the temple, it stands to reason that the homilist would have used the destruction of the temple in 70 CE to bolster the argument. But since the author is silent on the matter, some experts argue that Hebrews was written before 70 CE.

In fact, the author's argument and knowledge of the sacrificial system is based solely on Leviticus. The author never refers to the temple, but only to the tabernacle, the tent sanctuary that sheltered the ark of the covenant while the Israelites were wandering in the desert after the exodus from Egypt. Knowledge about the tabernacle comes from Exodus. The homilist displays no practical (or daily) knowledge of or concern about the Jerusalem temple at all—perhaps for good reason. If the author lived outside the land of Israel, the temple's role in both the author's and the audience's religious life may have been minimal. If they never had the opportunity to travel to Jerusalem to witness and participate in the temple sacrifice, their connection to it may have been tenuous. Finding "replacement" practices, behaviors, or modes of thinking may have been perfectly normal. We already know that other Jews living in Palestine and in the Diaspora developed alternatives to the Jerusalem temple, such as synagogues, sometimes called "temples," or outdoor worship by purifying water (Ps 137:2; Acts 16:13). Jews built some other temples: in Egypt on the island of Elephantine near Aswan (6th to 5th c. BCE); at Leontopolis in the Nile Delta (2nd c. BCE to 1st c. CE). Samaritans had a temple on Mount Gerizim (5th to 2nd c. BCE) and (later) a sacred site there (John 4:20-21). Nothing definitive in the text of Hebrews itself helps us prove one way or another whether the text was written before or after the Jerusalem temple's destruction in 70 CE.

Harold Attridge does not commit to a date, only giving the wide range of 60–100 CE as a possibility. Eisenbaum, on the other hand, makes a solid argument to date Hebrews at the end of the first century or the beginning of the second century (2005: 224–31). She gives three reasons (in this order):

1. The author of Hebrews is a second-generation follower of Jesus. The author admits to hearing the words of the Lord (Jesus) from *those who heard him* (Heb 2:3). Thus at least one generation is between Jesus and the author of Hebrews.

2. Our author is familiar with the gospel traditions of the crucifixion that developed only after the destruction of the temple in Jerusalem. Eisenbaum argues that the use of the Greek word *katapetasma*, meaning curtain or veil, at two places in the text (6:19-20;

10:19-20) displays awareness of the synoptic gospel tradition in which the veil, or curtain, in the holy of holies is ripped in two at Jesus' death by crucifixion (Mark 15:38//Matt 27:51//Luke 23:45). She states, "It is difficult to imagine that Jesus' crucifixion would have been linked to entry into the inner sanctum as an independent theological tradition [separate from the synoptic tradition] or that such a theological interpretation would have naturally come to mind prior to the destruction of the temple. Thus, I suggest that these two passages in Hebrews and their resonance with the tearing of the curtain in the synoptic gospels provide strong evidence for a post-destruction date for Hebrews" (2005: 229).

3. The themes and the elevated theological and christological style of Hebrews compare more favorably to early second-century Christian writing than to that of gospel texts or Pauline material. Unlike Paul's letters, which address specific issues within communities, second-century texts, like 1 Clement (and the Letter to the Hebrews), address broader theological themes that represent a second or even third generation's approach to the Christian message. This is not to suggest that the writer is not responding to a local situation, but as Eisenbaum states, "it might also be the case that the author is partly motivated by the very existence of other Christian literature" (2005: 230). In other words, Hebrews is more like a "theological essay" than an occasional letter to a congregation (2005: 230).

Luke Timothy Johnson represents a more traditional stance. He suggests a date sometime between 45 and 70 CE. Using the same material as Eisenbaum—the text itself—he arrives at a different conclusion. Where Eisenbaum suggests a late date because of silence regarding the temple (it was destroyed so long ago, and perhaps so far away, that it is a distant memory), Johnson claims that the silence is because the temple is still standing (38–39). Johnson sees the Christology of Hebrews as similar to Paul's (39), whereas Eisenbaum, as already noted, understands Hebrews to have more in common with texts that we know from the second century.

From our perspective, it seems most prudent to take Attridge's approach, which allows for the date of Hebrews to be either pre- or post-70 CE. However, for those who prefer to take a side, we prefer Eisenbaum's compelling arguments for a post-70 CE date in the first century. Based on the complex religious milieu caused by upheaval in Palestine and the wide variety of Judaisms in the Mediterranean area (see next section), we think her argument allows for a more inclusive reading of the text.

Introduction to Hebrews

Broader Cultural Context

No author writes in a vacuum; the author of Hebrews is no different. Hebrews is a product of various intersecting first-century worlds. Understanding these worlds gives us a better understanding of the text itself.

Hellenist, Greek-Speaking World

This is the world ushered in by Alexander the Great in the fourth century BCE, when all things Greek became the sign of high culture (much like France and French in the 18th and 19th c. CE). Across the Mediterranean world, the Greeks influenced everything from the style of government to education, philosophy, literature, and trade. In the first century CE, Greek was the language of good literature. While all the New Testament was written in Greek, most of the texts are in a common dialect, called Koine Greek. Hebrews surpasses them with what is the most sophisticated Greek in the New Testament. The text contains wordplays based on Greek terms that are not possible to convey in translation, and it is at home with the more complex grammatical constructions of classical Greek. Last, Hebrews also uses many of the classical principles of Greek rhetoric *[Rhetorical Habits of the Author, p. 249]*, another clue that the author and the congregation are well assimilated within the Hellenistic world.

Jewish Thought

Knowledge of the Dead Sea Scrolls, Philo, the Apocrypha, and other Jewish literature collectively called Old Testament Pseudepigrapha *[Jewish Literature in Antiquity, p. 238]* has made us aware of the variety of forms of first-century Judaism. This rich heritage speculates on the heavenly world, angels, the world to come, and the agents of God's intervention on the earth and at the end of time. All this literature provides insight into the thought world of Hebrews. Two specific literatures stand out:

- Philo's writing represents a philosophically oriented Judaism centered in Alexandria. Throughout this commentary we mention comparisons between Hebrews and Philo *[Jewish Literature in Antiquity, p. 238; Philo, Neoplatonism, and Hebrews, p. 245]*. Although quite different from each other, they interpret some of the same biblical texts.

- The Dead Sea Scrolls show some interesting parallels with Hebrews. These scrolls are a collection of documents, written

36   **Introduction to Hebrews**

or copied by a group called the Essenes. Both Hebrews and the Dead Sea Scrolls develop interpretations of the Melchizedek traditions; yet their theological conclusions are distinctive. Both sets of materials find significance in traditions about angels, Melchizedek, a messianic high priest, the tabernacle or temple, and the sacrificial tradition.

Early Believers in Jesus, the Christ/Messiah

The first believers in Christ were all Jews. Those sharing an understanding that Jesus was the Messiah were, at least early on, under the umbrella of what we may call Judaism. But the movement quickly spread to non-Jewish God-fearers and other people who did not identify with Judaism (Acts 13:16, 26). As it grew, distinctions developed between this movement and the parts of Judaism that did not recognize Jesus as the Messiah *[The Parting of the Ways, p. 243]*. Some Jesus-identifying groups thought variously about Jesus. When New Testament texts are read closely and comparatively, we can see different ideas about Jesus: just notice the differences between the Gospels of Mark and John. In the Gospel of Mark, Jesus is an enigmatic healer and casts out demons; he is reluctant to speak about himself as the Messiah. In the Gospel of John, Jesus speaks freely and at length about who he is and about his relationship with God.

Despite the differences, the life, suffering, and death of Jesus are central to most texts produced by Jesus' followers, including Hebrews. Most of the themes central to Hebrews are also present in other texts:

- The sacrifice of a sinless victim (Heb 4:14-15; 5:8-9; 7:26-28; 9:14). This theme also appears in 1 Peter (1:19; 2:22; 3:18) and is the basis for encouragement of a persecuted community in both writings.

- The exaltation of Jesus to God's right hand (Heb 1:3-4, 13; 5:6; 6:20; 7:3, 21c, 28; 8:1; 10:12-13; 12:2). Hebrews frequently cites Psalm 110, as do several other New Testament texts, in describing Jesus' position in the heavenly world. Two examples will suffice. In the synoptic gospels (Mark 12:36//Matt 22:44//Luke 20:42), Jesus quotes Psalm 110 to assert that the Messiah is someone more than the son (descendant) of David. In Romans 8:34, Paul uses it as a restatement of his gospel, that Jesus died and rose and is now sitting at the right hand of God.

Introduction to Hebrews

- Jesus as God's Word, Wisdom. Hebrews 1:1-3 shares with the Gospel of John, Philippians 2, and Colossians 1 a Christology based on personified Wisdom as found in Proverbs 8 and Wisdom of Solomon 7:25. These images in early Christian hymns were probably current in worship before the writings of Paul.

- Jesus as leader and example of faith. In Hebrews, Jesus is presented as the *pioneer of* faith and *salvation* (2:10), the one who has opened the way to the heavenly places (4:14), the one on whom we are to keep our eyes as we run *the race that is set before us* (12:1-2). First Peter 2:21 also poses Jesus as an example: "To this you have been called, because Christ also suffered for you, leaving you an example that you should follow in his steps." A similar teaching is implied in the Gospels when Jesus calls the disciples: "Follow me." The New Testament frequently speaks of Jesus' followers as followers of "the Way" (Mark 9:33; John 14:6; Acts 16:17; 18:26; 19:23; 22:4; 1 Cor 4:17; 12:31; Heb 10:20).

- Jesus as mediator of a new covenant (Heb 8:6, 8, 13; 9:15). Paul tells the Greek and Jewish Christians in Galatia that they are true children of Abraham and heirs to the promises of the old covenant (Gal 3:6-9). He assures the Corinthians that God has prepared them (Paul and Timothy) "to be ministers of a new covenant . . . of spirit," which gives life (2 Cor 3:6).

- Jesus as high priest brings a new covenant and the once-for-all sacrifice (Heb 4:14–5:8; 7:20-28; 9:11-14; 10:11-18). Although Hebrews is unique in applying this designation, Jesus offers an intercessory prayer for his disciples in John 17, giving himself as a sanctified offering (17:19). The "I am" statements in the Gospel of John are another way of stating that Jesus is the intercessor and way to God (14:6; etc.).

- Exile/exodus (Heb 3:7-19; 11:13-16; 13:1-15). First Peter 1:12-25 and 2:11 also speak to a group of Christ followers who see themselves as exiles and aliens in a foreign land.

- Faithfulness in the face of difficulties (Heb 3:1-6; 4:1-11; 11:1–12:2). Paul speaks to the Philippians about this as well in Philippians 1.

- The importance of community in living a faithful life (Heb 3:12-14; 10:19-25; 13:1-19). Much of 1 Corinthians is about how the members in Corinth can support one another despite their differences. Paul encourages the Romans to "instruct one another" (Rom 15:14); despite the many differences among the Galatians, he urges them to "bear one another's burdens" (Gal 6:2) and "work for the good of all, and especially for those of the family of faith" (6:10).

We know that Hebrews arose out of a deep engagement with the intersecting worlds of Judaism, Greek culture, biblical texts, and the developing movement of Jesus followers. This awareness allows us to engage with the text more fully as the early believers might have.

Is Hebrews Anti-Jewish?

One important recurring theme in Hebrews is that since Jesus has made the once-for-all sacrifice (7:27; 9:12, 28; 10:10), the need for the daily (or yearly) sacrifices of Levitical priests no longer applies. Jesus' saving act has ushered in a new covenant that replaces the old, obsolete covenant (8:13). The author of Hebrews offers the sacrifice of Jesus as a replacement for the sacrifices made on behalf of the people by priests. In other words, Jesus' better and onetime sacrifice is the replacement. Some experts call this a "replacement theology": one mode of sacrifice is replaced by another (Levine and Brettler 2017: 763–64). Hebrews is clear about this replacement with regard to sacrifice and covenant. Questions about the historical and religious context of this replacement theology posed in Hebrews will be discussed throughout the commentary.

Historically, however, Christians have read Hebrews through a supersessionist lens [*Supersessionist and Anti-Jewish Interpretations of Hebrews, p. 257*]. "Supersessionism understands Judaism not as a distinct religion from Christianity but rather as its prologue. In history, it is argued, Judaism *preceded* Christianity; moving forward, Christianity should *proceed* alone. Judaism paved the way, and now it should make way. This way of thinking has been extraordinarily influential in Christian theology" (Svartvik 2021: 34, emph. in the original). Additionally, by virtue of replacing Judaism, many surmise, the new religion, Christianity, is better than what it replaced. In the context of Hebrews, a supersessionist approach allows interpreters to apply their understanding about the relationship between Christianity and Judaism to the text: the new covenant (i.e., Christianity) replaces the old, obsolete covenant (i.e., Judaism). Therefore, Christianity is the superior religion. As the replaced religion, Judaism is considered inferior, a stepping stone to the

Introduction to Hebrews

new and better tradition. Throughout the two millennia of Christianity, many Christians have believed this to be the relationship between Christianity and Judaism. Christianity, foretold in the Old Testament, is the fulfillment of those Scriptures and therefore a better religion than Judaism. Judaism is incomplete; Christianity completes and therefore supersedes Judaism and its Scriptures. In other words, Christians have often *misused* the message of Hebrews to form a triumphalist and supersessionist narrative about Christianity.

Interpreting any ancient text like the Bible has its challenges. Its texts were written over hundreds of years by many authors in various regions of the ancient Mediterranean. Writers of biblical passages often use strategies that modern biblical scholars might question, such as taking an older scriptural text to prove an argument without considering the intention of the original text. The Letter to the Hebrews is a case in point. In chapter 8, the author argues that the new covenant ushered in by Jesus supersedes the old covenant. The author does this by using a text from Jeremiah 31 that announces a "new covenant." Subsequently, many Christians have generalized this passage, removing it from the discussion of sacrifice in Hebrews, then formulating a supersessionist understanding of the entire religion of Judaism, not just the facet under discussion in Hebrews.

On the contrary, *we* read Hebrews as a text that has deep connections with the Scriptures of Judaism and with Judaism itself. We firmly state that the text does not reject Judaism outright. Rather, it advocates for a new covenant that supersedes the old covenant *within* Judaism (see esp. the discussion about Heb 8:7-13).

However, we grant that some scholars of Hebrews, both Christian and Jewish, argue differently. The response to the destruction of the temple and thus of the sacrificial system looms large in this debate. After all, the temple was gone, and something needed to replace the ritual activity that ceased along with the temple's destruction. Beginning in the early second century CE, Jews developed a system of rabbinic commentary on the Torah that replaced the sacrificial system set up in it. Rabbinic Judaism, developed as a result, reinterprets the texts of the Torah (and the system they outline) to work in a world without a temple. In other words, Rabbinic Judaism replaced Second Temple Judaism but without negating it.

Those who argue for the inherent supersessionism of Hebrews compare the approach of rabbinic texts, none of which denigrates the earlier system, with the strategy the author of Hebrews takes. From this perspective, Hebrews takes a more radical approach (see "Guide to Reading" in Eisenbaum (2017: 461–62); and the essay *Supersessionist and Anti-Jewish Interpretations of Hebrews, p. 257*). If Hebrews was written after the destruction of the temple (see earlier discussion about the text's date), it too can be read as a replacement theology for temple sacrifice. These interpreters argue that despite its absolute dependence on and reverence for the Jewish Scriptures and its utter lack of criticism of Judaism as a religion, Hebrews is still a supersessionist text. It considers the sacrificial system set up in Leviticus to be inferior and replaced by the better, once-for-all sacrifice by Jesus. According to Hebrews, Jesus is the better high priest; he is sitting at God's right hand, lives forever, and is perfect. The mortal high priest is none of these things. And the original audience of Hebrews would have done well to remember this and continue in their faithful living. Therefore, these interpreters argue that Hebrews does, indeed, make a supersessionist argument that cannot be neglected or smoothed over (see, more recently, Levine and Brettler 2020: 171–77).

If, in fact, Hebrews carries this supersessionist assumption, what then? As we have suggested earlier in this discussion, the scholarly debate about the supersessionist aspects of Hebrews is not theoretical or merely academic. It is no overstatement to suggest that people's lives have been and are at stake over Christianity's understanding of itself. For many of us, the Bible is a crucial component to that understanding. So how can we be Christians in the twenty-first century who are both deeply mindful of the past and also seek to use the Bible as a companion, even when that companion provides challenges? We suggest that we let love be our guide. Hebrews draws to a close with the statement *Let mutual love continue* (13:1). What better way to begin, continue, and end a journey!

The Method of This Commentary

A great many assumptions have been read *into* Hebrews because of subsequent Christian interpretation of the text; we will provide insights that challenge those assumptions by attempting to draw out the meaning (exegesis) originally intended by the author. We do this through literary analysis and word studies in light of what we know about Hebrews' first-century context. No exegete is without bias, however, so we state ours up front and note its impact on our work with Hebrews. Our overriding intent is to interpret Hebrews in a way that does the least harm to Jews and Judaism.

Introduction to Hebrews

Assumption/bias	Impact
No ancient text can be truly understood outside its original context, so we need to be historically informed interpreters. In other words, we assume that the text was not written for us, so it is our job to understand what the author is saying, not to force the author to say what we want.	In the Explanatory Notes sections, we attempt to provide interpretations that, if read by the original audience, would have made sense. For example, we recognize the replacement theology (some will call this supersessionism) of Hebrews in terms of the sacrificial system, but this replacement theology does not represent a replacement of the entire religious tradition, which would be historically inaccurate and do injustice to the overall argument of Hebrews. The original audience (and the author!) would have been completely baffled by this approach.
The culture out of which the text arises is foreign to us as twenty-first-century people. We attempt to come to the text with humility and an open mind.	In the Text in Biblical Context sections, we provide some historical context that will help us understand why the Christian triumphalist reading is inaccurate.
Modern uses of any ancient text should be guided by values of love and inclusiveness that we believe Jesus exemplified.	We reject a Christian triumphalist interpretation of Hebrews because we believe it has no place within our own understanding of who we want to be as people of God. In the Text in the Life of the Church sections, we confront some of the missteps that Christians have historically taken with this text and discuss how it can be meaningful today.
Every English translation is an interpretation.	Sometimes we need to delve into the Greek words to gather a fuller sense of the real meaning of a passage.

The Essays

In addition to the material in the Explanatory Notes, The Text in Biblical Context (*), and The Text in the Life of the Church (+), short essays *[cross-references identified within italic brackets]* at the back of the book further explicate themes and concepts used throughout the book. They provide even more historical and literary context for Hebrews. For example, one essay provides a brief overview of important texts and authors *[Jewish Literature in Antiquity, p. 238]*. Another contains an introduction to the Greek translation of the Hebrew Bible and its use in Hebrews *[The Septuagint in Hebrews, p. 252]*. Another essay discusses the authorship and twentieth-century theories about the possibility of a woman author *[Priscilla as Author,*

p. 245]. We also address issues of atonement [*Atonement, p. 231*] and supersessionism [*Supersessionist and Anti-Jewish Interpretations of Hebrews, p. 257*] more directly in the Essays than in the commentary proper. When such topics arise in the commentary, we draw attention to the essays; however, they can be read separately at any time.

Using the Commentary: An Invitation

This commentary is for people who are curious about Hebrews. We have tried to make it engaging, void of the normal minutiae of scholarly commentaries. Thus we have attempted to distill and present the most important ideas from our own study and the wide range of commentaries so that people without knowledge of Greek or the historical background of the first century CE can still engage with the text. For people who want more detail, we recommend *The Jewish Annotated New Testament* (2nd ed., Levine and Brettler 2017) as a first step. This study Bible has good notes and introduction to the texts, especially for Hebrews, which were written by Pamela Eisenbaum, on whom we rely a great deal in this commentary. Its excellent essays provide considerable historical and religious background to the New Testament, which, at its core, is a collection of texts written by first-century Jews. We also list several commentaries and studies in the Selected Resources at the end of the book, as well as in the more extensive Bibliography. The scholarly discussion on Hebrews is extensive and deep; our bibliography only scratches its surface. We have used the NRSV in the quotations (for all biblical texts) unless otherwise noted.

Finally, after the anti-Semitic horrors and Holocaust of the mid-twentieth century, we cannot in good conscience read Scripture in ways that minimize the value of other religious traditions. There is difficult language in Hebrews, but it is our job as twenty-first-century Christians to understand its historical context and then to use the text with love within our own historical context. We invite you on that journey!

Hebrews 1:1-4

Prologue

Prophecy about the Son and His Place Next to God

PREVIEW

Good writers often open with a statement that attempts to pull their readers into the text and keeps them reading: *a prologue*. The author of Hebrews does exactly that here: *Long ago*, God spoke through prophets; but now *God has spoken to us by a Son* (1:2a, emph. added). The audience, whom the author will remind throughout the text about their ancestors of *long ago*, becomes part of the story. *[God] spoke to us by a Son* (1:2a, emph. added); that Son is more exalted than any angel. And having done his work on earth, he *sat down at the right hand of the Majesty on high* (1:3; cf. Ps 110:1). The author will return to the close connection between the Son and the audience throughout the text and will continually remind the audience that they play a role in the story.

First, though, our author needs to establish some basic understandings about the Son (identified as Jesus in 2:9). The first four verses are called the "prologue" or "exordium," a Latin word for "beginning." It presents the thesis and themes that appear throughout the text. The prologue also includes several literary techniques and rhetorical strategies that the author uses repeatedly. Finally, the prologue begins with a remarkable display of the author's use of language that continues throughout the text.

44   Hebrews 1:1-4

Now that the audience has heard how they themselves are central to the story through dazzling language and rhetoric, they are on the edge of their seats, ready to hear more!

OUTLINE

God Has Spoken by a Son, 1:1-2a
Nature and Work of the Son, 1:2b-3
The Son Is Exalted above the Angels, 1:4

EXPLANATORY NOTES

God Has Spoken by a Son 1:1-2a

The prologue establishes God's Son, Jesus, as the inheritor of God's wisdom and glory and his primacy as the once-for-all sacrifice and high priest. And although it is difficult to tell in English, the author uses rich literary language: the first Greek clause contains five words beginning with the Greek letter *pi*. The author expends great effort to use words that not only have the right meaning but also sound good when spoken aloud while demonstrating masterful sentence construction. The whole first paragraph is one sentence in Greek! Today, English professors might consider this bad form and label it a run-on sentence. Yet it contains many main and subordinate clauses, all of which relate to the other and build upon the other. These sentences have a circular nature: after a few introductory clauses, the author states the main thesis: *[God] has spoken to us by a Son* (1:2a). Eventually the end of the sentence returns to the subject, in this case the Son: *the name he has inherited [the Son] is more excellent than theirs* (1:4).

The prologue also contains an example of a rhetorical strategy *[Rhetorical Habits of the Author, p. 249]* that the author will use throughout the text: *synkrisis*, a Greek word that means "comparison." *Synkrisis* was a strategy used by many Greek rhetoricians to show the excellence of the subject at hand by comparing it to something else, not necessarily to denigrate what the subject was being compared to. A modern example is Mike Scott's poem "The Whole of the Moon." The final two lines speak of how the poet "saw the rain dirty valley," but the one whom he addresses "saw *Brigadoon*"; where he saw only a crescent, they "saw the whole of the moon."

These lines are indicative of the entire poem, in which the poet compares his own imperfect perception of the world with another person's better perception of it.

Hebrews 1:1-4

In Hebrews, the Greek word *kreittōn* (better) is a clue that the author is using *synkrisis*. It shows up in verse 4: *having become as much superior to [or better than] angels as the name he has inherited is more excellent than theirs.* The following verses will then be evidence that the name of the Son is better. Throughout the text, we will be on the lookout for this strategy; it appears at key points in the text.

While technically not *synkrisis*, verse 1 gives us a "that was then, this is now" comparison that sets the stage for the entire homily: in past times, God spoke through the prophets, but now God is speaking by a Son. The rest of the homily pertains to the message from the Son. This does not mean that the author disregards the prophets. On the contrary, the author uses them to great advantage throughout the text.

The writer of Hebrews hears all the Scriptures as the prophetic word of God, including history, poetry, wisdom, and ritual. The homilist sees Jesus as fulfilling all that God has revealed in them. Our author is not unique in this broad understanding of who prophets were and what the content of their message was. The biblical tradition itself considers Abraham (Gen 20:7), Moses (Deut 18:15), Aaron (Exod 7:1), and Miriam (15:20) as prophets. What Christians tend to call the Historical Books are named Former Prophets in the divisions of Jewish Scripture. In them, we find the figures of Deborah (Judg 4:4), Samuel (1 Sam 3:20), and Elijah and Elisha in 1 and 2 Kings. Our author sits squarely in this tradition by also reading the Psalms as prophecy of the coming Messiah.

The writer refers to the present time as *these last days* (Heb 1:2a). This theme shows up repeatedly in Hebrews. The last days refer to a new age of God's dealings with humanity that began with the coming of Jesus. While the exact nature of the last days is not the focus of the text (as it might be in Revelation, or even in some of Paul's letters), the writer firmly believes they have arrived (see Heb 2:5 about the *coming world* and the promises of rest in ch. 4).

God's effort to communicate with the people of Israel is a basic theme in Scripture. God creates the world by speaking. God speaks to Abraham, Isaac, and Jacob. God speaks to Moses in the burning bush and in the desert. God speaks to David and Solomon and other kings of Israel through visions, dreams, theophanies (visionary appearances of God), and prophets. Our author is continuing that tradition by claiming that God is now speaking through *a Son.* The rest of the text elaborates on this message.

It is important to read Hebrews as a text that understands Jesus not as canceling or eliminating the Prophets, but as amplifying,

46 Hebrews 1:1-4

validating, and fulfilling them. The Prophets, and indeed the entirety of the Jewish Scriptures, are foundational to the homilist's message.

Nature and Work of the Son 1:2b-3

Our author now sets up a confluence of statuses for Jesus. The writer has already established that God spoke by a Son (Jesus; 2:9). Through the use of Psalm 110, we see that this Son also sits at the right hand of God, giving him royal status (Ps 110 is called a "royal" psalm). In Hebrews, Psalm 110 functions to emphasize the place of royal honor and glory that God has given to Christ because of his suffering and his role as leader and forerunner, all of which provide access to God for those who follow. Psalm 110 was an extremely important text for Jesus followers in the first century CE and will appear with such regularity in this text (see, e.g., Heb 1:13; 5:6; 8:1; 10:12) that some commentators see Hebrews as an extended interpretation of Psalm 110 (L. Johnson: 72). See also comments about Psalm 110 in an essay [*The Septuagint in Hebrews, p. 252*].

Along with Psalm 110, the writer punctuates the text with a set of parallel poetic statements to introduce the glorified status of the Son. In addition to presenting the themes of the text and the rhetorical devices that emphasize the themes, the prologue also introduces the literary structures that will appear. In verses 2b-3, we see an inverted parallel structure, called a chiasm. In this arrangement, the first line parallels the last, the second parallels the second to last, and so forth. It looks like this (adapted): *a Son,*

A   *whom he appointed heir of all things* (1:2b)
   B   *through whom he also created the worlds.* (1:2b)
      C   *He is the reflection of God's glory* (1:3)
      C′   *and the exact imprint of God's very being.* (1:3)
   B′   *He sustains [bears] all things by his powerful word.* (1:3b)
A′   *When he had made purification for sins, he sat down at the right hand of the Majesty on high.* (1:3c)

Regardless of whether the author designed the text as a letter or a sermon, someone would have read it aloud, since most people in antiquity could not read. One can imagine a preacher delivering the sermon, pausing ever so slightly before reciting this small group of lines with a poetic flourish. It certainly would grab attention at the outset. You might imagine the audience as sitting up and taking special notice.

Hebrews 1:1-4

The themes of this faith statement might also intrigue the group of believers: inheritance and the exaltation of the Son. The Son is declared to be *heir of all things* (1:2b) and sitting *at the right hand of the Majesty on high* (1:3c). In the chiastic structure, these are A and A'. Roughly speaking, they refer to the Son's status given by God: the Son is the heir and is now exalted by sitting at God's right hand. In chapter 7, we will see our author emphasizing that Jesus is without genealogy in that he does not have the proper lineage to be a priest, yet he has inherited the priesthood anyway. In chapter 9, we also see that Jesus is the mediator, *so that those who are called may receive the promised eternal inheritance* (9:15). But not just Jesus inherits a special status. Throughout the text, the author reminds the audience that they share in this promise of inheritance as well. These reminders serve to encourage faithfulness (see chs. 11–12) and bolster their sagging spirits during difficult times.

Here B and B' expound on the role and nature of Christ. Thus B confirms a foundational belief about Christ: he had a hand in the creation of the world. Creation is not a major theme in Hebrews, although creation is referred to obliquely in 4:4-10 in relation to God's rest, and again in 11:3, where the worlds were prepared by the word of God. More importantly, it connects us with statements about Christ found in other literature. For example, John 1 contains another prologue expounding on the nature and identity of the Word (Christ), and Colossians 1:15-20 includes a hymn to Christ, "the image of the invisible God, . . . in whom all things . . . were created." Read in conjunction with C and C', we see that our author is also attributing to the Son the activities of personified Wisdom that show up in Jewish wisdom literature, especially Proverbs 8:27; Sirach 24:1-12; and Wisdom of Solomon 7:12; 21; 9:4 (cf. Genesis Rabbah 1:1).

Here B' adds a new twist to the audience's understanding of the Son with the statement *He sustains [or bears] all things* (1:3). This language makes reference to the priestly role that is so important in Hebrews. The audience may be assuming that the author is referring to the "cup" (death) that Jesus drank (Luke 22), but the author uses this language to elaborate on the sacrifice that Jesus carries as priest into the heavenly sanctuary (see Heb 9). Although the phrase "high priest" is not introduced until 2:17, the priestly function of making purification for sins is introduced here in the prologue to prepare the audience for its development more fully in chapters 5–8. This concept of Jesus as (high) priest is a distinctive aspect of Hebrews not found elsewhere in the New Testament. It is important to

48 Hebrews 1:1-4

recognize how the author develops that theme starting here in chapter 1.

Lines C and C′ elaborate on Jesus' nature as revelation. Jesus is both the *reflection of God's glory and the exact imprint of God's very being* (1:3), indicating that God's essence is revealed through the Son. The word used here, *imprint* (or *character*), is the same word used for the impression on coins or seals. Although it reveals the essence, it remains distinct from the original. These phrases take up the language and themes attributed to Wisdom in Proverbs 8:22-31, where Wisdom says, "The LORD created me at the beginning of his work, the first of his acts of long ago." The apocryphal Wisdom of Solomon 6–10 (cf. esp. 7:26) says, "For she [Wisdom] is a reflection of eternal light, a spotless mirror of the working of God, and an image of [God's] goodness." For more discussion on how early Jewish Christians used wisdom literature, see the Essays *[Jewish Literature in Antiquity, p. 238; The Role and Use of the Jewish Scriptures by Early Christians, p. 251]*.

The B and C lines work together to restate early Jewish-Christian thinking about Jesus *[Christology in Hebrews, p. 235]*. Jesus, the Son, is the reflection of God's glory and the imprint of God's being. In the Scriptures, *God's glory* (Gk. *doxa*) is commonly used to express a nonhuman, unearthly, and divine reality. Here our author is stating that it is also a characteristic of the exalted Son. Elsewhere in Hebrews, the author expresses the eschatological vision of Jesus *crowned with glory and honor* (2:9, quoting Ps 8), having brought *many children to glory* (Heb 2:10). Jesus also carries (bears or sustains) all things by his word. Jesus replaces Wisdom (Gk. *sophia*) as the bearer, glory, and imprint of God. While some New Testament authors see Jesus as the embodiment of Wisdom/Sophia (see esp. 1 Cor 1:24, where Paul says that "Christ [is] the power of God and the wisdom of God"), the homilist in Hebrews "submerges the origins of this christological language in the Wisdom tradition by never explicitly referring to . . . Wisdom/Sophia" (Beavis and Kim-Cragg: 5).

Simultaneously, the lines challenge the audience to expand their thinking by introducing new ideas about Jesus. The author shifts from the wisdom Christology that dominates the previous phrases to the introduction of the distinctive Christology of Hebrews, which presents Jesus as the great high priest. The prologue foreshadows themes that arise at great length through the rest of the text, especially in chapters 5–8: having established that the Son has all the familiar characteristics ascribed to Jesus in early Jewish-Christian

Hebrews 1:1-4

circles, the author now asserts that the Son (whom the author does not connect to Jesus until 2:9) also *made purification for sins* (1:3b), which is the role of a priest.

All these ideas are grounded in Scripture. Although we have reviewed the use of wisdom literature and Psalm 110, other psalms are important too. The statement *the Son whom he appointed heir of all things* (Heb 1:2b) is a clear reference to Psalm 2:8: "I will make the nations your inheritance, and the ends of the earth your possession." As with Psalm 110, it is a royal psalm, composed for the coronation of a king. But the writer of Hebrews has more in mind than the inheritance of an earthly kingdom: the inheritance that the Son, who is Christ/Messiah, has received begins with his sitting *at the right hand of the Majesty on high* (1:3)—not merely an earthly kingdom! Jesus the Son is heir not only of the earth, but also of the age to come!

The Son Is Exalted above the Angels 1:4

Our author writes enticing segues from one section to the next. Verse 4 explains that the Son is sitting at the right hand of God because he is superior to the angels in both name and position. It concludes the prologue and serves as an entry into the next section, which explores the relationship of the Son (Jesus) to the angels. It is somewhat ironic that Jesus, yet to be named, has already been identified as *Son*, who functions as heir and priest. The final verse of the prologue draws attention to this by claiming that it is not just the beings themselves (the Son, the angels) that the author will compare, but their names as well.

Names and naming play important roles in the Bible. A name in biblical language seldom refers simply to the word by which we identify a person. A name reveals the character and qualities of a person. Here the text confirms the name *Son*, familiar to all the readers. In the next section the writer compares the Son to the angels. Later, in Hebrews 6:10, the writer praises the audience for the love they *showed for his name in serving the saints* (ESV; the NRSV translates the Greek word for "name," *onoma*, as "his sake"). In 13:15, believers are challenged to offer a *sacrifice of praise* by confessing his name. In both instances, reference is made to the believers' loyalty to the *name*.

In the next section, we delve into why the author is comparing the Son to the angels. It is also the first comparison (*synkrisis*) that the author will handle. We will find more as we move through the text.

50   Hebrews 1:1-4

THE TEXT IN BIBLICAL CONTEXT

Wisdom, Kingship, and Priesthood in Scriptural Traditions

In Hebrews 1:1-4 we see a confluence of important biblical traditions: wisdom, kingship, and the priesthood. It is an excellent example of how the early church derived its teaching from those biblical traditions. We have identified ties to the creation story in the phrase "God spoke" (cf. Gen 1). The writer reminds us of the prophets through whom God spoke. We have identified the language of Wisdom in the descriptions of Jesus' role as creator and the messianic language in his role as heir. Like Wisdom, the Son radiates God's glory and bears God's image and character. Like the Davidic kings, the Son also fulfills the role of messianic king in Psalm 110:1, sitting at God's right hand.

Our author is not alone in identifying Jesus as God's Wisdom. The New Testament regularly transfers characteristics of Wisdom to the Son. Using the language of personified Wisdom in Proverbs 8:22-26 ("The LORD created me [Wisdom] at the beginning of his work. . . . Ages ago I was set up, at the first, before the beginning of the earth"), the prologue in the Gospel of John begins with the concept of Jesus as Word (Logos), "In the beginning was the Word [*Logos*]." Like Wisdom, Jesus came and dwelled among humanity, full of grace and truth. In Colossians 1:15-20 the author uses these same phrases from Proverbs 8:22-26 in a hymn to Christ ("He himself is before all things," Col 1:17). In 1 Corinthians 1:30, Paul writes that Christ Jesus "became for us wisdom from God." Thus, our author's identification of Jesus with Wisdom appears firmly within the context of Jewish Scripture and other teaching of the early church.

We find other echoes of biblical traditions. Our author says that the Son is a *reflection of God's glory and the exact imprint of God's very being* (1:3). "God's glory" is a sign of God's presence that originates in Exodus 16:6-7, when God promises that bread from heaven will rain from the sky and Moses tells the people of Israel that "in the morning you shall see the glory of the LORD, because he has heard your complaining." In 24:17, when Moses is on the mountain with God, he sees that "the appearance of the glory of the LORD was like a devouring fire on the top of the mountain in the sight of the people of Israel." Isaiah is familiar with God's glory, having seen it in a vision: "Holy, holy, holy is the LORD of hosts; the whole earth is full of his glory" (Isa 6:3). Later he promises that the "glory of the LORD shall be revealed, and all people shall see it together" (40:5). Like the author of Hebrews, other New Testament authors interpret Jesus as

Hebrews 1:1-4

the reflection of God's glory. Jesus tells the disciples in John 14:9, "Whoever has seen me has seen the Father." Paul declares that Jesus is the image of God (2 Cor 4:4; Col 1:15). The exalted name of Hebrews 1:4 also reminds us of Philippians 2:9-10, which declares that God "gave him the name that is above every name, so that at the name of Jesus every knee should bend."

Psalm 110 is useful for New Testament authors who wish to express the exaltation of Christ into God's glory. In the synoptic gospels, Jesus quotes Psalm 110:1 at his trial when asked whether he is the Messiah. Jesus replies, "I am; and 'you will see the Son of Man seated at the right hand of the Power'" (Mark 14:62//Matt 26:64// Luke 22:69). In Acts, Peter preaches about the exaltation of Jesus at God's right hand in his Pentecost sermon (2:33-35) and again in his sermon before the elders of Israel and the council (5:21-32). In his dying vision, Stephen sees the "glory of God and Jesus standing at the right hand of God" (7:55-56): here he is "standing" instead of seated. Paul uses Psalm 110 in his declaration of God's saving work on our behalf (Rom 8:34) and his affirmation of the power of the resurrection (1 Cor 15:25). It is reaffirmed in Ephesians 2:6, where believers are seated with Christ "in the heavenly places." Colossians 3:1 expresses a similar exhortation: "If you have been raised with Christ, seek the things that are above, where Christ is, seated at the right hand of God." Later apostolic teaching reaffirms the exaltation of Christ: 1 Peter 3:22 says that Jesus Christ has "gone into heaven and is at the right hand of God, with angels, authorities, and powers made subject to him." Revelation puts the words directly into the mouth of "the Amen," or Christ: "To the one who conquers I will give a place with me on my throne, just as I myself conquered and sat down with my Father on his throne" (3:21). The exaltation of Christ to God's right hand is a basic apostolic teaching.

Many of us are no longer familiar with the Wisdom of Solomon, Proverbs, or even many of the psalms, but we should assume that the early believers themselves—not just Paul, the anonymous gospel writers, and the author of Hebrews—were familiar with this material. This author and the audience were firmly established within the Jewish biblical tradition.

THE TEXT IN THE LIFE OF THE CHURCH

The Politics of Jesus as Son and Heir

For the early church, calling Jesus "Lord" and "Son of God" was not only a theological affirmation, but also a political statement. These

52   Hebrews 1:1-4

were official titles of the Roman emperor, as can be discovered in the Roman literature and inscriptions of the period. Jewish Christians claimed these titles for Jesus instead of the emperor. Their primary loyalty was to Jesus the Christ, not to the empire. In using these titles, they also affirmed a willingness to follow the teaching and example of Jesus.

Claiming that Jesus is the "image" or "impression" of God in Hebrews 1:3 is probably itself an act of resistance since the Roman emperor and his image were commonly regarded as a god. To use it for someone other than the emperor could have been dangerous. Using work by Darryl L. Jones about sermons as resistance literature, Jennifer T. Kaalund comments that Hebrews was an act of resistance against the Roman Empire: "As a sermon, it performs a particular task in the formation of identity: . . . the audience's response demonstrates a form of resistance to Roman imperial power" (88).

Later in Hebrews, we will see how the author emphasizes the importance of faithfulness, even in difficult times; that faithfulness can sometimes (maybe even *should* sometimes) make us feel like aliens. Our allegiances are not to the reigning powers on earth, but to God.

Because of that, we are outsiders. For now, we might think about how the spiritual—our belief—is manifested in our daily lives, both inwardly and as citizens of our neighborhoods, countries, and the world. What are we really saying when we profess Jesus as Lord, as Son and heir? What powers are we resisting when we confess Jesus to be "Lord" and "Son of God"? How does that confession shape our character and actions in our daily lives? In what way does it distinguish us as individuals, as local communities of believers, and as the broader Christian community?

The Prologue in the Revised Common Lectionary

Hebrews 1:1-4 is a lectionary reading for Christmas. The other readings that accompany this text include Isaiah 52:7-10; Psalm 98; and John 1:1-14. The passage from Isaiah is a joyful thanksgiving for the redemption of Jerusalem. Psalm 98 rejoices in the victory of the Lord and encourages singing praises and making "a joyful noise to the LORD" (98:4). The gospel reading is John's prologue, which begins, "In the beginning was the Word, and the Word was with God" (1:1). Hebrews 1:1-4 creates a bridge between the prophetic Scriptures and John with its opening *Long ago . . . , but in these last days*. Hebrews announces that God has spoken through a Son, and then the gospel elaborates on the Word itself. For Christmastime, the pairing of these two passages is an excellent opportunity for contemplating the mystery of God's incarnation in Jesus.

Using the Scripture index in *Hymnal: A Worship Book*, published by the Church of the Brethren, General Conference Mennonite Church, and the Mennonite Church in North America, we find three hymns that refer to Hebrews 1:1-4. The first, "Fairest Lord Jesus" (#117), is not an obvious selection. But one phrase captures the sense: "Jesus shines brighter, Jesus shines purer than all the angels heav'n can boast." Another, "At the Name of Jesus" (#342), alludes to Philippians 2 and Hebrews when it calls on the singers to bow their knees and call Jesus "Lord." The third hymn, "Lord, You Sometimes Speak" (#594), refers to Hebrews 1:2 with the phrase "Lord, you always speak in Jesus." While none of these hymns uses exact quotations of the text, they all use the text's understanding of Jesus as the Word, citing his name and status as Son in their own understanding of Jesus.

Part 1

Listen to What Is Said about Jesus and Follow His Example!

Hebrews 1:5–4:13

OVERVIEW

Living in a wilderness is difficult. Whether it is geographical isolation, extreme weather, or other conditions, a wilderness can create emotional, physical, and even spiritual strain. When we wrote these words during the COVID-19 quarantines, we were experiencing some isolation. The audience of the Letter to the Hebrews is also living in a kind of wilderness. They have chosen to follow Jesus, God's Son and pioneer of their salvation, but lately have shown a lack of faithfulness toward Jesus. In fact, they have become more like the faithless Israelites, whom the homilist uses as an example of how *not* to behave during a crisis. Using the experience of the ancient Israelites wandering in the desert, the homilist urges the congregation to remain strong and to live faithful lives. Jesus provides the example of faithful living. By following him, members of the congregation can enter the *real* promised land, where Jesus is already sitting at the right hand of God. That is true rest. God's Word, *living and active* (4:12), demands faithful attention and requires an accounting (4:13). Jesus is the pioneer who can lead to salvation, despite the wilderness conditions.

OUTLINE

The Son Is Greater than the Angels, 1:5–2:4
Jesus the Son Is a Human Being, like Us in All Things, 2:5-18
The Faithful Are to Enter into Rest, 3:1–4:13

Hebrews 1:5–2:4

The Son Is Greater than the Angels

PREVIEW

Why does the pastor spend so much time talking about angels? In the Scriptures, when angels speak, people listen. Powerful, spiritual, and heavenly, angels are God's agents; they speak for God and change people's lives. Three angels announce to Abraham and Sarah that they will become parents in their old age. An angel stops Abraham's sacrifice of Isaac. An angel appears to Moses at the burning bush. Angels are voices of authority in Scripture and for those who respect Scripture.

That was then. But now, *in these last days* (Heb 1:2), God has a new agent and voice of authority. Not just any agent, but God's Son. As God's Son, he is unlike any other heavenly being: he is superior in every way. To demonstrate the Son's exaltation and witness to his primacy over the angels, our author releases a long chain, or catena, of Scripture citations.

After the catena, the author concludes with a *synkrisis*, a comparison, issued as a warning: If transgressing the message declared by angels resulted in punishment, how much greater will the punishment be if the message from the Son is neglected!

58   Hebrews 1:5–2:4

OUTLINE

Catena: The Son Is Exalted above the Angels, 1:5-13
Summary: Angels as Servants, 1:14
Pay Attention! We Must Not Neglect This Salvation, 2:1-4

EXPLANATORY NOTES

Catena: The Son Is Exalted above the Angels 1:5-13

Why are angels so important to the writer and the original readers that ten verses are dedicated to ensuring the proper relationship between them and the Son? In the biblical tradition, angels serve several important functions: they appear as guardians (Exod 14:19; 23:20); they are intermediaries between God and humans, bringing important messages to such people as Hagar, Abraham, Lot, and Jacob (Gen 16, 18, 19, 22, 48), the mother of Samson (Judg 13), and Elijah (1 Kings 19). They are members of God's heavenly court, where they are often called "sons of God" (e.g., Gen 6:2). In later biblical literature, angels are guides or interpreters of the heavenly (or hellish) revelation (e.g., Dan 7:16). In the intertestamental Jewish literature (i.e., OT Pseudepigrapha, Apocrypha, and the Dead Sea Scrolls), interest in angels increased significantly. It is not surprising, then, that our homilist uses them in comparison to the Son.

This passage is one of contrasts: using Scripture, the author says something about the Son by comparing him to angels from other Scripture passages. In the following introductory phrases (emph. added), look for the implied "on the one hand, . . . but on the other." They come in groups of two.

> 1:5 For to which of the _angels_ did God ever say
> 1:6 And again, when he brings the firstborn into the world, he says
>   [to the firstborn]
> 1:7 Of the _angels_ he says
> 1:8 But of the _Son_ he says
> 1:13 But to which of the _angels_ has he ever said

The audience can hear the implied "on the one hand, . . . but on the other": by the end of the comparison in verse 13, they have clearly heard the message that, for sure, the Son is elevated above the angels.

This rhetorical device is *synkrisis*. It allows the author to affirm the opening thesis of Hebrews that in the past God has

Hebrews 1:5–2:4 59

communicated in a variety of ways, but the most recent and most complete is God's communication through God's human agent, *a Son*. The author makes the comparison using a catena, a set of scriptural passages (sometimes called "prooftexts") strung together in succession, one immediately after another. The chart illustrates how each quote in 1:5-13 (emph. added) is a different passage from Scripture. Together, they form a catena.

Verse	Introduction	Quoted text	Scriptural reference
1:5	*For to which of the* <u>*angels*</u> *did God ever say,*	You are my Son; today I have begotten you	Psalm 2:7
1:5	*Or again,*	I will be his Father, and he will be my Son	2 Samuel 7:14
1:6	*And again, when he brings the* <u>*firstborn*</u> *into the world, he says,*	Let all God's angels worship him	Deuteronomy 32:43
1:7	*Of the* <u>*angels*</u> *he says,*	He makes his angels winds	Psalm 104:4 (LXX)
1:8	*But of the* <u>*Son*</u> *he says,*	Your throne, O God, is forever	Psalm 45:6-7
1:10-12	And [of the Son he says]	In the beginning, Lord, you founded the earth	Psalm 102:25-27
1:13	*But to which of the* <u>*angels*</u> *has he ever said,*	Sit at my right hand until I make your enemies a footstool for your feet	Psalm 110:1

The author has compiled these specific texts to prove the supposition that the Son is greater than the angels. These specific Scripture passages originate from a royal context related to King David and his heirs. As in other early Jewish-Christian circles, our author interprets them to refer to the Son, meaning Jesus.

Most of the citations begin with an introductory phrase (emph. added) provided by the author to indicate that God speaks through the Scripture:

1:5 *For to which of the angels did God ever* <u>*say,*</u>
1:6 *And again, when he brings the firstborn into the world, he* <u>*says,*</u>
1:7 *Of the angels he* <u>*says,*</u>
1:8 *But of the Son he* <u>*says,*</u>
1:13 *But to which of the angels has he ever* <u>*said,*</u>

60 Hebrews 1:5–2:4

Notice how the passage opens with a series of rhetorical questions in verses 5-7, beginning with, "Did God ever say . . . ?" The answer is obvious: "No, God never said that to the angels." The writer expects the audience to actively engage the message and to have the answer in mind. After the opening question, the author builds his case with a set of additional Scriptures that relate to the first Scripture citation in 1:5 (2 Sam 7:14): *I will be his Father, and he will be my Son.* The argument is based on the premise that God's Son will naturally be more exalted than the angels who serve God.

The Scripture the author uses is important. Combined with the rhetorical devices, it packs a punch. Most of the passages that relate to the Son originate in a royal context. For example, the first citation is from Psalm 2:7. When a king of Israel was enthroned at Jerusalem, one of the titles he received was "son of God." *God* declares to the newly enthroned king, "You are my son; today I have begotten you" (cf. Heb 1:5). The enthronement of a Davidic king was equivalent to his adoption as God's son. We are familiar with this text because the gospel writers also use it at Jesus' baptism (Matt 3:17//Mark 1:11//Luke 3:22) and at the transfiguration (Matt 17:5//Mark 9:7//Luke 9:35). The second text, from 2 Samuel 7:14, quotes the promise of God through the prophet Nathan to David concerning his son Solomon, thereby establishing the Davidic covenant, God's promise that David's "son" will always sit on the throne. In Hebrews, the writer applies this promise to Jesus at his exaltation.

By the time Hebrews was written, these passages were also being used as messianic texts describing the one who will be raised up "to save Israel" (4QFlor I, 13). Acts 4:25-26 and 13:33 use Psalm 2 to refer to Jesus as Messiah. Revelation 12:5 and 19:15 use the same psalm to refer to the ruler who will rule with "a rod of iron." The author uses both the royal and messianic meanings and builds on them. Later in the text (Heb 5:5), the author quotes Psalm 2:7 (*Today I have begotten you*) again in an affirmation of God's appointment of Christ as high priest. However, since the language of bringing a child into the world is common for giving birth, one can also understand it as referring to the incarnation. In Luke 2:7, Jesus is called the "first-born" of Mary. It is not clear whether the homilist intended to designate one of these options or to include them all. The first readers of this text have already experienced *signs and wonders* and *gifts of the Holy Spirit* (Heb 2:4). They *have tasted the goodness of the word of God and the powers of the coming age* (6:5). These are all part of the coming world that has begun with Jesus' resurrection (or baptism or birth). Clearly, the coming age brought in by the Messiah is an idea

Hebrews 1:5–2:4   61

palpable to the author and the audience. Read in combination with
Deuteronomy 32:43—*Let all God's angels worship him* (Heb 1:6), the
next verse in the catena—we might interpret this as referring primarily to a nonearthly eternal world.

The author introduces the Scripture with the phrase *when he brings the firstborn into the world, he says* (1:6). Two words are in question: "firstborn" (Gk. *prōtotokos*) and "world" (Gk. *oikoumenē*). The most common use of *oikoumenē* in Greek literature and in the New Testament is in referencing the inhabited world of humankind. But as L. Johnson points out, the writer uses the Greek word *kosmos* for that meaning (79). If we read it in conjunction with Hebrews 2:5, which also uses *oikoumenē*, our author is probably talking about the world of the angels, the divine world. If that is the case, this passage refers to the introduction of the firstborn into the divine world of the angels and is more relevant to the Son's sitting at the right hand of God in that world, as opposed to the earthly, inhabited world.

God's firstborn oversees the earthly realm, the heavenly realm, and the age to come, where he will be worshiped and served by angels. Although our author does not use these texts, similar calls for heavenly beings to worship can be found in Psalm 97:7, "All gods bow down before him"; 103:20-21, "Bless the LORD, O you his angels, you mighty ones who do his bidding"; and 148:2, "Praise him, all his angels; praise him, all his host!" These psalms call for the angels to worship God. Here the writer has applied the exhortations to worshiping Christ, the Son.

An even better interpretation occurs when we combine it with what we know about the use of the word "firstborn" by other New Testament authors. In Paul's letters, "firstborn" is a figurative title for Christ (see Rom 8:29). Other writings refer to Jesus as the "firstborn from/of the dead" (Col 1:18; Rev 1:5). In Hebrews 12:23, the saints in heaven are called *firstborn* in reference to the resurrection. Thus, the primary uses of "firstborn" as a title for Christ speak of his resurrection and his role in the age to come.

Christ's resurrection and role in the age to come confirm the distinction between the angels and the Son. Building on the relationship established between the Son and the angels with the use of Deuteronomy, another comparison begins in verse 7 with a creative reading of Psalm 104:4. The psalm concerns the majesty of God as creator and affirms God's control over the natural world. It states, "[God] makes spirits his messengers, and flaming fire his ministers" (LXX). Our author reverses the subject and predicate: *[God] makes the angels winds . . .* (Heb 1:7). This rereading defines the angels as the

62   Hebrews 1:5–2:4

winds or spirits, and the servants as flames. Although such language conjures an imaginative notion of angels, it also establishes the angels as somewhat ephemeral and changeable, completely at the command of their maker. Angels now contrast with the authority and permanence of the Son's role.

The author's use of Psalm 45 immediately after that of Psalm 104 solidifies the distinction between the Son and the angels. Words like "throne" (45:6a), "scepter" (45:6b), and "anointed" (45:7b) describe the everlasting nature of the Son's position, creating a distinct contrast to the fleeting and impermanence of the angels as winds and flames of fire. The Son is royalty. His throne is *forever and ever*, and he is addressed as *"O God"* (1:8). The Son has a status the angels will never have *[Christology in Hebrews, p. 235]*.

The thought continues with the next Scripture, taken from Psalm 102:25-27, a lament psalm addressed to God as a call for help. The psalm ends with the verses cited in Hebrews, affirming the greatness and the eternal power of God in creating and sustaining the earth. Our writer interprets the psalm as words of God addressed to the Son. Repeating the themes of creating and sustaining the earth that appeared in the prologue (Heb 1:2-3), the emphasis remains on the permanent and eternal nature of the Son. Even the earth, God's creation, is impermanent compared to the Son: *But you are the same, and your years will never end* (1:12). The same kind of affirmation is made at the end of Hebrews in the statement *Jesus Christ is the same yesterday and today and forever* (13:8).

The catena closes with the same rhetorical question with which it began: *To which of the angels has God ever said . . . ?* (1:13). Not surprisingly, the author chose Psalm 110 to supply the answer: *Sit at my right hand until I make your enemies a footstool for your feet.* The author already alluded to this psalm in the prologue; now the first verse of the psalm is quoted in full here. As noted earlier, the author returns to Psalm 110 several times throughout the text. Here it confirms the Son's position of power at the right hand of God. The words paint a powerful image of a victorious monarch, whose enemies literally lie prostrate at his feet and figuratively serve as a footstool. The imagery here looks forward to the mention of Christ's victory over the devil in Hebrews 2:14-15 rather than looking backward to his relationship with the angels.

Summary: Angels as Servants 1:14

The summary verse is another rhetorical question, this time a reminder of the language of Psalm 104 in Hebrews 1:7. In contrast to

Hebrews 1:5–2:4   63

the Son, seated permanently in a place of honor at God's right hand, the angels are servants, and their service is *for the sake of those who are to inherit salvation* (1:14). Here and later in the homily (as in 9:15), the author includes the congregation as heirs, yet following the prime heir, the *Son*, the *firstborn*. The heirs mentioned remind us of the Son as heir in 1:2, 6.

Pay Attention! We Must Not Neglect This Salvation 2:1-4

This brief section, in which the author pauses to encourage the audience to pay attention, is sometimes treated as an interruption. It breaks the flow of discussion between two sections that seem to work together. In the preceding section the author has established the primacy of the Son over the angels; in the following section the author will continue that comparison between Jesus and angels, focusing on Jesus' humanity. Why then does the author pause here to focus on the dangers of neglecting or turning away from God's message (see also 4:1; 6:4-6)?

Think of a preacher who asks the congregation, "Are you with me?" Our preacher is using a similar strategy, making sure that, yes, the congregation agrees that they should *not drift away from* the message of salvation. Neglecting the salvation offered is serious. If members of the audience hear the message, they must respond. The preacher is checking to make sure they are paying attention by making three points about the message:

1. The *Son* delivered the message (Jesus, yet to be mentioned by name; 1:2; 2:3, 9).

2. That message was heard by the Son's followers and *was attested [secured]* for the present audience and the author by Jesus' followers (2:3).

3. It was also witnessed by God through signs and wonders (2:4).

The word the NRSV translates in 2:3 as "attested" can also be translated as "secured," or "valid" (Gk. *bebaios*), depending on the context. It resurfaces later in the text (as in 3:14; 6:19; 9:17). Here and elsewhere in Hebrews, it signifies a lasting "firmness" that had begun earlier and that the current audience confirms. In sum, the message delivered by the Son is valid. In fact, it has now become the greater message, since it has been delivered by the Son, not the angels. So if this is the case, how can the present audience *escape if they neglect such a great . . . salvation?* L. Johnson claims that this is a key moment in the text, foundational for moving forward (89).

64   Hebrews 1:5–2:4

Without clarifying and verifying that the audience is following these points, there is no reason to move forward.

This first chapter of Hebrews employs a remarkably creative display of Scripture to confirm a belief about the Son and his message. It is a classic illustration of a catena and how biblical material is used to create new meaning. The author has taken Scripture from another time and place to support the statement of belief in Hebrews 1:1-4: Jesus (not yet named) is God's Son, the heir appointed by God. Through Jesus, God created the world. By putting texts into the voice of God, texts originally addressed *to* God or a king, our author has appropriated the Scriptures to support the message about Christ in a new way for the sermon's audience. Many of us now may raise our eyebrows at the author's seeming disregard for the original meaning in several psalms and other Scriptures used for this catena, but we can also view the author's approach as a way to keep Scripture alive and constantly useful.

THE TEXT IN BIBLICAL CONTEXT

Hearing

Paying proper attention to the message of God is not just a concern in Hebrews; it recurs throughout biblical literature, where hearing is equivalent to obedience. With the warning "Let anyone with ears, listen!," Jesus calls attention to the fact that many people with ears are unable to comprehend the significance of what they hear and then respond with transformed lives (Matt 11:15; 13:9). In response to his disciples' question about his use of parables in Matthew 13:10-17, Jesus enigmatically quotes from Isaiah 6:9-10: "You will indeed listen, but never understand." Luke's version of this imperative is only slightly different: "Let anyone with ears to hear[,] listen!" (14:35). Jesus is using a long-established tradition from the Scriptures. In addition to Isaiah 6:9-10, the Shema of Deuteronomy 6:4 starts with "Hear, O Israel" and continues with how what they have heard is to be put into action: "You shall love the LORD your God with all your heart and with all your soul and with all your might" (6:5).

Appropriate hearing is also a theme of the Prophets and of wisdom literature. For example, Isaiah 50:5 says, "The Lord GOD has opened my ear, and I was not rebellious; I did not turn backward." And Jeremiah cries out, "Hear this, O foolish and senseless people, who have eyes but do not see, who have ears but do not listen!" (5:21). Similarly, the writer of Proverbs asks the audience to be "making your ear attentive to wisdom" (2:2). Recognizing the

Hebrews 1:5–2:4 65

importance of true listening, the psalmists ask God to listen and answer: "I call upon you, for you will answer me, O God; incline your ear to me; hear my words" (17:6). Finally, in a request for help for the nation, the writer of Psalm 44 reminds God, "We have heard with our ears, O God, our ancestors have told us, what deeds you performed in their days, in the days of old" (44:1). The Scriptures are a constant reminder of the importance of active listening!

Warnings

Hebrews 2:1-4 is the first of a series of warnings to the apathetic or disconsolate audience. Additional warnings appear in 3:7–4:10; 5:11–6:3; 10:26-39; and 12:25-29. Hebrews follows a long tradition in Scripture of bringing the message of God's judging the unfaithful and the message of God's grace. Some prophets give abundant calls to repentance and warnings to the people in relation to their faithlessness to God's covenants. For example, Isaiah warns Judah and laments, "Israel does not know; my people do not understand" (1:3); the prophet Amos warns Israel of impending judgment; and Hosea proclaims God's mercy but also warns against unfaithfulness.

Indeed, many biblical authors speak of the tension between God's grace and goodness, with warnings and stern reminders about the responsibilities required of the people of God. Jesus follows this tradition in many of the parables recorded by New Testament authors. For example, the pithy saying about salt in Matthew 5:13//Mark 9:50// Luke 14:34-35 gets to the heart of the matter: "You are salt of the earth; but if salt has lost its taste, how can saltiness be restored? It is no longer good for anything, but it is thrown out and trampled under foot" (Matt 5:13). Luke's version is even more vivid: If the saltiness loses its flavor, "it is fit neither for the soil nor for the manure pile. . . . Let anyone with ears to hear listen!" (14:34-35). Like Hebrews, Luke's version combines hearing the message with behavior. Our author's directive *to pay greater attention to what we have heard, so that we do not drift away from [the message]* (Heb 2:1) resonates with this parable.

Two other examples of parables with similar message will suffice. The parable of the tenants of the vineyard (Matt 21:33-45// Mark 12:1-12//Luke 20:9-19) closes with the words "the kingdom of God will be taken away from you and given to a people that produce the fruits of the kingdom" (Matt 21:43). The parable of the talents (Matt 25:14-30//Luke 19:11-27) warns the listener, "For to all those who have, more will be given, and they will have an abundance, but from those who have nothing, even what they have will be taken away" (Matt 25:29).

Paul's letters combine messages about God's grace with words of warning. Romans 11:17-24 uses the grafting of branches onto an olive tree as an allegory to check the presumption of Gentile believers. Paul says, "You stand only through faith" (Rom 11:20). He warns the Corinthians about the spiritual dangers of idolatry in 1 Corinthians 10 and about abuses of the Lord's Supper in 11:17-33, both of which concern the arrogance of so-called believers. Finally, in Revelation 2–3 we find seven letters to churches, each of which contains a specific warning. The Ephesians have endured, but "have abandoned the love you had at first" (Rev 2:4). The church at Smyrna is warned to remain faithful in their suffering (2:10-11), and the church at Sardis is commanded, "Wake up. . . . Remember then what you received and heard; obey it, and repent" (3:2-3).

Indeed, throughout biblical history, the people of God have been commanded to "wake up," listen, obey, and take on the responsibility that God gives them as people of God.

Angels

Many of the suppositions that undergird our author's discussion about angels and angelic powers arose in the Second Temple period and appear in Jewish writings known as the Apocrypha, Pseudepigrapha, and the Dead Sea Scrolls [Jewish Literature in Antiquity, p. 238]. A number of these texts feature the role of angels in the heavenly kingdom at some length. Jewish mysticism of the first century speculated about the role of angels around the throne of God and related their existence to the prophecies of Ezekiel and Daniel. The Qumran community, likely responsible for writing/copying the Dead Sea Scrolls, had an extensive treatise on the role of angels, which also included Melchizedek as an angelic, priestly figure. In addition to their role as messengers, angels were believed to control such phenomena as winds, stars, planets, countries, peace, healing, and death.

Much of our modern, limited understanding of the role of angels in antiquity comes from New Testament passages where an angel visits Mary (Luke 1:26) or Joseph (Matt 1:20) to announce their roles in the birth of Jesus. In Luke, an angel appears with a heavenly host to announce the birth of Jesus to the shepherds (2:8-14). While we might want to imagine the heavenly hosts singing beautiful Christmas carols, a "multitude of the heavenly host" is actually an *army of angels*. No wonder the shepherds are "terrified" (2:9)! If angels wield such power, we can see why some people may have worshiped angels, a practice that Colossians 2:18 warns against.

The New Testament text that has the biggest role for angels is Revelation. Multiple angelic roles occur. Each of the letters addressed to the seven churches begins with "To the angel of the church in [place-name]" (Rev 2-3). In chapter 7, angels are positioned at the four corners of the earth to hold back the four winds. The heavenly tabernacle has multitudes of angels standing around the throne (7:11) and blowing trumpets (Rev 8). An angel comes down to earth and delivers a prophetic scroll to John, which he then eats (Rev 10). Angels with trumpets use ritual bowls to pour out the wrath of God (Rev 17-18). In all these passages, angels serve as intercessors between humans and God. In summary, angels are crucial to John's revelation. Yet their sole purpose is to serve at the command of God.

The New Testament contains evidence of another important tradition regarding angels that directly impacts the understanding of our text. By the time Hebrews was written in the late first century, Jewish tradition had developed the idea that God gave the Mosaic law through angels. We can see evidence of this in Acts 7:38 and Galatians 3:19; both attest to an angel conveying the law to Moses. This tradition also appears in Jubilees, a noncanonical text providing an alternative account of how Moses received the law on Mount Sinai. In the Jubilees version, an angel is the purveyor of the law to Moses. Knowing this tradition makes Hebrews 2:2 more understandable: *For if the message declared through angels was valid ...* Therefore, if the law, which was declared via angels, merits the audience's reverence, how much more should they be in awe of the message given by the Son himself, validated with miracles and gifts of the Holy Spirit!

The Scriptures express no doubt about the existence or the importance of angels and spiritual experiences. From this brief survey, we understand angels to be powerful beings at the service of God. But because they are powerful beings, biblical authors call for caution: spirits should be tested to see whether they are from God (1 John 4:1). In telling of his own spiritual experience in 2 Corinthians 12:1-10, Paul does not boast of his visions, but only of God's grace. As the story in Genesis 6 relates, when angels go bad, they have their own power and can create chaos. Not every spiritual being is subject to God's will and purposes. So the author of Hebrews wants to ensure that the audience understands the true hierarchy and relationship between God, the angels, and God's Son. God's angels are ministering spirits, working for our salvation under the direction of the Son, who has revealed God's Spirit to the world.

68   Hebrews 1:5–2:4

THE TEXT IN THE LIFE OF THE CHURCH

Methods of Interpreting the Scriptures

The biblical passages cited one after the other by the preacher in this first chapter of Hebrews throw light on the variety of ways that Christians have used Scripture *[see the section on midrash in Rhetorical Habits of the Author, p. 249; The Role and Use of the Jewish Scriptures by Early Christians, p. 251]*. Ancient Jews and Jewish Christians often used Scripture as prooftexts. In this case, the author of Hebrews read and interpreted biblical passages in light of what was understood to be the significance of the life, death, and resurrection of Jesus.

Past generations used Scriptures like Psalms 2 and 110 in a variety of settings and derived the meaning of the Scripture from the context in which it was used. The traditional spiritual "O Mary Don't You Weep" is illustrative:

> O Mary, don't you weep, don't you mourn,
> O Mary, don't you weep, don't you mourn,
> Pharaoh's army got drown-ded,
> O Mary, don't you weep.

The song seems to refer to the Mary of Bethany. It deftly associates Jesus' raising Lazarus in John 11 with the triumph of Moses over Pharoah in Exodus. Dwight Allan Callahan states, "Here the Exodus, God's definitive deliverance in the Old Testament, signifies the Resurrection, God's definitive deliverance in the New. The figure of Jesus, unmentioned but ever present, correlates across the Old and New Testaments these two mighty acts of God, Exodus as escape from the death of bondage and Resurrection as escape from the bondage of death" (190). In the context of American chattel slavery, slavery and the desire for freedom from bondage gave Black people enslaved in the United States insight into the connections between these passages in ways nearly unthinkable to the enslavers.

This differs from the historical-critical approach that biblical scholars use to derive the original meaning from a scriptural text. The historical-critical method tends to begin with the assumption that the text has one meaning, the meaning assigned to it by the author or authors. The scholar's job is to determine that meaning. This requires an attempt at objectivity toward the text that leaves aside personal and social contexts. The consideration of the original context and social location of the author is important in determining the meaning of the text. In this commentary, we want to know

Hebrews 1:5–2:4

why the original author wrote the text, and we think it will help us understand the text if we know those things about the text.

However, even if we can derive the original meaning from a text, sometimes it does not satisfy a spiritual need that we currently have. Just as the lives of the author of Hebrews and the congregation were different from the lives of the psalmists, so our twenty-first-century lives are vastly different from those in the first century, when Hebrews was written. We bring different questions and needs to the text. If we use Scripture from a place of love and longing and not polemic, can we go wrong?

Hebrews 2:5-18

Jesus the Son Is a Human Being, Like Us in All Things

PREVIEW

The COVID-19 pandemic led to many existential crises. Cut off from friends, family, work, and other activities, thousands if not hundreds of thousands of people across the globe began to wonder what was meaningful in life and asked, "Why are we here? What does it mean to be human?" To answer those questions, some people reevaluated their priorities in life; others started gardens, learned new skills, or completed old craft projects that had been left undone in their attics for years.

Experiencing difficulties in life often brings on an existential crisis. In this passage, we learn that these Hebrews are also facing tests (2:18). They, too, might be asking these questions. The pastor, after beginning the sermon in such a lofty and even distant way, now "brings it home" to the congregation. Angels still serve as a comparator. But the human condition, which the congregation knows so well, now enters the scene. The Son, Jesus, the one who is greater than any angel, was human too. Jesus understands the mystery and the vagaries of the human condition.

The pastor explains what it means for the Hebrews that the divine Son, who is greater than the angels, became the human Jesus.

Jesus as the Son is willing to make himself lower than the angels to serve as high priest and make the sacrifice, a crucial aspect of this section. The interplay between his role as high priest and the suffering and death he takes on *as* high priest continues to be an important concept as we move through the text, and it is key to understanding Hebrews. All this was made possible because Jesus became fully human, thereby alleviating the suffering and death of other humans.

True to form, the author uses another passage from Scripture, Psalm 8. In its original setting, this psalm is a commentary on Genesis 1:26-28, "Let us make humankind in our image, according to our likeness," which raises existential questions regarding the place of humans within God's creation. In Hebrews, the author uses the psalm to focus on Jesus and his humanness.

As our author lays it out, the congregation begins to see that a fully human Jesus has suffered and through that suffering was perfected, or made complete, so that he could serve as the pioneer of salvation and free them and the rest of humanity from *the power of death* and *the fear of death* (2:14-15). Through his testing, he now helps those who are being tested.

Hebrews 1 emphasizes the close relation of the Son to the Father and his exalted status above the angels. The writer now names the Son as *Jesus* and begins to flesh out some of the main themes that surface throughout the text: suffering, perfection, Jesus as high priest and sacrifice.

OUTLINE

Psalm 8 as a Witness to Jesus' Glory, Honor, and Humanity, 2:5-8
Through His Suffering, Jesus Leads Us to Glory, 2:9-10
By Sharing in Our Humanity, Jesus Destroys the Power of Death, 2:11-18

EXPLANATORY NOTES

Psalm 8 as a Witness to Jesus' Glory, Honor, and Humanity 2:5-8

The first chapter insists that the message declared by the Lord requires greater attention than the message declared through angels. The author quotes a Scripture, then provides an interpretation that moves the argument forward. This section follows the same pattern. Finally, the author identifies *Jesus* as the referent of the Scripture passage and names him as the *pioneer* of salvation through his willingness to become flesh and blood, serve as high priest, and make a sacrifice (of himself) on behalf of everyone.

Picking up the theme from 1:2, *In these last days he has spoken to us by a Son,* our author continues to speak about a world that is something other than what the audience understands as current existence. Even though *these last days* are here, a *world* is still to come (2:5). The assurance about this world is that authority over it lies not with the angels, but with a greater power. We saw this in the quotation of Psalm 110:1 in Hebrews 1:13. Now, after the "interruption" of 2:1-4, the author reaffirms that statement using Psalm 8, another psalm in which *feet* feature prominently:

> What are human beings that you are mindful of them,
>   mortals that you care for them?
> Yet you have made them a little lower than God,
>   and crowned them with glory and honor.
> You have given them dominion over the works of your hands;
>   you have put all thing under their feet. (Ps 8:4-6)

Psalm 8 praises the majesty of God and God's creation, providing a small commentary on the creation story of Genesis 1:26-28: "Let us make humankind in our image, according to our likeness; and let them have dominion over the fish of the sea, and over the birds of the air, and over the cattle, and over all the wild animals of the earth, and over every creeping thing that creeps upon the earth." The psalm expresses a sense of wonder that even though humans are lower than God, God has chosen to be "mindful of them" (8:4) and has "given them dominion over the works of your [God's] hands (8:6). Like the Genesis text, the Hebrew version of the psalm uses the word "Elohim," one of many words for "God." Humans, male and female, created in God's own image, are only a little lower than Elohim, the divine.

Now the author of Hebrews reuses the psalm to say something about Jesus, not all of humanity. Not just enemies are used as a footstool (Ps 110:1, quoted in Heb 1:13); all of creation is now subject under the feet of Jesus, a vivid example illustrating the authority and exaltation of Jesus the Son. Since our author uses the Septuagint (LXX) translation of Psalm 8, with the word "angels" for the Hebrew Elohim, Hebrews 2:6-8 reads:

> *What are human beings that you are mindful of them,*
>   *or mortals, that you care for them?*
> *You have made them for a little while lower than the angels;*

you have crowned them with glory and honor,
subjecting all things under their feet.

It may be more difficult to see Jesus as the referent to this psalm in a modern inclusive translation. Ordinarily, inclusive translations do a wonderful job of making the text available to everyone. In this instance, however, the translation obscures the double meaning that the author of Hebrews develops. The original psalm is a meditation on how God has given humans, also called "son of man" (Ps 8:5 LXX), control over creation even though they are lower than the angels. When the psalm was translated into Greek, the words *anthrōpos* and *huios* were used. Both words are singular nouns, meaning "human" or "man" and "son," respectively. As Eisenbaum notes "The NRSV's attempt at gender inclusion masks the Christological connection" (2017:465). So if we were not concerned about inclusivity, the psalm should be translated grammatically this way: *What is man that you are mindful of him or the son of man that you attend to him? . . . You have made him for a little while lower than the angels.* The author of Hebrews uses the singular nouns to reinterpret their original meaning from a collective "humankind" to a singular Jesus. In this way, the Hebrews author reveals to the audience how they can see Jesus in this psalm, even though they may not yet be able to see the full picture of how everything is subjected to him.

Through His Suffering, Jesus Leads Us to Glory 2:9-10

The author now mentions Jesus for the first time. The previous section has focused on the exaltation and glorification of the Son, now identified as Jesus; this section compels the reader to focus on how Jesus has been perfected through *suffering*, a very human experience. This passage also sets up Jesus as the pattern for humans to follow. He is called the *pioneer* in verse 10. The Greek word *archēgos* has many different meanings. It can mean the founder of a nation or city, a leader, a scout of an army, or even an instigator of trouble! The meaning of the word depends on its context. In Hebrews, the immediate context in verse 10 is its combination with another closely related word, *agagontēs*, which means "leading." The NRSV offers the relevant text this way: *in bringing [leading] many children to glory, [God] should make the pioneer of their salvation perfect through sufferings* (2:10). Earlier translations, like the KJV, use *captain* instead of *pioneer*; some other versions use *author*. Either way, the important aspect is that Jesus, whether as leader, founder, captain, or author, leads or brings along the rest of humanity. And he is doing it by

74 Hebrews 2:5-18

means of his own suffering, which leads to his perfection. In leading, he provides the example for all humanity.

Verses 9 and 10 introduce the longer section in 2:11-18, which focuses more on Jesus' connection to the rest of humanity. First, though, the author needs to specify how Jesus established the human connection. To do this, Jesus had to make himself lower than the angels *for a little while* (2:9). The Greek word translated "for a little while" can have two different meanings: either temporal or degree. In the "original" psalm (Ps 8:5 LXX), the meaning is by degree (You [God] lowered him [man/son of man] a little lower than the angels). But most scholars agree that our author is using it here in a temporal sense: this Son was with God and creating *the worlds* (Heb 1:2); *was made lower* for a time to take on *the suffering of death* (not just any suffering!) *so that . . . he might taste death for everyone* (2:9; cf. Matt 16:28); then was *exalted* (Heb 7:26) to the right hand of God, enthroned, and *crowned with glory* (1:3, 8, 13; 2:9).

The word *taste* gives us a graphic depiction of Jesus' encounter with death. Tasting something entails ingesting it and in some way taking on the aspect of the thing tasted. That old expression "You are what you eat" comes to mind. Jesus suffered death. But through becoming death, he overcame it and had power over it. Taste is also a physical experience. It is the first step toward providing the body with nourishment; but if food does not taste good, we do not want to eat it. Jesus "ate" death anyway. Taste can also be intimate: if you focus on taste, you are experiencing not just the food but also the components of the food. The French word *terroir* describes this. The word is used to describe how wine takes on the taste of the environment where the grapes grew. Wine from the same variety of grapes can taste different when grown in France or in California; the *terroir*, the entire environment behind the grapes, makes the difference. Thus, by tasting death, Jesus not only became human; he also took on the full sense of humanness, the *terroir* of humanity.

The author does not stop there, however. Jesus has done this not just for himself but on behalf of all humanity. His death is *for everyone*. The phrases *for all* (2:9) and "for us" appear frequently in creeds or faith statements about Jesus in the New Testament. Paul states that "Christ died for us" (Rom 5:8) and that God "gave him [his own Son] up for all of us" (8:32). This theme quickly resurfaces at the end of the chapter as the author states that *Jesus free[s] those who all their lives were held in slavery by the fear of death* (Heb 2:15). The author repeats it throughout Hebrews (5:9; 7:27; 9:12, 28; 10:10, 20). The work of Jesus Christ was on behalf of all humanity.

Hebrews 2:5-18

But the prerequisite for his ability to effect salvation for others is Jesus' humanity. The author makes it clear that Jesus' suffering was the way that many are brought to glory: it was *fitting that God . . . should make the pioneer of their salvation perfect through sufferings* (2:10). This verse requires unpacking: Why is perfection necessary? Why is suffering necessary? Why is it "fitting"? Why does the author call Jesus a pioneer here, and what does that imply?

Perfection is a key theme in Hebrews *[Perfection in Greco-Roman and Jewish Thought, p. 244]*. It appears several times throughout the text (see also 5:9; 6:1; 7:11; 9:9; 10:1, 14; 11:40; 12:23). The Greek word *teleioō* means "to complete" or "bring to an end," as well as "to make perfect." It was applied to physical, moral, philosophical, and religious contexts throughout the Greco-Roman world (Peterson: 46). The exact meaning of the word depends on its context. In this passage, we see that to become perfect—to become qualified to lead his fellow humans to glory—Christ himself had to go through the process of becoming perfect. To become perfected, suffering must occur (see also 5:8-10; 7:28; 10:14; 12:2). We should not miss this close connection between suffering and the achievement of glory and perfection, both for Jesus and for *many children* (2:10). It establishes the argument for the rest of the text. Attridge describes Hebrews 2:9 as "one of the most characteristic and complex motifs of the text" (83). God perfects the agent of salvation (Jesus) through suffering; the perfection allows him to become the high priest (5:9; 7:28) and offer a sacrifice—himself—in the more perfect (heavenly) tabernacle (9:11-12). In other words, Jesus' being perfected happens through a process of human experience that prepares him for his office as heavenly high priest and intercessor for humanity in the presence of God. Jesus becomes high priest because of his human historical experience of suffering. So if this is how humans are also perfected and led to glory, it is fitting "that God allow the agent of salvation to suffer" (Attridge: 78).

Perfection thus communicates how the people of God can move out of a life of exile, a life of wandering in the desert, and into a life of glory. David Peterson says that Jesus' "life of obedience, . . . sacrificial death[,] and heavenly exaltation are the means by which he was perfected. Believers in turn are perfected by the very actions and accomplishments that perfect Christ" (186). The author of Hebrews states that it is God's purpose to have Jesus, the Son, open the way so that all humanity, called *children* in the NRSV (Gk. = *sons*) can come freely into God's presence.

76   Hebrews 2:5-18

Because of Jesus' actions and subsequent perfection, human beings now share in his relationship with God. They, too, are children of God. The pattern of Christ's life applies to others. Those who have attained perfection have reached a finished or completed state and now reside in glory with Christ.

In summary, Jesus is now identified as the Son from Hebrews 1. He was made *lower than the angels* to become an ordinary human so that he could taste death on behalf of all humanity. As the *pioneer* (leader/founder), he was made perfect through sufferings as an example. In this way, the author establishes the deep connection between Jesus and the rest of humanity: they are all children of God. The author does all this through an interpretation of Psalm 8 and introduces the recurring themes of perfection, suffering, and sacrifice.

By Sharing in Our Humanity, Jesus Destroys the Power of Death 2:11-18

Only through his humanness can Jesus, the exalted Son of chapter 1, fully experience suffering. But through that suffering he is made perfect and becomes the pioneer of salvation (2:10). The Son, now enthroned next to God's throne (1:8, 13), was earlier made lower than the angels in order to *taste death for everyone* (2:9). Humanity, suffering, and perfection combine to form the paradox that is the heart of the message.

Not surprisingly, our author opens this section with another collection of Scriptures, from Psalm 22 and Isaiah 8:17-18, to emphasize the suffering experienced by Jesus. The gospel writers use Psalm 22 to express Jesus' pain and sense of desertion in the passion story, as well as the experience of being mocked (Matt 27:27-54// Mark 15:24-34//Luke 23:32-49//John 19:17-37). It begins as an anguished cry of pain at abandonment by God (Ps 22:1). The psalm ends in praise that God "did not despise or abhor the affliction of the afflicted" (22:24). In somewhat of a twist, our author uses this portion of the psalm to emphasize the good news brought about by the suffering of Jesus: *I will proclaim [tell] your name to my brothers and sisters, in the midst of the congregation I will praise you* (Heb 2:12//Ps 22:22). Putting the words of the psalm into the voice of Jesus, the author proclaims God's name to all God's children. Surely the paradox is not lost on the congregation: a psalm that contains anguished words of suffering is also good news.

The final "words" of Scripture that Jesus speaks, *Here am I and the children whom God has given me* (Heb 2:13//Isa 8:17-18), announce the arrival of the children of God at the place of glory, where Hebrews 2:10 has started. In anticipation of future glory, Jesus announces that he has led his siblings to glory. It is a promise for the future and a reminder that Jesus is indeed the one who can bring God's children to glory. These words illustrate the rewards of faith and faithfulness, especially in grim times, that the author of Hebrews further develops in later chapters (2:17; 3:1-6, 19; 4:2; 11:1-39).

Note the emphasis on kinship throughout this passage. In addition to using nuclear-family language like "parent" and "child," our author also uses extended family phrases like *descendants of Abraham* (2:16). We know from other Christian texts that several writers considered themselves the spiritual children of Abraham and heirs to the promises (Luke 1:55; John 8:33; Rom 4:1-25; Gal 3:7). Our author comes back to Abraham in Hebrews 7; for now, our author uses "the children of Abraham" as a way of concluding that the work done by Jesus, as a human, was for humans. Jesus, in all his humanity, is the *one who sanctifies* (2:11). Those sanctified are the children of Abraham: they have God as the same parent and are the siblings with whom Jesus shares flesh and blood.

After establishing Jesus' humanity and kinship with the audience, our author in verses 14-15 explains the impact of Jesus' humanness: by facing death as a human, Jesus has conquered it *so that through his death he might destroy the one who has the power of death, that is, the devil, and free those who all their lives were held in slavery by the fear of death*. The writer does not explain exactly how Jesus' death liberates from fear, so we need to work that out ourselves. One might say that for anyone to be fully human, as Jesus has demonstrated, one must die. One cannot go through life avoiding death. The Hebrews author says such a *fear of death* amounts to being *held in slavery* (2:15). Instead, Jesus has gone through his human life looking death squarely in the face and living a fully human life as a result. His death is presented as voluntary, fearless, and faithful to God. By sharing our flesh and blood, he is our leader in how to live a fully human life. Paradoxically, leading a fully human life ushers humans into the divine presence. Because Jesus subjected himself to humanness, he gave others access to God's presence. Death holds no fear for us because it means coming fully into God's presence.

Believing that Jesus was fully human is not a new idea unique to the author of Hebrews. What is unique is the emphasis on his role as *high priest*, which the author introduces for the first time in 2:17. We know from the prologue that the writer is interested in the priestly role of the Son (1:1-3), which states that the Son has *made purification*

78   Hebrews 2:5-18

for sins. In this passage, the priestly role is further fleshed out. The human Jesus, as high priest, has made a sacrifice of atonement for the sins of the people. The high priest is responsible for overseeing the sacrificial system, and the high priest himself made a sacrifice once a year on the Day of Atonement. Two aspects of this priestly ministry are mentioned in these verses. First, he is *like* humans in every respect. The second is that he has made *a sacrifice of atonement for the sins of the people* (2:17). The theme of Jesus' sacrifice, mentioned only briefly here and in 1:3, anticipates what is coming in Hebrews 5–10. This anticipation is characteristic of the writing style of Hebrews. Elsewhere in the text, we find that one of the major qualifications of a priest is that he must understand human weakness from personal experience so that he can deal gently with the ignorant and wayward (5:2). Jesus inhabits the role of the high priest throughout Hebrews: a priest must make an offering for the sins of the people (5:3) by entering into the inner shrine on behalf of everyone (6:20), making intercession for them (7:25), and appearing in God's presence on our behalf (9:24).

But what does a "sacrifice of atonement" really mean *[Atonement, p. 231]*? In Greek, this word *hilaskomai* means "to expiate, atone, or make amends for sins." The ritual of sacrifice recorded in Leviticus 16 requires the high priest to atone, or make amends, for his own sins and that of the people by taking the blood of a bull and a goat as the sacrifice and sending a second live goat out into the wilderness (symbolically carrying their sins into oblivion). For the people, it is "a sabbath of complete rest" (Lev 16:31). Perry Yoder points out that the Hebrew word *kipper* behind the Greek implies "the *process* whereby a person makes amends," not the result (288). Based on the actions laid out in Leviticus 16, Yoder suggests that the best translation for *kipper* should be "cleanse" or "purify" (289). Our author gives the role of high priest who makes atonement (cleanses/purifies) to Jesus. Note again that this role was laid out in Hebrews 1:3: only after *he had made purification for sins [did the Son sit] down at the right hand of the Majesty on high.* He is also what is sacrificed. In Leviticus, the Day of Atonement is an annual Sabbath for the people. The author of Hebrews continues this understanding. Later in the text, our author speaks of *rest* as an aspect of the salvation available through obedience (see Heb 4:1-11).

Through the sacrifice of Jesus (the high priest), done on behalf of the people of God, the Sabbath (or rest) is available for the people. Thus 2:18 is a fitting summary to this difficult passage: *Because he himself was tested by what he suffered, he is able to help those who are being tested.* As

Hebrews 2:5-18

David DeSilva states, "Suffering as the path to perfection is fitting for the Son, the champion or pioneer, because it is the path that lies ahead of the many sons and daughters. It was therefore suitable for the Son to share fully, and triumph, in the human condition of frailty, vulnerability, and mortality in which all the sons and daughters share" (114). God sent Jesus to share in our condition because God recognized the suffering that is an inescapable aspect of our humanity.

THE TEXT IN BIBLICAL CONTEXT

Understanding Texts through Shared Scriptures

Psalm 8

By uncovering how the New Testament authors use their shared Scripture, we can learn something about the specific message of each text. This section of Hebrews is a good case in point. Other early Jewish Christians used Psalm 8 in connection with Jesus as well. In Matthew's Gospel, Jesus uses another portion of this psalm (8:2) to answer criticism from the Pharisees ("Out of the mouths of infants and nursing babies you have prepared praise for yourself," Matt 21:16). In his discussion of the resurrection of the dead in 1 Corinthians 15, and along with Hebrews, Paul uses the same combination of Psalms 110 and 8. He states, "For he must reign until he has put all his enemies under his feet" (1 Cor 15:25, citing Ps 110:1). Just two verses later, in 1 Corinthians 15:27, Paul continues, "For God has put all things in subjection under his feet," quoting Psalm 8:6. The author of Ephesians 1:20-22 also uses these same two passages in a discussion regarding the heavenly reign of Christ. Thus Hebrews is probably drawing on a shared practice of using specific texts to comment on the meaning of the life, death, and exaltation of Jesus Christ.

Hebrews 2:5-7 is much like Philippians 2:5-11, considered an early "hymn" to Christ. Although both contain a similar message about Jesus, the passage in Hebrews is clearly quoting Psalm 8, and the passage in Philippians is not.

Philippians	Hebrews
Christ became "human" (2:7),	*[He] was made lower than the angels* (2:9//Ps 8:4),
"humbled himself" (2:8), and	*now crowned with glory and honor* (2:9// Ps 8:5)
was "obedient to the point of death" (2:8).	*because of the suffering of death* (2:9).

80 Hebrews 2:5-18

Even though the sequence is different, we see similarities in how the two authors think of Jesus Christ. The contexts of the affirmations are different. Paul uses this early Christian hymn to remind the Jewish Christians in Philippi of the spirit of humility and submission to God that should characterize the relationship of Jesus followers to one another. In Hebrews, this psalm confirms Jesus' humanness.

Psalm 22

The gospel writers (cf. esp. Matt 27:46//Mark 15:34) use the "suffering servant" aspects of Psalm 22 in the passion story. "My God, my God, why have you forsaken me?" directly quotes Psalm 22:1. They pick up other aspects of Psalm 22 as well: dividing up the garments, casting lots, piercing the hands and feet, and great thirst. But that seems to be background information for our author of Hebrews. By quoting Psalm 22:22, *I will proclaim your name to my brothers and sisters* (Heb 2:12), our author focuses on a message of strength and endurance despite the suffering.

Understanding Texts through Shared Themes

Christ's Suffering Was for All

Another theme explored in this passage and throughout Hebrews is that Jesus' life, suffering, and death were for everyone. Many verses in the New Testament affirm that what Christ did was for all, for many. In Mark's report of the Last Supper, Jesus says of the cup he offered them, "This is my blood of the covenant, which is poured out for many" (14:24). In Luke 22:19, both the broken bread of his body and the cup poured out are for "you" (plural). In John 6:51, Jesus says, "The bread that I will give for the life of the world is my flesh." Similar language is in 1 Corinthians 11:24.

Vicarious Suffering

Closely related is the theme of vicarious suffering. One of the basic "Christian" confessions is that "Christ died for our sins" (Rom 5:6, 8; 1 Cor 15:3; Gal 1:4). Early Jesus followers used the suffering servant songs, especially Isaiah 53:4-5, to express their understanding:

> Surely he has borne our infirmities
> and carried our diseases;
> yet we accounted him stricken,
> struck down by God, and afflicted.
> But he was wounded for our transgressions,

Hebrews 2:5-18

crushed for our iniquities;
upon him was the punishment that made us whole,
and by his bruises we are healed.

The idea was not new to believers: it also shows up in other ancient Jewish texts. For example, in 4 Maccabees, an apocryphal book in some versions of the Septuagint and continuing as a part of Orthodox Scriptures, we find Eleazar the priest, his wife, and their seven sons who were martyrs under the persecution of Antiochus IV in the second century BCE. The writer affirms the meaning of the entire family's suffering: "They became, as it were, a ransom for the sin of the nation. And through the blood of those pious people and the propitiation of their death, divine Providence preserved Israel, though before it had been afflicted" (4 Macc 17:21-22 NETS). The author of Hebrews is aware of this writing. Early Anabaptists followed suit since they read and valued Maccabean literature, yet with discretion. We will examine this further in our discussion of Hebrews 11 and 12:1-3.

THE TEXT IN THE LIFE OF THE CHURCH

The Nature of Jesus

Hebrews bears witness to the variety of expressions for Jesus that were used by early Jesus followers. So far, our homilist has declared that Jesus is the Son, *appointed heir of all things* (1:2), a *reflection of God's glory and the exact imprint of God's very being* (1:3). He was *made a little lower than the angels* (2:7, 9), but also *shares flesh and blood* (2:14) with his brothers and sisters. He is the *high priest in the service of God, to make a sacrifice of atonement for the sins of the people* (2:17). Our author is bringing together a set of understandings about Jesus, creating or following a Christology composed out of what were separate lines of thought [*Christology in Hebrews, p. 235*].

In the second century and later, those who professed Jesus as Christ hotly debated the nature of Jesus. Was he completely divine and only *seemed* to have a body (the central conviction of Docetism, from the Greek word *dokeō*, "to seem/appear")? Did he remain fully human but was adopted as the Son of God at baptism (Adoptionism)? Did the divine Christ enter the body of Jesus at baptism and leave it right before his death on the cross (Separationism)? These types of thinking about Jesus sometimes fall under the heading of "Gnosticism" [*Gnosticism, p. 237*]. Early Jesus followers, including Gnostics, found evidence for these Christologies, and many other versions of them, in the writings of Paul and in the Gospels. If one reads the biblical manuscripts closely enough, one can find ambiguity about the nature of Jesus even within the same text. Sometimes scribes, the people (men and women!) who copied the texts from one manuscript to another, changed the text to fit their own idea of what the nature of Jesus really was (Ehrman: 3–4).

During the first several hundred years of what we now call Christianity, nothing was settled in thinking about Jesus. Although we can construct a narrative that makes it look as though there were a solid line of thinking from Paul to the Gospels and up through the early Middle Ages, counting everything else as a perversion of that, in reality there was a wide variety of thinking about the nature of Jesus. The large number of New Testament manuscripts (well over five thousand!) are evidence of that *[Textual Variants, p. 260]*. The range of thinking about Jesus naturally led to variety in the manuscripts reflecting that thinking. This fact adds to the miraculous nature of the text itself: it not only speaks truth about God and Jesus; it also bears witness to the nuances among early Jewish Christians as they discovered, wrote, and copied those truths.

The manuscripts of Hebrews are a case in point. One important textual variant occurs in 2:9, an example that illustrates the possibility of a scribe modifying the text to remove any misunderstanding about the nature of Jesus at his death. Almost all manuscripts say that Jesus was *made lower than the angels . . . so that by the grace of God he might taste death for everyone* (emph. added here and next). However, two manuscripts (and some citations from church fathers) say *made lower than the angels . . . so that apart from God he might taste death for everyone* (thus in a typical Bible, a footnote indicates that some "ancient authorities" read *apart from God*). Bart Ehrman argues compellingly that *apart from God* is the original and is therefore the better reading (171–76). His argument relies on the contents and subject of Hebrews itself (as opposed to the overwhelming manuscript evidence in favor of *by the grace of God*). In this passage the author is emphasizing Jesus' fully human nature. He left the divine realm and was made lower than the angels so he could taste death, as every other human does. His separation from the divine realm combined with his fully human nature made his sacrifice work. The original text *apart from God* underscores the full humanity of Jesus to make this point. However, in the second and early third centuries, when the debate about Jesus' nature was raging, *apart from God* could be distasteful to those arguing for what became the orthodox understanding of Jesus: that he was fully human *and* fully divine, from birth to death. To remove opportunities for wayward interpretations, scribes modified the text to match the developing orthodox sense.

Perfection through Suffering

As members of Anabaptist congregations who regularly take the towel and the basin (John 13:1-20) to enact our belief that we should live a life of servanthood, we believe part of our obligation as followers of Jesus is to work to end the suffering of women, children, people of color, and other historically marginalized groups who suffer physical and mental trauma because of personal or systemic violence. But we also live in a culture that sees little value in personal sacrifice. In fact, our culture promotes ease and comfort in all aspects of life. We have gadgets that heat our cars before we get inside them in the winter and loud leaf blowers that use gas and create noise pollution just so we don't have to use our arms to rake leaves. Our culture routinely disregards notions of sacrifice to obtain personal goals.

But suffering is a reminder of our humanity. Even the most privileged suffer in some way, if only in the experience of death. Hebrews declares that suffering made Jesus a complete, mature human being. Without experiencing humanity in its fullest and most perfect state, Jesus would not have been equipped to minister to others. This understanding of Jesus' suffering contrasts with certain theories of atonement assuming that an angry God required a bloody sacrifice to appease God's anger toward sinful humanity (e.g., Anselm) [Atonement, p. 231]. Instead, we see here that for Jesus, suffering was an essential factor in being a fully human being and thus able to relate positively with and minister to other humans.

Jesus has walked in our shoes. Suffering and sacrifice that require giving up our own selves to understand someone else equips us to reach out and minister to others. Full maturity depends on integrating self-sacrifice into our faith and our trust in God.

Hebrews 3:1–4:13

The Faithful Are to Enter into Rest

PREVIEW

In Hebrews 2, Jesus was "demoted" to earthling status and became our pioneer. The existential crisis about what it means to be human was resolved by giving Jesus as an example of a well-lived human life. Having lived, suffered, and tasted death as a human, he now is *crowned with glory and honor* (2:9). But before the congregation gets comfortable in thinking that this sermon is only a teaching about the nature of Jesus and what it means to be human, they discover that they themselves are now the subjects of the homilist's words. In chapters 3–4, the audience receives a heavenly calling: Jesus has made humanness meaningful. This allows the homilist to challenge them to become *holy partners in a heavenly calling [and] consider that Jesus ... was faithful* (3:1-2). Jesus has provided the example of a well-lived human life. Now the congregation must follow with their own faithful life, the end of which is a promise of heavenly rest. Before that, though, lies a life of responsibility and faith. Jesus has responded and now sits at God's right hand. Will they?

Employing the same literary and rhetorical strategies established at the beginning of the text, the author uses yet another biblical passage as an illustration, this time Psalm 95. The homilist uses the Israelite experience in the wilderness to elaborate on the importance of remaining *faithful* (Gk. *pistos*, 3:2) during difficult times and the resulting *promise of ... rest* (Gk. *katapausis*, 4:1) for those who are

Hebrews 3:1–4:13

faithful to God. The author continues to use *synkrisis* (comparison) and to rely on biblical interpretation. We remember that *synkrisis* works to build up the subject and does not necessarily denigrate the comparator: the author uses both Moses and the Israelites as comparators to elevate Jesus and the audience. This section closes with an intriguing exhortation about the word of God and the inevitability that each person must give a personal account (or word) to God.

This passage is often described as an "interlude" because it connects the themes from the first two chapters (Jesus the Son, as figure par excellence) to the remainder of the text (Jesus as high priest and savior of the faithful people of God).

OUTLINE

Jesus Compared to Moses, 3:1-6
The Holy Spirit Is Speaking Today, 3:7-11
Exhortation to the Audience, 3:12-19
The Rewards of Faithfulness, 4:1-11
Accountability to the Word of the Living God, 4:12-13

EXPLANATORY NOTES

Jesus Compared to Moses 3:1-6

The author now asks the congregation to consider Jesus in light of Moses rather than the angels. Like the angels, Moses was a looming figure in antiquity. He led the Israelites out of Egypt, delivered the commandments to them, started them on their journey to the Promised Land, and interceded with God on their behalf. His faithfulness rivaled that of Abraham, and he had direct access to God on several occasions. Our author refers to two of these moments in this passage. First, our author refers directly to Numbers 12: God confronts Miriam and Aaron after they "spoke against Moses because of the Cushite woman" (12:1). In what can only be described as a scene of sibling rivalry, they ask, "Has the LORD spoken only through Moses? Has he not spoken through us also?" (12:2). God quickly corrects them with the response: "I the LORD make myself known to them [prophets] in visions. . . . Not so with my servant Moses; he is entrusted with all my house. With him I speak face to face—clearly, not in riddles" (12:6-8). In other words, God is saying that Moses is special, so Miriam and Aaron need to remember their more limited roles.

Our author uses the language from this passage in Numbers to talk about Jesus in light of Moses. The author focuses on the use of the Greek word *therapōn* for the word "servant" in the Septuagint of

86   Hebrews 3:1–4:13

Numbers 12:7-8 *[The Septuagint in Hebrews, p. 252]*. The English word *therapy* derives from this word. In antiquity, this term often indicated the healing service of a priest in a temple setting, especially those associated with Asclepius, the Greek god of healing (cf. Lev. 14). Moses is designated a servant-healer in *God's house* (Heb 3:5). Although Aaron was technically the priest for Israel, Moses served the priestly function of advocate and intercessor with God for the people. Moses was the servant par excellence: no intermediary was between God and him. He spoke to God directly for the entire house of God, all the Israelites.

This relationship between Moses and God, however, is that of servant and master. In this role, Moses is *to testify to the things that would be spoken later* (3:5). For our author, those later things are Jesus and his salvific and priestly role. Yet Jesus assumes these roles not as a servant of the house but as a son. Jesus' role as a son who is also servant (therapist), savior, and priest exceeds the roles given to Moses by God. Moses was *faithful in all God's house as a servant. . . . Christ . . . was faithful over God's house as a son* (3:5-6, emph. added).

Who or what is the house, according to the homilist? Is it the audience, or at least those in the audience who are confident and bold? Perhaps more than any other writing in the New Testament, Hebrews insists on the urgency of perseverance in living a faithful life. On several occasions our author exhorts the audience to hold fast to boldness or confidence (3:14; 4:14; 6:18; 10:23). Those who are confident and bold become the actual structure of God's house, the foundation, the bricks, and the mortar—the solid structure. Visualizing those who have remained confident as the house itself gives us a good image of how our author expects the audience to be interrelated and connected. A solidly built house with Jesus over it will not fall.

The Holy Spirit Is Speaking Today 3:7-11

Our author continues: they will be God's house as long as they *hold firm the confidence and the pride that belong to hope* (3:6). Our author then speaks to the audience through the words of Psalm 95:7-11, in which the psalmist begs the Israelites not to *harden your hearts* (Heb 3:8, quoting Ps 95:8). Originally, the psalm appealed to a generation of Israelites living hundreds of years after those who fled Egypt, urging them not to be like the desert generation, who hardened their hearts and therefore did not enter the Promised Land. Behind the psalm are previous events described in Exodus 17 and Numbers 12 and 14, in which Moses plays an intercessory role. In these passages,

Hebrews 3:1–4:13

the Israelites complain about the lack of water (Exod 17:1-7), Aaron and Miriam conspire against Moses (Num 12), and the people threaten to replace Moses with another "captain" (14:1-4). In these stories, God's anger is mollified by Moses, who intercedes sometimes for the Israelites in general and sometimes specifically for Aaron and Miriam, lessening the consequences of their unfaithful behavior. In Hebrews, the psalm becomes a warning to *hold fast/firm* (3:6, 14; 4:14). Through the voice of the psalmist, our homilist warns the worshipers not to harden their hearts. He reminds them of the Israelites' rebellion in the desert at Massah and Meribah, where they "quarreled and tested the LORD" because they had no water (Exod 17:1-7). The LXX version of the psalm has translated these place names as "rebellion" and "testing," playing on their Hebrew roots. The psalm correctly picks up the accusation of the original texts when the Israelites complained, put God to the test, and finally rebelled when they should have entered the Promised Land.

Psalm 95 begins as a hymn of praise to the power of God, then becomes an invitation to worship and hear God's voice. But it moves quickly to words of warning about the consequences of unfaithful behavior. Its meaning applies equally to those who first heard the psalm and the current audience of Hebrews: Don't harden your hearts to the voice of God. Listen. Pay attention! *Take care, brothers and sisters, that none of you may have an evil, unbelieving heart that turns away from the living God* (Heb 3:12).

Exhortation to the Audience 3:12-19

Our author uses an attention-grabbing rhetorical device, taking lines from Psalm 95 (7b-11) that begin with the word *today* (95:7b// Heb 3:7b). Since this is a word spoken by the Holy Spirit, it has contemporary relevance for our author. The "Hebrews" who are receiving these words from their pastor are to hear the words as a challenge in their own context. They too must decide. The contemporary significance of the Scripture is emphasized in 3:13, 15; and 4:7 as the author repeatedly refers back to the opening of this portion of the text: *today.*

Another rhetorical device is the structure of 3:16-19. This paragraph includes a series of questions characteristic of diatribe, used in public settings to morally exhort an audience. Through a series of jabbing questions, the homilist cajoles the audience into confronting their own unfaithful behavior by reminding them of the Israelites' rebellion in the wilderness. Unfaithfulness, sin, disobedience, and rebellion are all highlighted by a series of questions posed to the congregation. Who heard but were *rebellious*? The entire generation (3:16). With whom was God *angry*? Those who *sinned* (3:17). Who did not enter God's *rest*? Those who were *disobedient* (3:18). These questions cajole the audience into faithfulness. God rescued the ancient Israelites from slavery in Egypt and, with the Egyptians in pursuit, helped them pass through the sea. God miraculously provided them with food and water. They received God's law at Mount Sinai. Yet they disbelieved and rebelled when the time came to enter the land! The audience of Hebrews has also experienced God's miracles and wonders in their midst (6:4-6). They, too, have received the promises of God. The point of this illustration should be amply clear to them. Their pastor sees that they are facing a similar moment of decision as God calls them to move forward; this is not the time to be unfaithful.

Last, this section begins (3:12) and ends (3:19) with the use of the Greek word *apistia*. Many English translations, including the NRSV, translate this word as "unbelieving" (3:12) and "unbelief" (3:19). However, that is misleading and incorrectly influences our understanding of the text. The author has already used the root *pistis* in 3:2, describing Jesus as *faithful*, which is much truer to the central meaning of the word, not just in this text but in the Greek language overall. This is key to how the word should be translated in the rest of the passage (and the text as a whole). Jesus (and Moses) are both described as *faithful* to God in the early part of chapter 3, so based on the context alone, the translation should continue with the same basic meaning. This is especially the case here: the author is holding up the faithfulness of Jesus and Moses as examples that the people should follow. Translating *apistia* as "unbelief" moves the focus of the passage to a private or intellectual sphere rather than keeping it in a more public or covenantal sphere. To make sure the audience understands this, the author comments on the *unfaithfulness* (AT) of the ancient Israelites in the wilderness: the consequences of their rebellious, unfaithful nature and actions kept them wandering in the wilderness for forty years, unable to find the *rest* promised them at the outset of their journey.

The author concludes the extended interpretation of Psalm 95 with a series of rhetorical questions that emphasize the responsibility of the Israelites and the contemporary audience. *Who heard and were rebellious* (3:16)? The answer: the past and present house of Israel. The author compares the contemporary congregation with the ancient Israelites who wandered in the desert for forty years, calling their wandering *the rebellion* (3:15).

The homilist uses the words of the psalm to emphasize that faithfulness is a *communal* matter. Keeping the house maintained is a collective responsibility. They are partners with Christ and with each other in that activity. Notice that the homilist tells them to *exhort one another every day* (3:13) and be *partners of Christ* (3:14), participating in Christ's own faithfulness. This act of faith counters the warning that none of them should have a *faithless heart that turns away from the living God* in 3:12. Holding *firm to the end* (3:14) is an act of faithfulness that does require a measure of belief. But more importantly, it requires trust and confidence—in God and in each other. Acting unfaithfully as individuals will yield consequences for the entire group. Building blocks make up the house in 3:6; when one crumbles, the entire house is soon to follow.

The Rewards of Faithfulness 4:1-11

The community our homilist addresses is one that, like the ancient Israelite community, may struggle with obedience. Our homilist uses the promise of God's rest as an incentive to spur the congregation to faithfulness. The promise of rest (Gk. *katapausis*) now becomes a major theme of the text. In 3:11-4:11, the homilist repeats a form of the word eleven times, beginning with its use in Psalm 95 (in Heb 3:11). The word "rest" also signifies the Sabbath, to which the homilist refers in 4:4 with a quotation from Genesis 2:2, *And God rested on the seventh day from all his works.* The two important questions most scholars wrestle with are what our homilist means by "rest" and when the congregation will experience God's rest.

One of the first things to note is how many times the word "rest" is coupled with the verb "come into," or "enter": ten times in 3:18–4:11 (DeSilva: 153). Our author uses different tenses of the verb. Sometimes the verb is in the present (e.g., in 4:3): *For we who have believed enter that rest*; sometimes the verb is in the infinitive form and combined with another verb in the present tense (e.g., in 4:11): *Let us . . . make every effort to enter that rest.* So is the rest now or in the future? Both Attridge and DeSilva understand the rest to be a future reality not yet fully available to the congregation (Attridge: 123; DeSilva: 156). The homilist's use of the word *today* from the psalm in 4:7 does not suggest that the congregation can enter into rest at the present moment. Rather, it is an invitation, or even a command, that *today* is the day to be faithful so that God's rest remains available to them as individuals and as a congregation (DeSilva: 153).

In other words, God's rest is available to the congregation on God's time. And rest itself is an eschatological condition, of which

90 Hebrews 3:1–4:13

the audience has only a glimmer in the present moment. The work required of the congregation is to remain faithful today so they can experience God's rest. While the psalm implies a geographical place (the Promised Land) where the Israelites go to experience rest, Hebrews "calls attention consistently away from any such geographical and nationalistic conception" of rest (DeSilva: 159).

The use of Genesis 2:2 in Hebrews 4:4 suggests that God's rest—the rest our author expects the congregation to seek—is something more than a geographical location. God's rest is more than the rest in the land, as implied in the example of the rebellious Israelites. In fact, our author is clear that the place Joshua reached was not the place of real rest, for *if Joshua had given them rest, God would not speak later about another day* (4:8).

For our author, *rest* is a condition, not a place. It has more to do with a state of being than with a physical location, such as the Promised Land. We might consider Joshua and his rest as a metaphor for the rest that Jesus offers. Not coincidentally, Joshua and Jesus are the same name. Joshua (Yeshua) is the Hebrew version; Jesus is the Greek form of the name. Joshua led the people to a place, but Jesus will lead them to an *eternal* (9:15) condition (4:10). The Promised Land as a metaphor is important for our audience. Regardless of their place of birth or ancestral home, they now find themselves in a "wilderness situation" by virtue of their association with the Jesus movement. The rest for which they should be striving is not a place but the attainment of God's glory. Centuries after Joshua, the psalmist called the Israelites to enter God's rest as the Israelites in the wilderness had failed to do. Now Hebrews provides assurance that the promise of rest is still open to them today. God's rest was provided, beginning on the seventh day of creation, a Sabbath still open for the people of God.

This offer of real heavenly rest can be attained only through obedience. This is key for our author, who expresses that sentiment in negative terms in this passage, using the Greek word *apeitheia* in 3:18 (participle form); 4:6; and 4:11, which the NRSV translates as *disobedience* in 4:6 and 4:11. The English word *apathy* derives from this word. In Greek, it means that someone is without conviction or lacking the will or ability to be convinced. Therefore, they are disobedient. Anyone can enter God's rest since it is still available, but only those who are not disobedient can enter. It is not a purely individual matter. Our author is appealing to the group, using another group as a negative example, and seems to be saying, "Do not emulate the ancient Israelites who were disobedient, who failed to be

Hebrews 3:1–4:13   91

convinced to live faithfully and ended up wandering in the desert. Instead, *today*, you should exhort one another in an effort to remain convinced or obedient so that you can attain the real rest, the real Sabbath, which God will give."

What is rest for our author? Attridge and others suggest that a "precise interpretation" of what our author means is difficult to determine, but we must understand "rest" in relationship to other "related soteriological motifs in Hebrews itself, motifs such as inheritance of the promise, glorification, and perfection" (Attridge: 128). Together, these motifs make up what our author thinks of as salvation: entering into the presence of God and sharing in communion with God. This is not just an individual endeavor: one's ability to achieve rest is directly connected to the group's ability to be *united by faith with those who listened* (4:2). Listening to God's word has been a repeated theme since the beginning chapters of Hebrews (e.g., see 1:1; 2:1). In chapter 4, it is tied directly to the ability not just of individuals to arrive at rest, but also of the group to do so.

This passage provides another piece of evidence that the religious milieu of both the readers and the author of Hebrews includes deep traditions of biblical interpretation based on the Jewish Scriptures. To bring a message to the contemporary audience, the preacher uses allusions from the creation story to interpret the "rest" in Psalm 95. Just as the catena of verses strung together in Hebrews 1 says something about the Son, so here the author collects verses to make a statement about the promises for those who are faithful. Several commentators (e.g., Attridge, L. Johnson, and Boyarin [2016]) consider how the author creates catenae to be closely related to early forms of midrash [*Rhetorical Habits of the Author, p. 249*], a type of biblical interpretation developed by Jewish rabbis in the second to sixth centuries CE. The specific technique used by the author in this passage is called *gezerah shawah*, in which one passage is used to interpret another with similar words. In this case, the author uses Genesis 2:2 to interpret what "rest" means in Psalm 95:11. *Rest* is no longer just what was achieved through Joshua in the Promised Land: now it is God's rest, a heavenly rest, the eternal *Sabbath* (Heb 4:9).

If rest is something to strive for, something not yet fully achieved, is there any rest for the author's congregation as they struggle with their present reality? As the author reminds the congregation by recalling Genesis 2:2, God rested on the seventh day (Heb 4:4). As the people of God, God's Sabbath remains for them (4:9). There must be some sense in which faithfulness, holding fast,

92 Hebrews 3:1–4:13

and maintaining hope and confidence are already part of the promised rest of God. Those who believe and faithfully persevere are already *partners of Christ* (3:14) and members of his household (3:6). They are able to enter directly into the presence of God and fellowship with God, where there is rest. As L. Johnson says, "Hebrews makes clear that [entering into God's rest] is a matter of hearing, trusting, and obeying a gift already given through Christ. Humans who accept this gift 'cease from their works' not in the sense that they cease human effort, but in the sense that, like God, their works are no longer a striving to fill a need, but share in an outpouring of abundant life" (130).

Last, the homilist urges the congregation to *make every effort to enter that rest, so that no one may fall through such disobedience as theirs* (4:11). The homilist uses a compound Greek word in this verse, built on *deigma*, which means "pattern" or "example." The same word later occurs in relationship to earthly worship as *a sketch and shadow of the heavenly things* (8:5) and *sketches of the heavenly things* (9:23). The author is using a "typological" reading of the Jewish Scriptures: they are an earthly sign for a spiritual meaning. In this passage, the author is reading the experiences of the wilderness generation in the same way. But the NRSV translation obscures the meaning somewhat. David Hart's translation reads *Let us strive, therefore, to enter into that rest, so that no one should fall, after the same* pattern *of disobedience* (emph. added). As L. Johnson puts it, "Just as the earthly, material realm is an 'example' of the heavenly, so is the past an example for the present" (131).

Accountability to the Word of the Living God 4:12-13

This brief passage suitably closes the argument thus far: God's word has taken center stage. (For an excellent discussion of this passage, see L. Johnson: 131–37.) In graphic language, our homilist describes God's *word* as *living and active, sharper than any two-edged sword* (4:12). God's word is not just an account of the ancient Israelites' wandering in the desert: it is also meant for the people of God today and is *living*. Likewise, this *word* names Jesus as God's Son and places him on the heavenly throne, above the angels (1:5, 13). God's word is active. As a two-edged sword, it pierces, *divides soul from spirit, joints from marrow, [and] . . . is able to judge the thoughts and intentions of the heart* (4:12). The implication is that God's word, and therefore God, is powerful enough to penetrate into the innermost being of a person. That sentiment is confirmed in the next clause: God's word is able to *judge the thoughts and intentions of the heart* (4:12). In other words, no one can hide from God: we are all *naked and laid bare* (4:13). Therefore, by the very nature of God and God's word, we must render an account of our lives.

Translated as "account" in English, the last Greek word in the sentence is *logos*. It is a wordplay because the Greek word *logos* has a dual meaning in this passage. It is both God's *word* or message (4:12) and an *account* (4:13) that everyone needs to give to God. The Greek word *logos* appears regularly in the text *[Logos, p. 242]*. No one English word can capture the meaning of this Greek term. Differing contexts require various English words to capture the sense. When our author uses *logos*, it usually implies something more than just "word," which is why translators have used the English word "message" and other terms in trying to convey the sense of the passage. The following chart summarizes the translations and meanings that appear in Hebrews for *logos* (underlined words are the translation of *logos*).

Reference	Translation (NRSV)	Meaning from context
2:2	the <u>message</u> declared through the angels	Angels relay God's message but are not the message.
4:2	the <u>message</u> they [the Israelites] heard	The message is the good news.
5:11	We have <u>much to say</u> that is hard to explain	Literally, there is a *great logos* that is hard to explain.
5:12	<u>oracles</u> of God	This refers to Scripture.
6:1	<u>basic teaching</u>	The author defines what is meant by basic teaching: instructions about baptism, laying on of hands, resurrection of the dead, and eternal judgment.
7:28	<u>word</u> of the oath	This points to the oath sworn by God in Psalm 110:4: "You are a priest forever."
12:19	The hearers beg that not another <u>word</u> be spoken to them	The author refers to the Sinai experience: Exodus 20:19, "Do not let the LORD speak to us."
13:7	Remember . . . those who spoke the <u>word</u> of God to you	The *word* includes the lived faithfulness of their leaders: that is the message.
13:22	my <u>word</u> of exhortation	This sermon itself is the word of exhortation.

94   Hebrews 3:1–4:13

In a "subtle manipulation of language in the shift of meaning of logos" (Attridge: 136), our author has used God's *word* to create accountability to God and God's *word*. Having done so, the audience may now be ready to hear the message about God's Son, Jesus.

THE TEXT IN BIBLICAL CONTEXT

Our author has used the themes from Numbers 12–14, Psalm 95, and Genesis 2 to speak with the audience of Hebrews about Jesus and their response to him. Seeing how our author uses these texts helps us understand Hebrews in its broader cultural background, even if we do not know specifics about its immediate context.

The Word

As with other New Testament writers, the author of Hebrews follows a precedent set by the Jewish Scriptures in describing the Scriptures, or God's word, as *living and active* (4:12). Isaiah 49:2 and Wisdom of Solomon 18:15-16 use language that speaks of God using the mouth as a "sharp sword." Isaiah 55, another vivid passage, illustrates this idea. The prophet compares the word to the rain and snow that give life to the earth by providing "seed to the sower and bread to the eater" (55:10). The Lord says, "My word goes out from my mouth; it shall not return to me empty, but it shall accomplish that which I purpose" (55:11). In Acts 7:38, Stephen speaks of "living oracles" given to Moses on Mount Sinai. Also, 1 Peter 1:23 speaks of "the living and enduring word of God," the gospel "announced" to the readers (1:25).

In Hebrews, the active power of the word is described by a graphic, even violent, metaphor: *sharper than any two-edged sword* (4:12; cf. Rev 1:16; 2:12). Other New Testament authors use similar language. Ephesians 6:17 says the word of God is "the sword of the Spirit." According to Revelation 19:11-16, from the mouth of the Word of God "came a sharp sword with which to strike down the nations." Hebrews says God's word is *piercing*, or penetrating (4:12). The Greek verb occurs only here in the New Testament, but a similar idea appears in the Wisdom of Solomon, which says that in addition to being "holy, unique, loving the good," Wisdom is also "penetrating through all spirits that are intelligent, pure, and altogether subtle" (7:22-23). The language means that God is able to discern the thoughts and intentions of the inner being and to make fine distinctions of judgment. God's word to us helps us make those discernments as well.

Hebrews 3:1–4:13

The Wilderness

The wilderness experience after the exodus from Egypt is one of the most important themes in all of Scripture. In Hebrews, it is used as an example of faithlessness. Our author is not alone in that understanding. We have already seen our author's extensive use of Psalm 95:7-11; other texts ranging from Ezekiel 20:1-31 to Psalms 78:5-67 and 106 also describe the wilderness experience in negative terms. For example, Ezekiel has a long diatribe against Israel because, during many periods in its history and in the wilderness, it "did not observe my statutes, and profaned my Sabbaths" (20:16). Various psalms have similar sentiments, describing, as does Hebrews, the Israelites as rebellious, unfaithful, stubborn, and disobedient. Psalm 78 retells the experience of the Israelites in the wilderness and emphasizes their rebelliousness: "They tested God in their heart by demanding the food they craved. They spoke against God" (78:18-19). Psalm 106 is another rehearsal of the many sins committed by Israel during their years of wandering, including a reference to the same "waters of Meribah" (106:32), or "testing," which both Psalm 95 and our author use.

Instead of the unfaithfulness of the Israelites, other psalms focus on the faithfulness of God in the wilderness. Psalm 105, a companion piece to Psalm 106, praises God for rescuing Israel from slavery and keeping them safe during the exodus:

> He spread a cloud for a covering,
>   and fire to give light by night.
> They asked, and he brought quails,
>   and gave them food from heaven in abundance. (105:39-40)

Psalms 135 and 136 praise the Lord for the acts of wonder throughout the history of the people, including their time in the wilderness:

> O give thanks to the LORD, . . .
> who led his people through the wilderness,
>   for his steadfast love endures forever. (136:1, 16)

The prophet Hosea has a beautiful passage (2:14-23) in which the people of Israel have been called to the wilderness to renew their covenant with God. Using language of marriage, the text reads, "I will take you for my wife in faithfulness; and you shall know the LORD" (2:20). In these texts, the wilderness is seen as the place where God has displayed that faithfulness.

96   Hebrews 3:1–4:13

Other New Testament authors use the wilderness experience as illustration. In 1 Corinthians 10:1-13, Paul employs a typological reading to count the Israelites as a negative example, much like the writer of Hebrews. The Israelites were protected by the cloud, they passed through the sea, they ate spiritual food, and they drank spiritual (God-given) drink from the rock (Christ). But they put God to the test: they became idolaters, they indulged in orgies, and many of them were destroyed by serpents. Paul says, "These things happened to them to serve as an example, and they were written down to instruct us, on whom the ends of the ages have come" (1 Cor 10:11). The sermon preached by Stephen in Acts 7 recounts the history of the Israelite people and how they disobeyed God and were unfaithful, much as the Psalms do.

All these texts use this experience to illustrate faithfulness or the lack of it. Notice that the Israelites are rarely described as *unbelieving* (cf. Acts 14:2; Heb 3:12). The biblical examples of rebelliousness and disobedience clarify that we should translate *pistis* here as "faithful," not "faith" or "belief"; and *apistia* as "unfaithful" (3:19), not "unbelieving." The authors focus on the *actions* of God or the Israelites, not as much on beliefs of the people themselves. Hebrews stands on the shoulders of this tradition.

Jesus and Moses

Comparisons between Jesus and Moses (3:1-6) in the New Testament are both direct, as in this passage, and indirect, in the form of subtle allusions. In the Gospel of Matthew, we see both types of comparisons. In the Sermon on the Mount (Matt 5–7), Jesus expands the law of Moses to "fulfill it" (5:17). But more subtly, the Jesus of Matthew is portrayed as a new Moses. For example, the gospel contains five sections of teaching, all ending with the words "when Jesus had finished" (7:28; 11:1; 13:53; 19:1; 26:1). Many interpret this as a parallel to the five books of Moses, or the Torah. Some aspects of the lives of both figures are similar. The infant Jesus is endangered, as was the infant Moses. Both Jesus and Moses receive or give out the law to the people. At the transfiguration, described in all three synoptic gospels, Peter, James, and John see Jesus on the mountain with Moses and Elijah.

The Gospel of John creates a sharper divide. Its prologue states the overall message: Moses brought the law, but Jesus brings grace and truth (1:17). Unlike Moses, the bringer of the law, Jesus *is* the truth, the Word, and the means of salvation. In 3:14-15, Jesus says, "Just as Moses lifted up the serpent in the wilderness, so must the

Son of Man be lifted up, that whoever believes in him may have eternal life." John 6:31-35 compares the manna that the Israelites received in the wilderness to the bread of life from heaven: Jesus. Finally, in a dispute about whether healing on the Sabbath is legal, Jesus effectively reduces the role of Moses even in giving the law (7:19-24). At issue for our purposes is how Moses' influence is minimized. Even though "the law" (i.e., Moses) allows for circumcision on the Sabbath, it was not really Moses who "gave them circumcision," but the patriarchs (Abraham, Isaac, and Jacob). Moses did not even provide circumcision! Jesus, however, heals the sick.

The Sabbath Rest

The Sabbath is an important biblical theme that pervades both biblical and intertestamental Jewish texts (Attridge: 127, 131). God commands the people to remember the Sabbath and keep it holy (Exod 20:8-11; Deut 5:12-15). As Attridge notes, the Sabbath rest in noncanonical texts like Jubilees and Pseudo-Philo is marked by "praise and thanksgiving directed toward God" (131). This is attested by Philo as well when he recounts the activities of an ascetic group in the Egyptian wilderness, the Therapeutae, who think of the Sabbath as a "most complete festival" (*On the Contemplative Life* 4.36), which includes a group assembly and the breaking of their fast with a simple meal. In Revelation, those "who had been slaughtered for the word of God" (6:9) are given a white robe and "told to rest a little longer, until the number would be complete" (6:11). Later, when everyone is assembled, the angels, elders, and the four living creatures worship God and sing (7:9-12). In these texts, rest from work does not imply inaction, but active attention toward God. Those at rest in heaven (6:11) continuously sing praises to God (Attridge: 131).

Like Hebrews, Jesus interprets the Sabbath as a gift and a blessing to be accepted. In Matthew, the Sabbath discussion includes stories and teachings and begins with the invitation "Come unto me, all you that are weary and carrying heavy burdens, and I will give you rest" (11:28). This invitation is followed by a Sabbath healing, which ends with a word from Jesus: "The Son of Man is lord of the sabbath" (12:8). Mark 2:27 provides an expanded version of this teaching: "The sabbath was made for humankind, and not humankind for the sabbath, so the Son of Man is lord even of the sabbath." The Sabbath is not a burden to be imposed on humanity, but a rest: we are invited to enter that rest by coming to Jesus.

98   Hebrews 3:1–4:13

THE TEXT IN THE LIFE OF THE CHURCH

Hold On!

Houses are designed to withstand the outside elements and keep those inside safe. The safety of the physical structure provides opportunities for love and companionship inside. But once the physical structure is damaged, safety is difficult to maintain. As *God's house*, the Hebrews are urged to *hold firm* what belongs to *hope* (Heb 3:6). They are asked to *exhort one another every day* (3:13) so they as a group can keep the house structurally sound. If they take collective action *today* amid the wilderness of whatever difficulties they are experiencing, they will achieve the promised rest.

The mixed image of the people of God as a *house* wandering through the *wilderness* is jarring. They did move a literal house, the tabernacle, for forty years. Yet both authors, the psalmist and the preacher of Hebrews, remind their audiences about the real and figurative house of God, the people (Heb 3:4-6). In the case of Hebrews, they are partners with Christ in living out the word of God.

But the challenges are enormous: a small band of people, away from any permanent home, are struggling to find the home they were promised. It is easy to lose faith. But without faith and faithfulness, without each other and without God, they are lost and homeless.

The words of the spiritual "Hold On!" recall this experience:

> Keep your hand on that plow, hold on!
> Noah, Noah, let me come in.
> Doors all fastened and the windows pinned.
> Keep your hand on that plow, hold on!
> Noah said, "You lost your track,
> can't plow straight and keep a'lookin' back . . . "
> Keep your hand on that plow, hold on!
> If you want to get to heaven, let me tell you how,
> just keep your hand on that gospel plow, hold on!
> If that plow stays in your hand,
> it'll land you straight in the Promised Land.
> Keep your hand on that plow, hold on!
> (many variations; first printed in the Cecil J. Sharp Collection, 1917)

These lyrics use two other biblical passages, the flood and Luke 9:62, to express the same sentiment about holding fast that we see in Hebrews. Noah and his family built the ark as a house/barn to withstand a big storm. The ark is now battened down, and those not part of the building process cannot get in when they might want to. Keeping their hands on the plow, moving forward, is the only way.

The origins of the song "Hold On" are unclear. Some describe it as a spiritual; others notice its use in the struggle for civil rights. If the song rose out of an enslaved African community, we might think they had little in common with the audience of Hebrews. But both were minority groups, living in strange settings, with little hope for rest in their earthly lives. Their main resources were each other and their faith. They had to find collective ways to remain strong despite unbearable odds. Sharing songs and sermons about keeping the community strong through faith helped keep both groups on course so they could find their way to the promised land of freedom and rest.

Part 2

Jesus' High Priesthood

Hebrews 4:14–7:28

OVERVIEW

It is difficult to maintain one's faith journey without support from a community. The reminder about the wandering Israelites, who had the best of intentions, is good. God delivered them from slavery in Egypt, but that did not excuse them for rebelling in their journey toward the Promised Land.

Now the preacher introduces a strange concept: Jesus as high priest. The congregation knows that Jesus does not have the correct lineage to be high priest: he is not a descendant of Aaron, from the tribe of Levi. Rather, he is a descendant of David, from the tribe of Judah. Only Aaron's descendants can be priests. To counter this objection, the preacher lays out a different kind of high priest by relying on biblical traditions about Melchizedek based on the books of Moses, Psalm 110, and traditions that arose in Second Temple Judaism. Jesus is already sitting at the right hand of God, and the psalm says that the one who sits there is a priest belonging to "the order of *Melchizedek*" (110:4, emph. added). Hereditary (earthly) lineage is secondary to the heavenly priestly order, which transcends any earthly category. The earthly high priest makes offerings only for himself and the people on the Day of Atonement. However, Jesus goes further: he offers himself.

Jesus the high priest is both sacrificer *and* sacrifice. Amid all this, the preacher continues to exhort the readers into greater faithfulness; theory without practice is empty and meaningless.

OUTLINE

Jesus: Son and Great High Priest, 4:14–5:10
Grow Up! (A Message on Group Identity), 5:11–6:20
Jesus the Son Is Foreshadowed by the Priest-King Melchizedek,
7:1–28

Hebrews 4:14–5:10

Jesus: Son and Great High Priest

PREVIEW

Three notions—high priest, without sin, boldness—take the audience farther along the path of exploring Christ's role in their salvation. The core of this brief passage is an exhortation to approach Christ. The passage reminds the audience why and how they can be bold. Jesus, the great high priest, is sitting on the throne, having experienced very human temptations (tests). He can fully sympathize with them in their own struggles toward obedience.

Our author's argument rests on two psalms we have already encountered in Hebrews 1: Psalms 2 and 110. The interpretation of these psalms forms the focus of the entire text, not just this section. Here the homilist brings them together to proclaim Jesus as *Son*, *high priest*, and *source of... salvation*. These psalms serve as sectional divisions within the text. In some outlines of Hebrews, the quotation of Psalm 2:7 in Hebrews 5:5 is considered the close of the long introduction that started in 1:5 with the same text. Similarly, the reappearance of Psalm 110 in 5:6 is thought to be the start of the extended discussion regarding Jesus as high priest, not ending until 7:28.

104   Hebrews 4:14–5:10

OUTLINE

Approach the Throne of Grace with Boldness, 4:14-16
The High Priesthood, 5:1-10
    5:1-4   Every High Priest
    5:5-10 Jesus as High Priest

EXPLANATORY NOTES

Approach the Throne of Grace with Boldness 4:14-16

This brief section transitions between the christological ideas presented by the homilist earlier in the sermon and the explication of the new idea the homilist brings: Jesus as high priest. The homilist deftly sums up the features about Jesus already presented:

> Jesus is exalted (4:14).
>   He has passed through the heavens (1:3-4).
>   He sits at the right hand of the throne (1:13).
> Jesus is the high priest (4:15).
>   He is a merciful high priest (2:17).
>   He is high priest of our confession (3:1).
> Jesus is God's Son (4:14).
>   God spoke to us through a Son (1:2).
>   The angels worship him (1:6).
>   The Son's throne is forever (1:8).
> Jesus was human and experienced testing (4:15).
>   He was made lower than the angels (2:9).
>   He shared flesh and blood with humans (2:14).

Picking up from Hebrews 1, identifying the Son as the one who sits enthroned at the right hand of God (1:3, 13); and the second chapter, naming Jesus as high priest (2:17), here the author begins to develop this Christology about Jesus: he is both the high priest and Son, yet very human. Our homilist has reminded the audience that Jesus is *the apostle and high priest of our confession* (3:1).

Jesus is also the *pioneer* (2:10). He, too, has experienced temptation and testing. Because of that, he is totally sympathetic to the human condition. However, he is without sin. We should pause and think about this in more detail. Our author is keen on emphasizing Jesus' sinlessness, which is deeply connected to his being made perfect through sufferings (2:10) and his faithfulness to God (2:17-18). It is a stark contrast to the earlier people of God in 3:7-11 who hardened their hearts and rebelled on the day of testing. The use of the word *testing* in 4:15 reminds the audience of the testing in the wilderness. The Israelites failed because they rebelled and were unfaithful. As we move through this passage, we see that Jesus succeeds because, throughout the testing, *Jesus* has remained obedient. The relationship between Jesus' sinlessness and his obedience and faithfulness is unmistakable. In 2:1, the readers are reminded not to *drift away*. Later, the homilist urges them not to *be hardened by the deceitfulness of sin* (3:13). The preacher says to the congregation, *We have become partners with Christ, if only we hold our first confidence firm to the end* (3:14). With this same boldness and confidence, they should now feel free to *approach the throne of grace* (4:16).

Beginning with this passage, the author repeatedly reminds the audience about the benefits of drawing near to, or approaching, God (esp. 7:25; 11:6; 12:18, 22). As Attridge has pointed out, drawing near, or approaching, God is an important motif in Hebrews (141). The verb *proserchōmetha* (*let us . . . approach*; 4:16) is a "hortatory subjunctive," a form used as an author exhorts a group to action. The passage feels similar to Leviticus 9, which exhorts the congregation to approach the tent with the required offerings, after which the priest (Aaron) offers the sacrifices. Moses says to them, "This is the thing that the LORD commanded you to do, so that the glory of the LORD may appear to you" (9:6). Indeed, after the people follow the command and the sacrifices are made, they experience the presence of God (Yoder: 103). In a similar fashion, the Hebrews congregation will find God's *mercy and . . . grace to help in time of need* (4:16).

These are words of comfort to a congregation that might be struggling. The homilist is telling the congregation that Jesus' own experience as a human has enabled him to understand their own frailty. Despite the majesty and glory bestowed upon him as God's Son, he knows the human condition. The otherworldly sovereign has been replaced by an approachable mediator. Now as high priest, he is giving the congregation the opportunity to receive mercy and grace, gifts that Jesus can bestow on them when they approach the throne with boldness (DeSilva: 183).

The High Priesthood 5:1-10

Our homilist does a masterful job, seamlessly moving from one idea to another. Hebrews 4:14-16 is a good example of that, summarizing the message up to that point while also introducing the important theme of Jesus as high priest in chapter 5. It introduces the next section: the qualifications of a high priest and how Jesus meets those qualifications. Laid out, it looks like this (with artificial headings so the sections are clear):

106

I. Introduction (4:14-16)
   A The Son of God, Jesus, is high priest. (4:14)
   B The Son sympathizes with our weaknesses. (4:15)
   C The Son provides mercy and grace. (4:16)
II. Definition of High Priest (5:1-4)
   C′ The high priest offers gifts and sacrifices for sins. (5:1)
   B′ The priest deals gently with the ignorant and wayward because of his own weakness. (5:2-3)
   A′ A true priest is called by God. (5:4)
III. Jesus, the new high priest (5:5-10)
   A″ Christ, the Son, was also appointed high priest. (5:5)
   B″ Jesus offered prayers for himself with cries and tears. (5:7-8)
   C″ Jesus is a source of eternal salvation. (5:9-10)

Because the individual elements within each section are assigned letters and arranged in a visual manner, we can see several things. Each section includes roughly the same three themes:

A *who/what* the high priest is
B *how* the high priest behaves
C *what* the high priest offers

The arrangement is technically called a chiasm. Laying out the qualifications of a high priest in 5:1-4 as "definition of high priest" allows the superior qualities of Jesus to be highlighted in the last section.

5:1-4 Every High Priest

The author emphasizes the similarities between a "normal" high priest and Jesus (later in the text, the author sharply contrasts Jesus' role with the Levitical priests). In this middle section, the author defines what a high priest is and describes the characteristics of a high priest. Wedged between the first and third sections, it affirms the statements made in 4:14-16 about Jesus and then lays out the qualifications so that the final section, in yet another restatement, confirms that Jesus has met and exceeded those qualifications.

The duties and characteristics of high priests can be listed as follows:

- Priests are chosen from among the people. The author reminds the audience that if the priest is to be the representative of people before God, he himself must be fully human. Though it may have been self-evident to the audience that priests are fully human, it is important for the author to remind the audience that Jesus, too, was fully human. This qualification emphasizes the fully human aspect of Jesus.

- Priests oversee *things pertaining to God* (5:1) on behalf of the people. We saw this phrase in 2:17, the basic meaning of which is that the priest is in charge of worship. They offer gifts and sacrifices for sins. While the focus of Hebrews is on offering sacrifices for sins, priests also gave offerings in thanksgiving and as dedications, some of which were voluntary offerings to please God. Others were mandatory "firstfruits" offerings (on Lev 2:1–3:7; 23:9-21; and the many rituals of thanksgiving stipulated for the Israelites, see Yoder: 50–54, 230–36).

- They are to *deal gently* (5:2) with ignorant and wayward people. The verb translated as "deal gently" in the NRSV is a synonym for 4:15's phrase "to sympathize with." It can also mean "deal with in a measured way" to express that the priest, who also has human failings (see next point), recognizes feelings in the people he is serving and determines to deal fairly with them, with sympathy and understanding. The text specifically mentions people who are ignorant and wayward, not those who, like the ancient Israelites in Hebrews 3, consciously rebelled against God.

- The priest himself is *subject to weakness* (5:2). The emphasis on the human characteristics of the priest is important to the overall project of the author, to have a fully human Jesus. He offers sacrifices for himself as well as for others (5:3). If the high priest is human and subject to failings, he must also make sacrifices for himself before he can do so for others.

- The high priest is called by God to do this work, not by people. Only God can call the high priest. Although this is the biblical model, it became especially corrupted in the Hellenistic period, when the Maccabees installed themselves as high priests in place of the Zadokites (2nd c. BCE; the author refers to the *biblical* model of high priesthood and not to the first-century reality: this is further evidence that the biblical text is the guiding force, not current events).

5:5-10 *Jesus as High Priest*

Now we come to the passage that is a real transition point. The author reintroduces the biblical proof from Psalms 2 and 110,

108 Hebrews 4:14–5:10

initially introduced at the beginning of the text, to reaffirm Jesus' status as the Son and the Christ claimed in chapters 1–4. The author then uses that material to further develop the argument about Jesus as the high priest, starting in chapter 7. In Greek, Hebrews 5:7-10 is one long sentence with several subordinate clauses. The two basic premises are in simple declarative statements in 5:8 and 5:9b:

He learned obedience (5:8a).	He became [the] source of eternal salvation (5:9b).

The way the passage is constructed in Greek underscores that in order for Jesus to learn obedience, he first offered up prayers and reverently submitted. As a result of his reverent submission, he suffered, was made perfect, and was called high priest. Having done these things, he became the source of salvation.

Having offered *prayers and supplications* (5:7a)	*having been made perfect* (5:9a)
having been *heard because of his reverent submission* (5:7b)	having been *designated [or called] a high priest by God according to the order of Melchizedek* (5:10)

Jesus exceeds the qualifications of high priest. He also brings new meaning into the office of high priest. For example, like Aaron, Jesus was appointed by God. But even better, Jesus is God's Son. Jesus offered prayers and supplications, yes. But now he is also the answer to those prayers because he is *the source of eternal salvation* (5:9).

We might think for a bit about what salvation means for our author [*Atonement, p. 231*]. This is the second time that the author has connected salvation to perfection and suffering. Attridge considers the presentation of salvation by the author as "complex" (66). Indeed, it is difficult to pin down the precise meaning of salvation. In Hebrews 4, we examined the idea of rest as a reward for obedience. Here, salvation is connected to perfection, the notion of completion or fulfillment. It is not passive. Only through voluntary suffering (5:8) did Jesus learn to obey and become a source of salvation. The author has declared that God made Jesus, *the pioneer of their salvation* (2:10), *perfect through sufferings.* That sentiment is repeated here. In that same passage, salvation is associated with the *coming world*, not yet available; but the author is urging the community to be ready to enter it (2:1-5). We see the same idea in this passage as well: salvation is *eternal* (5:9).

Hebrews 4:14–5:10

This is not just abstract thinking about the nature of Christ. Many commentators (cf. Thompson 2008: 117–18) believe that the way the author talks about Christ is a pastoral response to the needs of the community. The pastor has asked them to *take care* (3:12) and *exhort one another every day* (3:13) so that their hearts are not hardened and they hold their *first confidence firm to the end* (3:14). In the same way, this passage reminds them to *approach the throne of grace* (4:16) so they can find grace and salvation in their time of *need*. Clearly, the author is exhorting the audience to remain strong. The audience is invited to find comfort and encouragement in the characterization of Jesus, the Son, as a high priest who, like *every high priest* (5:1), is sympathetic and has faced similar hardships. Through those hardships, they will find Jesus and salvation.

As for the mysterious figure of Melchizedek, the high priest mentioned in 5:10 (and Ps 110:4), this verse serves as an appetizer to the main meal that our author serves up in chapter 7. Stay tuned!

THE TEXT IN BIBLICAL CONTEXT

A Great High Priest Who Has Passed through the Heavens

The description of Jesus as passing through the heavens in Hebrews 4:14 is reminiscent of the heavenly journeys taken by Enoch (Gen 5:24), Elijah (2 Kings 2:1-12), and Paul (2 Cor 12:1-10). About Enoch, Genesis tells us only that "God took him." First Enoch, a collection of revelatory traditions about Enoch that was written over the course of the third to first centuries BCE, narrates the heavenly journey taken by Enoch after "God took him." Second Kings describes something potentially similar when "a chariot of fire" came down and took Elijah, who "ascended in a whirlwind into heaven" (2 Kings 2:11). Paul was "caught up into Paradise and heard things that are not to be told" (2 Cor 12:4). The experience was so "exceptional" that in order to keep him grounded, Paul was given a "thorn . . . in the flesh" (12:7).

Although Ezekiel does not have a journey, he sees visions of heaven (Ezek 1). In Ezekiel's first vision, he sees four-winged creatures, a wheel beside each one, and "something like a throne" above each creature (1:26). Daniel 7:9-10 picks up themes from Ezekiel 1 in describing the Ancient One and the heavenly realm. Ezekiel and Daniel describe the heavenly realm as full of awe, power, and glory. Was our homilist thinking about these thrones with the phrase *throne of grace* in Hebrews 4:16? Scholars do not know, but those descriptions of heavenly realms are lurking in the background of the

110   Hebrews 4:14–5:10

use of Psalm 110 and the author's repeated affirmation that Jesus is seated at the right hand of God.

The High Priesthood

The priesthood in ancient Israelite society was limited to "Aaron and his sons" (Exod 29:30). The process by which entry into the priesthood was ritualized is laid out in Exodus 29:1-35 and in Leviticus 8–9. The role of the priest was cultic: priests were to serve God, the tabernacle, and the people (Yoder: 306). Detailed instructions are laid out in Leviticus for how the priests, from Aaron down to ordinary priests, were to perform their duties and behave properly.

However, neither Exodus nor Leviticus mentions the high priest specifically, even in the discussion of Yom Kippur in Leviticus 16. Both texts refer only to "Aaron" (see Yoder: 152–59), with Aaron serving as the prototypical high priest. The high priest's role is mentioned in later biblical texts (e.g., Num 35:25; 2 Sam 8:17; 1 Kings 2:27, 35). In time, the role was given to Zadok and his line of firstborn descendants (1 Kings 2:27, 35). In these texts we see the high priest anointing the king and acting as his closest advisor. In the Hellenistic period, the high priest took on an even greater political role. In fact, a foreign Seleucid king, Alexander, appointed a (Jewish) Hasmonean, Jonathan, as high priest (1 Macc 10:18-22). This practice continued through the Hellenistic period and into the first century CE. For example, Herod the Great appointed six high priests. Since biblical priests were never appointed, certainly not by foreigners (which many Jews considered Herod to be), this was a major corruption of the office.

Although the New Testament does not critique the appointment of the high priest, we observe a close working relationship between the high priest and the Roman authorities. After questioning Jesus, the high priest hands him over to Pilate. The Essenes were critical of the alliance between the high priest and the Romans (and wanted the line of Zadok restored). With their alternate ideas, Essenes understood the figure of Melchizedek as both a heavenly and messianic priest, a kingly priest. Our author has much more to say about Melchizedek later in the text, as will we.

THE TEXT IN THE LIFE OF THE CHURCH

Suffering in the Revised Common Lectionary

Our Christian ancestors were sensitive to the theme of suffering and developing a faithful response to it. Suffering is treated thoroughly

Hebrews 4:14–5:10

in the group of lectionary readings for Year B, the fifteenth Sunday after Pentecost.

First Reading and Psalm	Alternate First Reading and Psalm	Letter	Gospel
Job 23:1-9, 16-17 or Psalm 22:1-15	Amos 5:6-7, 10-15 or Psalm 90:12-17	Hebrews 4:12-16	Mark 10:17-31

The readings for this Sunday are about seeking God in difficult times or with difficult questions. The book of Job struggles with the foundational question of God's role in people's suffering. Job lost his wealth, his family, and his health. His friends tried to convince him that it was because of his own wickedness. In response, Job wants to confront God directly and lay out his case, but he does not know where God is. Job is terrified, but he still has faith that God will keep him from the darkness.

The prophet Amos calls the people to "seek the LORD and live" (Amos 5:6) because they are living unrighteous lives. In fact, they have turned justice into wormwood, a foul-tasting substance, and will be accountable to God for their "transgressions" (chs. 1–2) and cruelty.

The gospel text is the parable of the rich man who sought out Jesus to ask what he needed to do to inherit eternal life. When pressed, Jesus told him that he should give away all his possessions to the poor. After the man left, knowing that he was unable to do this, Jesus taught about the difficulties of entering the kingdom of heaven. His disciples argued with him. Peter told him that they had already left everything to follow him. Jesus replied that in this world, those who follow him would receive the things they had forsaken a hundredfold (e.g., houses and family) "with persecutions." "In the age to come" they will receive "eternal life."

The cost of discipleship can be high. Sometimes we suffer because we do the right thing. The rich man walked away, shaking his head: he loved his "possessions" more than "eternal life." The disciples were expecting rewards for giving up their possessions. How do we handle hardship, especially when it involves our attempts to live faithfully? The author of Hebrews exhorts the audience to remember that Jesus is the high priest who can *sympathize with our weaknesses* (4:15) and who *learned obedience through what he suffered* (5:8). Jesus pioneered this path to salvation. Will we follow?

Hebrews 5:11–6:20

Grow Up! (A Message on Group Identity)

PREVIEW

Insult . . . warning . . . exhortation . . . teaching.

Insult. The author undoubtedly intends to shock readers into paying close attention by accusing them of infantile behavior and attitudes. First, they ought to be teachers, but they are still infants needing milk (5:11-12). Second, they are unskilled in righteousness and cannot eat solid food because they lack the training and therefore the maturity to distinguish good from evil (5:13-14).

Warning. The use of metaphors related to food and athletics, common in antiquity, creates a powerfully packed insult. The congregation is full of infants, requiring milk (implying a lack of autonomy and reliance on one's mother). Unable to eat regular food, they also are flabby because of their lack of physical training. The two metaphors are brilliantly melded into a single message for the audience: "Grow up! We don't have time to waste on material we've already covered!"

Exhortation. We should read this entire section as an aside to the overall christological thesis of the work [*Christology in Hebrews, p. 235*]. Beginning with verse 11, the author leaves aside the discussion about Jesus as the high priest according to the order of Melchizedek and exhorts the readers to a more mature practice. The author waits to pick up the discussion of Melchizedek until the last

Hebrews 5:11–6:20   113

verse in chapter 6, where he repeats, almost word for word, what he said in 5:10. The main goal of this section is to encourage the audience by way of insult, exhortation, warning, and teaching to "keep the faith" so they can receive the promises from God, just as Abraham did.

Teaching. Only after the homilist gets the full attention of the congregation can teaching occur. The congregation can move forward in understanding and faithful practice only when they realize their responsibilities. The homilist exhorts them to be like properly cultivated ground, which soaks up falling rain, rather than like soil that produces only thistles (6:8).

OUTLINE

Insult and Shame: Move On to Maturity, 5:11–6:3
Warning: It Is Impossible to Restore Those Who Have Fallen Away, 6:4-8
Exhortation: Persevere Because God Is Just, 6:9-12
Teaching: God's Promises Are Sure, 6:13-20

EXPLANATORY NOTES

Insult and Shame: Move On to Maturity 5:11–6:3

Our author has *much to say that is hard to explain* (5:11) about Jesus' role as a priest according to the order of Melchizedek. But the congregation cannot understand because they have become *dull in understanding.* The author must build in periodic pauses to remind them that they are *heirs of the promise* (6:17) given to Abraham, called to live their lives in a foreign land (real or metaphorical). Two previous asides (2:1-4; 4:1-13) deal with similar issues of encouragement to keep the faith. These pastoral encouragements (coupled with stern warnings) work in tandem with the christological thesis. Their focus is Jesus, the pioneer, and their faithful work is done in community.

The author continues some of the language from the preceding chapter. Perfection, or maturity, is a key goal in following the example of Jesus. Remaining infantile and underdeveloped is not an option for our author. Practice trains their faculties (6:1). The Greek word for "trained" is *gymnazō* (5:14; 12:11). Literally, it means to "exercise." While the author does not specifically mention suffering, physical and mental training implies a certain amount of self-denial and sacrifice. But this audience has not even trained enough to eat solid food! They would recognize this short passage as an insult after

114   Hebrews 5:11–6:20

receiving the message that Jesus, the Savior, has reached perfection through much more difficult circumstances (2:10).

The point is that the "Hebrews" are *unskilled in the word of righteousness* (5:13). They have not developed the muscle for it through practice. It is unclear what this means in the context, or even what the *good* and *evil* are (5:14), since the author left off at 5:10 with the teaching about the priesthood of Jesus. What sort of ethical implications does the author intend in that teaching? Later in this chapter, we read that the author wants *each one of you to show the same diligence* as God *so as to realize the full assurance of hope to the very end* (6:11). Once again, we see a melding of two goals in this text: (1) the author wants to teach about the priesthood of Jesus and his role as Savior; and (2) the author also wants to instruct readers on individual and group behavior. Perhaps their ability to comprehend a difficult teaching about Jesus is indicative of their overall ability to maintain their faith in other ways.

The group is at an impasse in their faithful response to Christ, and their preacher is imploring them to move on. Moving on to perfection (or maturity) requires moving past the basic teachings about Christ (6:1-3):

1. *Repentance//faith*

2. *Instructions about baptisms//laying on of hands*

3. *Resurrection of the dead//eternal judgment*

It is not that they are to forget what they have learned by way of belief (#1), rituals (#2), or thinking about the end times (#3), but that they are to add to it. They are to build on their elementary education. It is not clear why the author refers to baptism as *baptisms* (pl.; cf. 1 Cor 15:29; Heb 9:10). We know from the Gospels and other ancient texts that Jews practiced baptisms and washings (John 3:22-23; 4:2; 5:7; Eph 5:26). Jesus' forerunner, John the Baptist, was baptizing people as they confessed their sins (Matt 3:6). In the Hebrew Prophets, water is used as a method of purification. The Lord promises the house of Israel, "I will sprinkle clean water upon you, and you shall be clean from all your uncleannesses" (Ezek 36:25).

The Didache, a late first-century text, provides instructions for the eucharist and baptism. But we do not know to what practices or instructions this passage is alluding. The same applies to laying on of hands. In the New Testament, laying on of hands was used for healing (Matt 9:18; Mark 5:23; Luke 13:13; Acts 9:12; James 5:14-15), receiving the Holy Spirit (Matt 19:13; Acts 8:17, 19; 28:8), and blessing various forms of ministry and leadership (Acts 6:6; 13:3; 1 Tim 4:14;

Hebrews 5:11–6:20

2 Tim 1:6). Belief in resurrection and eschatological judgment was so pervasive among many Jews and Jewish Christians that it would have been considered a somewhat elementary belief. By the end of 6:3, the homilist is encouraging the congregation to move past these elementary teachings toward a more mature faith, *if God permits.*

Warning: It Is Impossible to Restore Those Who Have Fallen Away 6:4-8

God's permission, ironically, is based on whether the person is poised to receive it. We might hear a bit of incredulity in the pastor's voice at this point. About those who have already *repented, been enlightened,* received *the heavenly gift* (via baptism or laying on of hands?) of the *Holy Spirit* (cf. the dove's descent at Jesus' baptism), and experienced a foretaste *of the world to come*—how can such persons still mismanage and fall away? It is as though they are *crucifying* Jesus *again* (6:6)! Warnings in this section come in the form of reminders of how their lives have changed through their encounter with Christ.

The author uses a series of images to describe the life of a Jesus follower. First, they have been *enlightened* (6:4; lit. *"those who have been given light, or have been illuminated"*). They have received the message about Jesus. In the Gospel of John, Jesus *is* the light (8:12). Light is a favorite metaphor for the presence of God in the Gospels and in the Jewish Scriptures. Both the burning bush (Exod 3) and the transfiguration (Matt 17 and parallels) come to mind. In the second century, enlightenment became a common expression for baptism. Although the term probably does not have that technical sense here, we can understand how later Christians came to use it in that way, given its connection to baptism both here and in the Gospels.

Second, they have *tasted the heavenly gift* (Heb 6:4). Tasting is a common metaphor for experiencing and savoring something. *The heavenly gift* could serve as a reminder of the manna provided by God to the Israelites in the wilderness. Paul issues a similar sentiment in 1 Corinthians 10:1-13 as he warns the hearers not to fall away (10:12). Even though the Israelites tasted the manna, they still did not make it to the Promised Land! They are an example *not* to be followed!

Third, they have *shared in the Holy Spirit* (Heb 6:4). The word used, *metochos,* is the same term the author used in 3:1, where the hearers are called *partners in a heavenly calling;* and in 3:14, where they *have become partners of Christ.* Hebrews emphasizes the partnership they share with each other (see also 2:4).

116   Hebrews 5:11–6:20

Fourth, they have *tasted the goodness of the word of God* (6:5). God's speaking (the word) is an important theme in the first four chapters (1:1-2; 2:3-7, 12-13; 3:7-11; 4:3, 12). As these passages suggest, the word of God includes both God's promises and God's acts. All who received this message had experienced such powers when the gospel was brought to them (2:4).

Finally, those who have *fallen away* are *crucifying again the Son of God and are holding him up to contempt* (6:6). The Greek word *parapiptō*, translated as "fallen away," means "to miss," or "go astray." While the author does not exactly accuse the readers of going astray, the author is warning them that they are close to doing so.

DeSilva's comments on this passage shed some light. He suggests that the homilist is "appealing to the topic of gratitude" toward Jesus, their benefactor. To turn or fall away from their benefactor, who has made the once-for-all sacrifice, is dishonorable and shows a lack of gratitude toward the benefactor. It also denies the one doing so the benefits of what was given freely and makes them no longer available. In that sense, the benefits are unrecoverable (238). It then causes a "tension between themselves and the Son," the benefactor (239). In other words, the homilist is working hard to encourage the members of the congregation to stay the course and reap the benefits promised to them. Those who turn their backs to God cannot reap the benefits while leaving. Our author is reminding them of the choice they have to stay focused and taste the reward.

After using words such as *tasted* and *shared*, implying a meal-based context, the homilist closes this section with an agricultural metaphor in 6:4-6. They are like the ground that produces thorns and thistles and needs to be *burned over* (6:8). Instead, they need to be like the ground that can soak up the rain and produce good crops. The only alternative to moving forward is falling away, and our author reminds the audience of this.

Exhortation: Persevere Because God Is Just 6:9-12

From insult to warning, our homilist now proceeds to exhortation. The sharp words of insult and warning are followed by pastoral words of assurance and encouragement. Our author is *confident of better things, . . . things that belong to salvation* (6:9) for the congregation. The author provides a theological justification for this, *For God is not unjust* (6:10). The congregation has done good work through love *in serving the saints* (6:10). In other words, they are *not* like those who go astray, but like people focused on salvation. In fact, they have been and still are focused on salvation. Through diligence, they will realize *the full assurance of hope to the very end* (6:11) and will remain *imitators of those who through faith and patience inherit the promises* (6:12). Just as the insult and warning are strong, so now are the words of assurance!

We can get a better sense of the pastoral values the author is espousing by delving a bit more into this passage. Faith, or faithfulness, hope, and love are central. *Love* is made manifest by *serving the saints* (6:10), both in the past and present. Later in the text (10:32-34 and 13:1-3) the author specifically lists how this has happened: being partners in persecution, visiting each other in prison, and showing hospitality. *Saints* (holy ones) is a term commonly used for believers in Christ. Acts calls those who believe "saints" (9:13, 32, 41; 26:10). Paul addresses several of his letters to "the saints" (Rom 1:7; 1 Cor 1:2; 2 Cor 1:1; Eph 1:1; Phil 1:1; Col 1:2) and expresses hope that the recipients of his letters will minister to the needs of the saints in Jerusalem (see esp. 2 Cor 8:1-9:15). In other words, mature faith involves acts of love toward the saints as one's co-congregants and co-religionists.

The author deeply values spiritual growth. Although the NRSV in 6:11 reads, *And we want each one of you to show the same diligence*, the Greek verb *epithymeō* behind the English "want" is stronger and more intense. It expresses personal passionate desire, intense longing for, and even coveting. It might be better translated, *We earnestly desire* . . . The congregation is being addressed not with apostolic authority but with deep pastoral concern. For the homilist, spiritual growth implies action. We saw this earlier in the passage as the author admonishes the audience that the only way to advance to eating solid food is through training (5:14). Now they need to be reminded that continuing diligence is necessary if they are to retain their hope for the future. Faith and confidence in God are not passive characteristics. They are not mere ideas, but actions that require practice through perseverance. As practice is given to faith and trust in God, hope is renewed.

The homilist also has an eschatological mindset. In other words, the homilist looks forward to the end time, when the plans, purposes, and goals of God will be fully manifest in the world. Like most of the New Testament, Hebrews sees Jesus' ministry as initiating the "age to come" (2:5; 6:5). The Hebrews, having *tasted the goodness of the word of God and the powers of the age to come* (6:5), are already participants in the coming age. Now they are called to hold fast to their faith and hope until it is consummated. Their faithfulness and diligence will be a manifestation of God's kingdom and part of bringing the new age to its consummation.

118   Hebrews 5:11–6:20

Hence, there is no room for *sluggish*ness (6:12), which, not coincidentally, is how the passage started in 5:11. It is the opposite of striving, zeal, diligence, and self-discipline, the virtues our author desires for them. Instead, they should be *imitators of those who through faith and patience inherit the promises* (6:12). In chapter 11, the author catalogs a long list of the faithful who have lived by God's promises. Its brief introduction shows that they have examples of people who have already lived faithful lives: they can imitate those saints—the most sincere form of flattery and highly recommended by our author! While not named specifically here, the Israelites to follow (many in Heb 11) are those who lived by their *faith*. The author has shifted from using forebears as a source of negative examples earlier in the text to flagging positive examples.

Teaching: God's Promises Are Sure 6:13-20

Our author closes this section with the most positive example of a forefather who has inherited the promises: *Abraham*. For early followers of Jesus, Abraham is a principal example of a person who lived by faith and hope. For our author, Abraham's defining characteristic is that he *patiently endured* and thereby *obtained the promises* (6:15). Living as though God's promises are being completely realized, as Abraham did, allows one to claim the promise that God gave him. Abraham never fully claimed the land of Canaan or saw how the nations were blessed through his faithfulness. But he remained faithful. The Hebrews should do likewise. Because God is *unchangeable*, the promises and the oath given to Abraham regarding the promises are also *unchangeable*. The author and the Hebrews have taken refuge in that unchangeability.

The phrase in 6:18, *we who have taken refuge*, implies that, like Abraham, the homilist and the congregation are refugees. Based on other passages in Hebrews in which the homilist makes special note of the outsider status of either Abraham or the congregation itself (11:13-16), the author is drawing attention to their group identity as special followers of Christ. They consider themselves in some way to be outside the current world order. As refugees, separated from the rest of the world, it is imperative that they be able *to seize the hope that [God has] set before* them (6:18). They have already been exhorted *to hold [krateō] the confession* in 4:14; now in 6:18 they are called to *seize [krateō] the hope*. Although 6:18 does not identify *the hope*, this probably means Jesus: *a hope that enters the inner shrine behind the curtain, where Jesus . . . has entered* (6:19-20). For our author, there is no hope without Jesus and, as in the following chapters, no lasting access to God.

Hebrews 5:11–6:20   119

The author has moved from insult to warning, then exhortation, and back to the teaching regarding Jesus, who has made the priestly offering of himself. He is the advocate, the forerunner, the one who brings hope. Now the author is ready to fully discuss Jesus' role as priest according to the order of Melchizedek in chapter 7. Once that priestly role is laid out, the author develops the priestly Christology and explores how Christ is the pioneer and perfector of our faith.

THE TEXT IN BIBLICAL CONTEXT

Agricultural Motifs

The pastor uses vivid agricultural metaphors in Hebrews 6:7-8 to describe the results of the ill-used blessing from God. The ground that drinks up the water and produces a useful crop receives a blessing. A crop of useless thistles is *on the verge of being cursed* (6:8). The Jewish Scriptures use agricultural motifs in various ways, some of which the pastor may have been pondering while preparing the sermon. We explore three examples. It is unclear whether these specific passages are behind the agricultural metaphors in 6:7-8. But all the passages demand a level of responsibility from the people of God similar to what our pastor is demanding.

Because of Adam and Eve's sin, the ground will bring forth "thorns and thistles." As humans "eat the plants of the field," they will need to "toil" to sustain themselves (Gen 3:17-18). No longer is the relationship between humans and earth straightforward; they will need to exert themselves to bring life out of the earth.

Deuteronomy 11 lays out the rewards of obedience to the Israelites. If they are obedient, they will be able to "occupy the land" into which they are crossing (11:8). The land is "flowing with milk and honey" (11:9) and "watered by rain from the sky" (11:11). Unlike Egypt's desert and necessarily irrigated fields, the land of Israel has hills and valleys blessed with seasonal rain, producing grain, grass, grapes for wine, and olives for oil. Diligent work and faithfulness to God are required to ensure that the land yields its promise. The work involves "loving the LORD your God, and serving him with all your heart and with all your soul" (11:13), not getting distracted by false gods. Otherwise, the land will no longer yield its bounty.

Isaiah 5:1-7 presents a poem about the relationship between the land, people, and God. In this beautiful and profoundly moving poem, an owner mourns his vineyard, which does not bear good grapes. A vineyard was often used as a metaphor for a lover in

120   Hebrews 5:11–6:20

Israelite poetry; here it represents "the house of Judah and the people of Israel" (5:7). Since this carefully tended vineyard produces only wild grapes instead of good ones, the owner has no recourse but to abandon it, let it be overcome with briars and thorns, and call on the clouds to "rain no rain" (5:5-6). The poem closes with a social application: "The LORD . . . expected justice but saw bloodshed; righteousness but heard a cry!" (5:7).

Our pastor continues the expectations set in the Jewish Scriptures by asking the congregation to be cultivators of the promises sown by Abraham and earlier people of faith.

Abraham

Early followers of Jesus the Christ traced their genealogical roots to Abraham. In a spiritual sense, Abraham was the father of the faith, the receiver of the covenant. Paul presents Abraham as the ancestor of the faithful in Romans 4. According to Paul, Abraham and all his spiritual descendants were made righteous through his faithfulness (4:13). In Galatians 3, Paul insists that the promises God made to Abraham were to all his offspring. Paul insists on this because of what was going on among the Gentile Galatians who were attempting to practice the Judaic law. Paul was opposed to this, deeming it unnecessary. For Paul, Abraham received the promise prior to the law's being given to Moses. Gentile followers of Jesus should therefore remember that it is this covenant that they inherit (3:15-18). Hebrews also uses the theme of Abraham's faith, though "Judaizing" practices are not at issue for our pastor. As with Paul, God's oath regarding the promises is unchangeable. Unlike Paul, the author of Hebrews does not seem to have any difficulties regarding "the law." Other than sacrifice, a major topic in upcoming chapters, we do not know enough about the Hebrews audience to specify their stance on observing the law of Moses.

In the Jewish Scriptures, Abraham's name often occurs in reminders of God's promise regarding the land of Israel. For example, God tells Moses, "I will bring you into the land that I swore to give to Abraham, Isaac, and Jacob" (Exod 6:8; cf. Deut 9:5; Josh 24:2-3; Neh 9:7-8).

In contrast, "Moses" is often used as shorthand for what we call the Pentateuch, the five books attributed to Moses. Outside the Pentateuch, Moses the person is often called God's "servant" (e.g., see Neh 1:7-8). New Testament writers continue both approaches; when quoting the Pentateuch, they sometimes write "Moses said" as a shorthand for the law and, therefore, their code of behavior.

Hebrews follows Nehemiah in understanding Moses to be God's servant (3:5).

THE TEXT IN THE LIFE OF THE CHURCH

Baptisms and Laying On of Hands

One of the hallmarks of Anabaptism is adult, or believers, baptism. Over the centuries, many Christians have been adamant about the appropriate methods of baptism. Some denominations have experienced divisions over this practice. Christian denominations have criticized other churches for their understandings and practice, making claims and counterclaims about infant baptism versus believers baptism or immersion versus pouring. The words of Hebrews 6:1-3 should give us pause. Anabaptists today can maintain a practice without losing sight of what is most important. Can we move on from the basics to a deeper understanding of what it means to be a follower of Christ? Baptism is the public declaration of a person's intention to live in community in solidarity with Christ. By what fruit do we know the intention is being upheld and that the person and community have moved on together to greater faithfulness?

At some point in life, you or a family member may have experienced a threatening illness. Perhaps you asked for the laying on of hands before surgery or at some other crucial moment in the illness (6:2; cf. Mark 8:23; 1 Tim 4:14; James 5:14). You may have been present or participated as a family member or clergy in the service. The power of that act can be palpable. As a community of believers, we know that the laying on of hands can provide healing when we are faced with challenging, even life-threatening, situations. It might seem out of step with the rest of society, although in the twenty-first century many people who understand the healing act of touch use various methods to heal the body and soul. In any of these practices, ancient or modern, the evidence of healing comes afterward. What does it mean to be healed? Can we move on from our illness to live a more faithful life?

Repentance of Apostates

Apostates are people who have turned away from God. Throughout Christian history, many conscientious Christians have suffered great anxiety over scriptural texts that speak of an unforgivable sin, or sin unto death, or the impossibility of repentance. A strong awareness of their own sinfulness has made them doubtful and fearful of how God would deal with them. In his spiritual biography *Grace Abounding*, John Bunyan agonized that by his carelessness he might have reached a point where repentance was no longer possible. The warning texts of Hebrews hung over him like a dark cloud. Might he be like Esau (12:16), who sold his birthright? He trembled with fear lest he *fall into the hands of the living God* (10:31). Was he one of those who had crucified the Son of God again and held him up to contempt? Only with much searching and prayer was he able to hear the positive word and assurances of other texts.

It took Bunyan years of struggle and continual prayers and supplications on his part to understand that sinfulness and apostasy are very different. Interestingly, another passage in Hebrews seemed to get him over the hump: 12:22-24. There the reader is encouraged to go to *Jesus, the mediator of a new covenant*. When he realized that he had access to that experience, he was freed from the terrifying fear and wanted to share such freedom with others. Bunyan's diligent seeking of God helped him realize *the full assurance of hope* (6:11). Peter, who turned his back on Jesus, also returned to receive forgiveness and acceptance (John 21). Both examples suggest that living a faithful life is a daily decision in the same way that apostasy, separation from the community, and denial of faith are daily decisions. Repentance is always possible.

Too much emphasis has been placed on these few verses in Hebrews. The overall message of Hebrews is one of promise and encouragement: Christ is sitting at the right hand of God and has made it possible for us to have eternal rest with him. Sometimes it is difficult to remain enlightened, to walk in the light. As people in communities of faith, we can remind each other that God's grace is always available if we just remember to face toward it.

Hebrews 7:1-28

Jesus the Son Is Foreshadowed by the Priest-King Melchizedek

PREVIEW

What is so important about Melchizedek? On what basis is he qualified to be high priest? And why is it important that Jesus belong to Melchizedek's order? Up to now, the author has repeatedly called Jesus a *high priest*. We find the title in 2:17; 3:1; 4:14, 15; 5:1, 5, 10; and 6:20. Three times he adds to the title the additional phrase *according to the order of Melchizedek* without explaining what that means (5:6, 10; 6:20; cf. 7:1, 10, 11, 15, 17).

However, in calling Jesus a high priest, the author faces a staggering problem either ignored or postponed up to now. Since Jesus is not from the tribe of Levi, he is not even eligible to be a priest, let alone a high priest! A big oops? No. Here finally, at the beginning of chapter 7, the author is ready to offer a careful argument that provides the answer to that problem: Jesus is the kind of priest that Melchizedek was. This is not just a concession or a weak attempt to find a loophole. The author makes the case that the ministry of the Aaronic priesthood was limited and ineffectual. A different kind of priest was needed, a more effective priest. The author turns to that argument in chapter 7.

124   Hebrews 7:1-28

The homilist has cleverly divided this chapter into three subsections by using a rhetorical device called *inclusio*, a strategy that creates sections of text by using the same word (or a form of it) at the beginning and end of the section.

7:1-10   Melchizedek *met* (*synantaō*) Abraham.
7:11-19 If *perfection* (*teleiōsis*) was attainable through the
         Levitical priesthood . . .
7:20-28 A better hope was confirmed with an *oath* (*horkōmosia*).

Throughout the chapter, the writer uses Genesis 14 and Psalm 110 as the backbone for developing the argument that the heavenly priesthood granted to Jesus is superior to that of the Levitical priesthood because it was first granted by Abraham to a similar figure, Melchizedek, when they *met*. More importantly, unlike other priests who *offer sacrifices day after day*, Jesus did this *once for all when he offered himself* (7:27), a more *perfect* sacrifice (7:11, 19, 28).

This was promised by God through an *oath* in Scripture: "The LORD has sworn and will not change his mind, 'You are a priest forever according to the order of Melchizedek'" (Ps 110:4).

The themes established in these units are intricately connected through the use of midrash, an ancient Jewish interpretive strategy *[Rhetorical Habits of the Author, p. 249]*, and another rhetorical strategy called *synkrisis* (comparison), to establish the superiority of the priesthood of Jesus, through Melchizedek, over that of the Levitical priesthood.

OUTLINE

When Melchizedek Met Abraham, 7:1-10
    7:1-3   Midrash on Melchizedek
    7:4-10   Elaboration on Melchizedek's Greatness
Perfection Is Attainable through Jesus' Priesthood, 7:11-19
An Oath Confirms Jesus' Everlasting, Holy, and Perfect Priesthood,
      7:20-28
    7:20-22   Confirmed by an Oath
    7:23-25   Eternal
    7:26-28   Holy and Perfect

Hebrews 7:1-28   125

EXPLANATORY NOTES

When Melchizedek Met Abraham 7:1-10

7:1-3 Midrash on Melchizedek

The writer uses the first ten verses of chapter 7 to establish the greatness and the priority of Melchizedek over other priests. Because Melchizedek *met* Abraham and received tithes and then blessed him (7:1-2), by extension he also met Levi (who was in Abraham's loins at the time), as well as the hereditary Levitical priests after him (7:9-10). Since Jesus came from the tribe of Judah, not Levi, the author cannot base Jesus' priestly status on genealogical grounds. Instead, the author uses biblical material in Genesis 14 and Psalm 110:4, along with other ancient Jewish traditions that mention Melchizedek, to establish the credentials of both Melchizedek and Jesus as high priest. The author claims that because Melchizedek is without genealogy or *end of life*, he resembles the *Son* (Jesus) and *remains a priest forever* (7:3), thereby establishing the superiority of both Jesus and Melchizedek over Levitical priests.

Our author begins by establishing the foundational knowledge about Melchizedek in 7:1-3. *Resembling the Son of God, he remains a priest forever* (7:3). The solution for our author in using Melchizedek is that neither Melchizedek nor Jesus is a priest through normal means. Although not of the tribe of Levi, Melchizedek has been given a priestly status. And the author of Hebrews wants to assign that status to Jesus. We can see the author working out the problem of Jesus' ancestry in this brief passage.

The chapter opens with a cursory summary of the meeting between Abraham and Melchizedek as given in Genesis 14:17-20. King Melchizedek met and blessed Abraham as Abraham was returning from defeating various raiding kings. Abraham gave one-tenth of his possessions to Melchizedek in return. Our author leaves out a lot of details recorded in Genesis and replaces them with ancient Jewish traditions about Melchizedek's name and origin. To establish the priority of Melchizedek's priesthood, our homilist uses another biblical text that mentions Melchizedek, Psalm 110, to inform the Genesis story. Concentration on Psalm 110 allows the homilist to (1) assume a nonbeginning and everlasting status for Melchizedek; (2) establish a priesthood based in a historical event (Abraham meeting Melchizedek); and (3) establish the resemblance of Melchizedek to the Son (110:4).

126   Hebrews 7:1-28

Many scholars consider this passage to be a midrash, but merely quoting biblical verses and interpreting them is not midrash. It becomes midrash when the writer uses a *second* biblical text to interpret the one under scrutiny. Here the writer uses Psalm 110, commonly understood as a royal messianic psalm, to interpret the Genesis passage. This brief but powerful section closes with the phrase *resembling the Son of God, he remains a priest forever* (Heb 7:3). This phrase belongs neither to the Genesis story nor to Psalm 110. Rather, in true midrash form, it is an interpretive statement by which the author reiterates the point made in Hebrews 5:5-6, where the author has joined Psalms 2:7; 110:1; and 110:4 to identify the Son, seated at God's right hand and high priest forever after the order of Melchizedek. Both Melchizedek and Jesus are the true priests; Abraham has established their priesthood, which lasts forever because they have *neither beginning of days nor end of life* (7:3). The rest of the chapter lays out three pieces of evidence that support this claim: (1) Abraham's tithing to Melchizedek implies that his descendants also give tithes to this priest; (2) the immortality of these superior priests allows the attainment of perfection; and (3) an oath confirms this priesthood.

7:4-10 Elaboration on Melchizedek's Greatness

The homilist continues with an immediate declaration of the significance of Melchizedek. When he met Melchizedek, Abraham recognized Melchizedek's greatness. And through this encounter, Levi, a descendant of Abraham and the ancestor of priests, met and recognized the greatness of Melchizedek as well. Drawing on the speculative expansion of Psalm 110:4 to identify Melchizedek as a heavenly being (see TBC), Hebrews 7:8 reminds us that *he lives*. Because he lives forever, a priest like Melchizedek is superior to the Levitical priests, who are merely mortal. And because Abraham gave him tithes, his descendants, who were in his loins, also tithed. This includes the Levites, the tribe assigned the priestly office in Israel and commanded by the law to collect tithes from the people (in Lev 27, priests assess the value of the tithes; Num 18:20-32 explains how the people of Israel are to give their tithes to the priests to support their work). Since Melchizedek met and received tithes from Abraham, he also met and received tithes from Levi. According to the writer of Hebrews, the one who blesses is superior to the one being blessed: so this establishes Melchizedek's superiority over Abraham and his descendants (yet within the biblical tradition are many instances when the "lesser" being blesses the "greater").

Hebrews 7:1-28

Perfection Is Attainable through Jesus' Priesthood 7:11-19

In the middle of the chapter, the author returns to the concept of perfection (*teleiōsis*). A major theme in chapter 2, the author brings it to the forefront again in the context of the work of the priests *[Perfection in Greco-Roman and Jewish Thought, p. 244]*. The section begins with the claim that if the Levitical priesthood had been effective, it would have made the people perfect. It closes with the statement that *the law made nothing perfect* (7:19). What the author means by perfection is not completely obvious; it probably "combines elements of maturity and moral growth (see 5:14), . . . overcoming sin (9:27; 10:4), . . . cleansing the conscience (9:9), [and] entering into a state of holiness through an opening to God's power and presence through faithful obedience (5:7-10; 12:1-2)" (L. Johnson: 185–86). The author believes that the Levitical priesthood was not adequate to accomplish all this. If it had been, another kind of priesthood would not have been necessary (7:11). Based on a reading of Psalm 110 that is repeated in Hebrews 7:17 the author finds this priesthood in the order of Melchizedek, not that of Aaron (from whom the Levitical priesthood descended).

To argue this claim, the writer relies on the rhetoric device called *synkrisis* (comparison). *Synkrisis* begins in this section and continues through the end of the chapter. The comparison is between the two types of priesthood and how they derive their usefulness and their power.

Aaron/Moses	Melchizedek/Jesus the Son
old	new
mortal	everlasting
continuing	once and final

The Levitical priesthood derives its usefulness from the law given to Moses, with generations of mortal men inheriting the ability to *serve at the altar* (7:13). This is also restated at the end of the chapter, in 7:28, with the claim that *the law appoints as high priests those who are subject to weakness*. The priesthood of Melchizedek, on the other hand, has been given the upper hand by the psalmist, who has declared a new order in which the high priest is *a priest forever* (7:17; Ps 110:4). According to our homilist, this promise from the psalmist is *the abrogation of* (or some form of annulment, canceling by official or legal means) the earlier commandment (7:18).

128   Hebrews 7:1-28

The author closes this section with the same theme with which it started—perfection and the inability of the previous priesthood to attain it—and includes an affirmation that *a better hope* (7:19) will enable people to approach God. That better hope is the priesthood of Jesus Christ and the promise of perfection.

We want to be careful not to read supersessionist thinking into this passage [*Supersessionist and Anti-Jewish Interpretations of Hebrews, p. 257*]. We cannot and should not generalize about Jewish practice based on our author's approach to the sacrificial cult. Elsewhere in Hebrews our author implies a positive (or at least neutral) approach to the Sabbath (4:9) and to the collection of tithes in 7:5 (cf. Regev: 277).

Eyal Regev suggests that the Hebrews author is attempting to reconcile the belief that Jesus is the heavenly high priest with the law of Moses. The law itself has changed because of the change in the priesthood. He asserts, "It is possible to see the change in the Law as an explanation after the fact for the change in the priesthood" (277–78). As he states,

> It is possible that Hebrews' alternative cult of Christ as the high priest and sacrifice does *not* derive from a rejection of the Law. It defies the sacrificial law not because of a general or outright rejection of the precepts of the Torah, but transforms the temple cult owing to a more specific religious concern that results from only partial rejection of the Law. (278)

As high priest, Jesus does not annul the Mosaic law but changes understanding of it (cf. Matt 5:17, where Jesus declares that he has come "to fulfill . . . the law").

An Oath Confirms Jesus' Everlasting, Holy, and Perfect Priesthood 7:20-28

7:20-22 Confirmed by an Oath

From the promise of perfection through "the better hope," the author closes the chapter with several additional comparisons between the two priesthoods. The oath uttered by God in Psalm 110:4 and repeated by the author in Hebrews 7:21 looms large in the author's argument in these comparisons. Since the oath (in the psalm) came many years after the law was given to Moses, the oath takes priority. The author begins and ends the chapter with this important point: it is crucial to the argument that the congregation be convinced of the priority of the oath. The author relays the story

Hebrews 7:1-28 129

of Abraham, introduced in 6:13-20, in which the oath of God is the double guarantee of certainty and of God's faithfulness to Abraham and his descendants. Most likely the original audience of Hebrews also knew about other oaths in the biblical tradition, including God's swearing that Moses' generation would not enter the Promised Land (Num 32:11; Heb 3:18) and the promise to Noah after the flood (Gen 9:9). They would know that God kept those promises (sealed with an oath), so this promise from Psalm 110:4, that Jesus will be a priest forever, is sure to be kept as well.

Jesus is the guarantee of the oath (Heb 7:21-22). In ancient society, parties put up a "surety" or guarantee that a pledge would be kept. The writer claims that Jesus himself is the guarantee that God will keep the promise laid out in Psalm 110:4. The phrase *better covenant* deserves special scrutiny. The term *covenant* (Gk. *diathēkē*) has multiple meanings, depending on the context. It can mean "testament" in the sense of a will. In this case, it means "a binding agreement, a promise." To complete the agreement, God also puts up a guarantee, a surety that God will keep the promise. That *guarantee* is *Jesus*, the seal that the oath will be kept (Heb 7:22).

7:23-25 Eternal

The term *better* (Gk. *kreittōn*), sometimes translated as "superior," is the adjective modifying *covenant* or *agreement*. The author poses this as a statement of fact and not as a polemic against the Levitical priesthood by using comparison (*synkrisis*) to distinguish the two priesthoods. A fuller analysis of what he means by a *better covenant* appears in the next chapter; the author completes chapter 7 by comparing how the priesthood of Christ is better.

Most important, Jesus' priesthood is everlasting, *forever* (7:24). The author uses an "on the one hand . . . but on the other" structure in 7:23-24 to compare the Levitical priests, *many in number* and impermanent because of *death*, and Christ, one and eternal. A limit of the Levitical priesthood was that mortal men fulfilled the duties and passed away. Consequently, many priests served. Now Christ is high priest, the only one, and he remains *forever*. Because Christ's priesthood is *permanent*, he can go beyond the impermanence of the Levitical priesthood and the limited abilities of the mortal men serving in it. This section closes in poetic fashion, lost in English translation. The author uses the root *pan* (Gk. = *all* or *every*) to emphasize the "always" nature of Christ's priesthood. Christ *is able for all time to save [Gk. sōzein . . . panteles] those who approach God through him, since he always lives [Gk. pantote zōn] to make intercession for them* (7:25).

130   Hebrews 7:1-28

7:26-28 *Holy and Perfect*

In this final paragraph, Jesus becomes both the one who sacrifices and the one sacrificed. Once again, relying on *synkrisis* (comparison) to state the message about the superiority of Jesus, the final verses offer the following parallels.

Levitical priests	Christ
daily sacrifices	once for all
sacrifice for themselves and others	he himself is the sacrifice
appointed by the law	appointed by an oath
subject to weakness	holy, blameless, undefiled

The author sets up several distinctions in this final section. First, the *holy* and *blameless* Christ (v. 26) is compared with the mortal high priests, who are *subject to weakness* (v. 28). Second, the priests *offer sacrifices day after day*; Christ's sacrifice is *once for all* (v. 27). However, this contrast is based on the author's mixing of daily sacrifices and the yearly sacrifice that happened on the Day of Atonement *[Atonement, p. 231]*. Only on the Day of Atonement was the high priest required to make a sacrifice for his own sin. Daily sacrifices did not require this (see Lev 16 for more on the Day of Atonement; also Lev 1–7; Exod 29:38-42; Num 28:3-8 for regulations of daily offerings), leading some scholars to suggest that the author did not have firsthand experience of the temple workings but relied solely on knowledge of the biblical material (C. Koester 2001: 368; see also Attridge: 214).

Most important, the nature of the sacrifice is different (Heb 7:26-27). Christ is not just the high priest who sacrifices: *he himself* is also the sacrifice, yet needing to be offered only once. This is the heart of the distinction of Christ's priesthood that the author of Hebrews has been emphasizing in the chapter. His *priesthood* is of a new order: it is everlasting. Now the writer focuses on an additional element of Jesus' *sacrifice*: it is *once for all* (Gk. *ephapax*). This is where the entire text has been headed. The word *ephapax* appears in only two other books in the entire New Testament (Rom 6:10; 1 Cor 15:6; cf. *hapax* in 1 Pet 3:18). In Hebrews, it appears three times: 7:27; 9:12; 10:10. In chapters 9–10, the author uses a related word, *once* (Gk. *hapax*; 9:7, 26-28; 10:2; 12:26-27), to discuss the sacrifice made by Christ compared to those offered by the Levitical priests. This all indicates that the author is emphasizing the worth of the sacrifice (daily/yearly;

Hebrews 7:1-28

or *once for all*). The author returns to this theme several times in the rest of Hebrews, usually comparing Christ's sacrifice of himself with the Levitical priests' sacrifices.

We can see how the nature of the sacrifice is compared in chapters of Hebrews:

	Levitical priests	Christ
Frequency	Daily (7:27)	Once for all (7:27; 9:26-28)
For whom?	For himself, then others (7:27)	Just for others (7:27)
With what?	Unblemished animals daily (10:4)	His own body once for all (10:10)
Where	At the tabernacle daily (7:27; 9:6); in its holy of holies once a year (9:7)	Entered heaven once for all (9:12)
Outcome	Worshipers cleansed temporarily (10:2)	Sanctified once for all (10:10)

The chapter closes with a summary of the homilist's argument: the oath made by God in Psalm 110:4 appoints the perfected Son as priest (Heb 7:20-21). Having established the Son's priority through this oath, the author can explain how covenant (ch. 8), ritual (ch. 9), and sacrifice (ch. 10) change because of Christ's priesthood.

THE TEXT IN BIBLICAL CONTEXT

Melchizedek

Why should the writer of Hebrews base a Christology on Melchizedek, a figure mentioned only twice in the Jewish Scriptures (Gen 14; Ps 110) [*Christology in Hebrews, p. 235; The Septuagint in Hebrews, p. 252*]? The figure of Melchizedek is expanded in the literature of Second Temple Judaism, catching the imagination of writers in various ways. In addition to the biblical texts about Melchizedek, we also have at least four separate sources with distinct interests:

1. 11QMelchizedek, among the Dead Sea Scrolls, was copied and preserved by a community of separatist Jews called Essenes (Vermès: 500–502). This scroll, dated to around 50 BCE, gives the archangel Melchizedek the role of leading heavenly angels in fighting against the angels of darkness, liberating the captives of Belial, and functioning as *judge* in the end time—thus *not* as a priest. From the Dead Sea Scrolls [*Jewish Literature in Antiquity, p. 238*], we know that the Essene community developed an eschatological worldview that pitted themselves as the Sons of Light against the Sons of Darkness (all

132   Hebrews 7:1-28

other Jews and the enemies of Israel). We can see the special interests of the Essene community in this understanding of Melchizedek as having a leading role in the end-time events.

2. Philo. In his *Allegorical Interpretation* (3.79–82; see Yonge: 59), Philo, a first-century Jew of Alexandria (Egypt), treats Melchizedek as a symbol of divine reason. He uses the meaning of his name ("king of righteousness") to compare righteousness, peace, and divine law to a despot who represents lawlessness and war. Philo's goal is to reflect on the human soul. He does so by interpreting characters in Genesis as allegories of the soul [*Philo, Neoplatonism, and Hebrews, p. 245*].

3. Josephus, in his *Jewish Antiquities* (1.177–182), writes briefly of Melchizedek. A first-century Jew born in Jerusalem, Josephus was a leader in the Jewish Revolt against Rome until he switched sides, a historian, and an advisor to Emperor Titus from 71 CE onward. In his work chronicling the history of the Jews, Josephus summarizes the passage from Genesis and adds a translation of his name: "King of Righteousness." Our Hebrews author builds on this collective imagination and uses it to make a new claim about Jesus as the everlasting high priest.

4. Second Enoch, a pseudepigraphical text (Charlesworth 1983: 196–213), describes the ascent of Enoch through ten heavens and establishes his descendants as members of the priestly class. Its last chapters (69–73) contain a birth narrative of Melchizedek and posit him as a priest before his own ascent into heaven. This book has been dated anywhere from the first century BCE to the tenth century CE. Because 2 Enoch has Enoch's descendants as a pre-flood priestly class, it may point to an alternate tradition within Judaism of how (and whom) God appointed priests. Nir, a brother of Noah and descendant of Enoch, becomes priest. His barren wife miraculously gives birth to Melchizedek, who is then taken up into the heavens before the flood. This is how Melchizedek can continue as priest after the flood. According to Andrei Orlov, 2 Enoch may reflect divisions among Jews during the Second Temple period regarding how animal sacrifices should be conducted: this text recounts a different process (33–34). Thus the figure of Melchizedek represents a competing tradition of priesthood and sacrifice within Judaism.

The use of Melchizedek in Hebrews to expound on Jesus' role as ultimate and eternal high priest is another reminder that our homilist is operating squarely within the framework of first-century CE Judaism. In later centuries, Christians lost their connection with Judaism and thus failed to understand that our author is writing within that context. The elevation of Jesus as high priest is not to condemn an entire religious tradition, but to put forth a more permanent sacrificial system than the one the Levitical priests managed. James Thompson says it best:

> The author addresses the universal temptation to substitute human mediators for the ultimate high priest. . . . The distinctive feature of the high priest according to Melchizedek is that he abides forever (7:3, 16, 24-25). . . . The eternal high priest provides the hope that is the "anchor of the soul," security for a vulnerable people (6:19-20). He offers God's guarantee (7:22), and he "always" intercedes (7:25) insofar as his sacrifice is final (7:27). Thus the knowledge that the high priest according to the order of Melchizedek is eternal provides the stability for a people whose world is shaken. (2008: 164–65)

Priests in the Jewish Scriptures

A superficial look at Scripture may suggest that the ancient Israelite priesthood was monolithic and clearly delineated. However, the situation was much more complex than that, and we can speak only in general terms here. It is challenging to sift through the many layers of Jewish Scriptures written and edited over hundreds of years to uncover practices during any one historical period represented in those texts. The following explanation, summarized from Lester Grabbe (1995), is a good introduction. See also Yoder's accessible discussion of the work of priests as laid out in Leviticus 7–10 and 16.

The primary role of the priest was as cultic specialist. The priest's job was to offer sacrifices (see Yoder's BCBC commentary on Lev 1–9 for a clear explication). Priests' duties included caring for the tabernacle or temple's furnishings (e.g., Num 3:5-10), providing music for worship (e.g., 2 Chron 5, 7), performing divination (Exod 28:30), acting as judges (Num 5; Deut 17:8-13), and teaching, learning, and studying the Lord's "statutes" (Lev 10:10-11). As indicated by the brief survey that follows, no single biblical source lays this out in a straightforward manner. Scholars have developed this understanding of the priesthood by sifting through the Pentateuch, the Prophets, the Historical Books, and the Psalms.

In addition to the variety of duties, some of the sources indicate different types of Levites, depending on one's actual genealogical heritage. Leviticus and Numbers lay out two classes: priests are those who descend directly from Aaron (a Levite), who serve at the altar; and a lesser order, other Levites from the tribe of Levi, who help the priests but do not actually approach the altar. The basis for this understanding is found in Leviticus 8–10 and 16, which concern the installation of the priests and high priest; and Numbers 3:5-10, which outlines the duties of other Levites. Deuteronomy 10:8-9 confirms that priests are to come from the tribe of Levi and stipulates their lack of "allotment or inheritance" of agricultural land (other than pasture), but does not distinguish between types of priests and often uses the term "Levitical priests" to encompass all of them.

Another complicating factor is that these same Scriptures witness to people (all men, of course) who became priests without the proper genealogical background. Two of the most familiar figures are Samuel and Zadok. Samuel was not of the tribe of Levi, but of Ephraim (1 Sam 1), and was given by his parents to Eli, a Levitical priest. First Samuel narrates Samuel's priestly education and service, culminating in his anointing Saul as king. Incidentally, Samuel also served as judge and prophet, two other roles that priests perform. (Several prophets were also of the tribe of Levi.)

Zadok was the high priest who anointed Solomon as king. His descendants were the high priests at the temple in Jerusalem until the beginning of the Hasmonean period, around 153 BCE. His complicated genealogy remains a puzzle. Not until 1 Chronicles 6:8-12, a text probably written during the Second Temple period (533 BCE–70 CE), is Zadok's genealogy mapped out in such a way as to clarify that he comes from the tribe of Levi. Ezekiel's vision of the temple in Ezekiel 40–48 follows the division of labor laid out in Leviticus and Numbers but makes clear that the only priests to offer sacrifices are in the Zadokite line.

Priests during the Second Temple Period and in the New Testament

It is difficult to construct exactly how priests worked during the Second Temple period (539 BCE–70 CE). First Chronicles 23–26 details the division of labor between the descendants of Levi and the other tribes. In the first centuries BCE and CE, we need to rely on such sources as 1 and 2 Maccabees, Josephus, Philo, and the New Testament to understand how priests worked during the period when Jesus lived.

In the Persian period (536–333 BCE), the lack of a king in Israel resulted in gradual growth in the importance and influence of the high priest. In time he became not only the most important spiritual figure in Israel, but also the most important political figure. When the Maccabeans wrested political power from the Seleucids in the second century BCE, they could not afford to have their subjects look to an alternative figure (the high priest) for spiritual and political leadership: when they assumed kingship, they also assumed the role

Hebrews 7:1-28

of high priest, combining both roles in one person. Although they were from the tribe of Levi, they were not Zadokites. In response, some of the Zadokites rejected the Jerusalem priests and the whole system of worship represented by the temple and withdrew to the wilderness to become Essenes.

Thus, the Jerusalem priesthood was responsible for governing the nation of Israel. When the Hasmonean Dynasty (i.e., the Maccabeans) fell to the Romans in 63 BCE, Rome realized that they needed to control the high priesthood. The high priest was head of the temple and responsible for the spiritual welfare of the people. He was also responsible for governing Judea and collecting Roman taxes, which many Jews thought were oppressive. Even though the high priesthood was traditionally a hereditary position maintained for life, *Rome* appointed the high priests in the first century. They retained their position only by doing what was pleasing to Rome. Long before Jesus' ministry, the high priests were seen as collaborators with Rome. We can see this at work when agents of the high priest arrest Jesus: the high priest questions him and then sends him to Pilate, to have him crucified.

The Gospels speak of another class of priests, the Sadducees. In Matthew, Sadducees are often paired with Pharisees (e.g., Matt 3:7; 16:1, 6, 11-12) as groups who deeply oppose the ministry of Jesus. The Sadducees object to his teaching about the resurrection (Matt 22:23//Luke 20:27//Mark 12:18) and actively persecute Jesus and his followers.

While a cursory reading of the New Testament may lead us to form negative judgments about priests, we should be cautious. Neither Jesus nor his followers repudiated the priesthood or the sacrificial system, even though we know from other sources that such groups as the Essenes considered the high priests and the entire government as illegal. According to the Gospels, Jesus directs people he has healed to show themselves to the priests for sacrificial ceremonies of purification (Mark 1:44; Luke 17:14). In Luke 1:5 we also have a wonderful story about Zechariah, the father of John the Baptist and a priest from the order of Abijah. Luke's narrative confirms much of what we already know about the priesthood. Priests took turns serving in the temple. We see Zechariah doing just that in Luke 1:8. We know that priests acted as diviners (e.g., Num 5:12-31). While offering incense, Zechariah received a prophecy through a vision (Luke 1:12). Acts 6:7 informs us that "many of the priests became obedient to the faith." Only by reading the text closely do we see the wide variety in priests' behavior.

136 Hebrews 7:1-28

Jesus as intercessor is a common theme in the New Testament. In Luke 22:32, Jesus prays for Peter that his faith may not fail. In John 17, Jesus prays for all his disciples. Paul reminds his readers that Jesus is at the right hand of God, making intercession for us (Rom 8:33-34). The theme may be traced to Isaiah 53:12, where the servant of the Lord makes intercession for the transgressors. Here the writer directly relates it to his role as high priest.

Priests in the Greco-Roman World

In the Greco-Roman world, access to gods through sacrifice and other types of religious devotion was generally not restricted to a certain class of professional priests. In Roman civic religion, priests came from the senatorial, or elite, class of people. Their job was to make sure that the public worship of the gods was carried out in an orderly fashion. On the other hand, Egyptian worship was centered in a temple, much as with Judaism (until 70 CE), with priests performing daily rituals, including sacrifices. Depending on where one lived and what gods were worshiped, the experience of priests would have been different from that assumed by Hebrews.

THE TEXT IN THE LIFE OF THE CHURCH

Priesthood in the Christian Church

In early Christianity, the term "priest" did not come into general use until the latter part of the second century. In the first century and early second, elders (presbyters) and bishops were charged with oversight of churches (see 1 Timothy). First Clement 40–41 (usually dated to ca. 96 CE) mentions bishops and presbyters but says little about their exact roles.

The descriptions of these positions correspond more closely to the operation of synagogues than they do to practice in the temple (destroyed in 70 CE). Only in the third and fourth centuries did the term "priest" (Lat. *sacerdos*) begin to be used for bishops and presbyters. Starting in the early Middle Ages, church fathers laid out the primary work of the priest: to ordain, baptize, instruct, and distribute the eucharist. During the Reformation, many Protestant Reformers rejected the title of priest for their leadership because of its association with the mass. The Reformers spoke of "the priesthood of all believers," calling all Christians to ministry.

The priesthood of all believers has little to do with the role of Jesus as a high priest according to the order of Melchizedek in Hebrews. To speak about the priesthood of all believers, the

Reformers invoked a passage from 1 Peter 2:9, calling the people of God a "royal priesthood, a holy nation." Some Protestant churches, especially the Anabaptists, interpreted the priesthood of all believers as a call for all in the church to minister in the world. As a community of God, we are to be "priests" to each other.

Hebrews 7 in Anabaptist Thought

During the sixteenth and seventeenth centuries, confessions of faith were written by Anabaptists and distributed among Anabaptist groups to bring them together or to delineate between groups (Koop: 9). Many early confessions contained statements of practice regarding baptism, the ban (church discipline), and the Lord's Supper; later confessions took on more theological and christological issues. A case in point is one of the longest confessions, titled "Confession of Faith according to God's Word," or the "Thirty-Three Articles," from a group now called Old Frisians, written in 1617. It was a response to the publication of martyr stories that included Anabaptists from all around Europe, regardless of doctrine. Conservative Anabaptists from Holland rejected this universal approach and wrote a separate martyrology with the Thirty-Three Articles as an introduction to the work. The Thirty-Three Articles use Hebrews 7 in chapter XIX on the "office of Christ." The document outlines several "offices" that Christ has: prophet, king, and, quoting Hebrews 7, high priest. The Articles confirm Christ's dual role as high priest and as sacrifice, stating that "he has fulfilled and transformed the Levitical Priesthood" (Koop: 221).

Dirk Philips, an early Dutch Anabaptist, used Hebrews 7 at some length to think through the incarnation of Jesus. On Hebrews 7:3, 16, Dirk (son of Philip, a Catholic priest) interprets what the writer of Hebrews says about Melchizedek as a "figure" of Jesus. By this he means that the Melchizedek character symbolizes a certain aspect fully realized in Jesus. Dirk wrestles with the mystery of the incarnation and the nature of Jesus as fully human and fully divine. In a lengthy discussion of theological matters in his *Enchiridion* (handbook), he uses Melchizedek to affirm "the divinity and humanity of Jesus Christ the Son of God" (Dirk 1992: 139). Although Melchizedek had earthly parents, his genealogy was not explained in Genesis "in order that he might correctly be compared with the Son of God as one among those who truly was on earth, loved, served, and offered himself just as a human being, and yet was not from the earth, but from heaven." However, Jesus is the "genuine Melchizedek" (140).

138 Hebrews 7:1-28

As Read in the Revised Common Lectionary

For the second time, Hebrews 7:23-28 appears in the lectionary along with Job (42:1-6, 10-17). Psalm 34:1-8 and Mark 10:46-52 also appear on the twenty-third Sunday after Pentecost in the Year B cycle of readings. Psalm 34:8 encourages people to "taste and see that the LORD is good." After all Job's trials, God confirms to him that he has been heard and seen. The gospel reading is the story of blind Bartimaeus, whose sight is restored by Jesus. These three passages share an affirmation: God provides a multisensory experience that allows us to witness God's goodness. Hebrews 7:23-28 affirms this saving grace of God by emphasizing the holy, blameless, undefiled, separated-from-sinners, and exalted status of Jesus, who intercedes for us.

Melchizedek as Other

Melchizedek was an outsider. From the beginnings of the biblical narrative, the people of God have struggled with what it means to be God's chosen people. But Abraham recognizes the presence of God in an outsider named Melchizedek, a practice that continues with Jethro, a Midianite priest who gives counsel to his son-in-law Moses (Exod 18); Rahab of Jericho, who protects Israel's spies (Josh 6); and Ruth, the Moabite great-grandmother of David (Ruth 4).

Christianity has struggled with openness to outsiders. The New Testament begins with outsiders in Joseph's genealogy and with the magi from a foreign land and different religious background, traveling to Bethlehem to pay homage to the baby Jesus, the Christ (Matt 1–2). The magi see the truth present in Jesus. We, too, know of faithful people in other religious traditions who not only seek the divine, but also experience God and the sacred in profound ways that transform lives. They, too, are followers of truth. If we can allow those outsiders to be the new Melchizedeks among us, we will find additional blessings as we travel through life.

Part 3

Jesus' Priestly Ministry in a New Covenant

Hebrews 8:1–10:18

OVERVIEW

Does something new necessarily make the old obsolete? And if something is obsolete, is it rendered unusable or unnecessary? Having established Jesus as the new high priest according to the order of Melchizedek, the pastor now uses the themes of priesthood, tabernacle, and sacrifice to talk about a new covenant based on Jesus—a covenant that Jeremiah already spoke about, which replaces the one delivered to Moses. Descriptions of the tabernacle may help us understand how the new covenantal system works. The new covenant reworks the old so that Jesus, the sacrifice, is now also the priest. Because Jesus' blood has been spilled once for all, a place of sacrifice is no longer needed.

Today's readers must imagine how these passages may have been understood by the original readers. We examine how modern Christians can understand and incorporate these ideas into our theology and practice without falling into thinking that Christianity is, by its very nature, superior to other religions, especially Judaism, because of this new covenant. Many of our Christian forebears learned this supersessionist approach from the early church [Supersessionist and Anti-Jewish Interpretations of Hebrews, p. 257]. Supersessionism has generated a great deal of destructive behavior by Christians toward Jews. How can we use these passages of Hebrews to celebrate our place in the new covenant while also cherishing and maintaining the "old"?

Some commentators find the central focus of Hebrews 8:1–10:18 to be sacrifice (e.g., Attridge: 225); but Mary Ann Beavis and HyeRan Kim-Cragg, L. Johnson, and Susanne Lehne stress the centrality of the covenant. Without minimizing sacrifice as important to the author of Hebrews, we follow Beavis and Kim-Cragg, L. Johnson, and Lehne in their approach to this section. The new covenant, so eloquently expressed in Jeremiah 31, culminates what this author has been developing throughout Hebrews. The new covenant is at the center of the text and its central idea. Observing this structure encourages us to ask, How can we uphold the "new" while cherishing the "old"?

OUTLINE

Christ Is High Priest and Minister of a New Covenant, 8:1-13
The Two Covenants, 9:1–10:18

Hebrews 8:1-13

Christ Is High Priest and Minister of a New Covenant

PREVIEW

The COVID-19 pandemic caused many of us to rethink how we do things. One of those things is church itself. We may have gotten used to "going to church" one or more times a week. But suddenly, "church" was gone and replaced by people in boxes on the computer screen or live-streaming video of one or two people in a sanctuary. We had to reconsider what "church" was. It was not the building, but the people. We still had "church," but we had to find new ways to express it.

Chapter 8 reconsiders the idea of covenant. The old becomes new. Themes discussed earlier in the text now crystallize as part of the new covenant:

- the eternal high priest seated at the right hand of the heavenly throne in the true sanctuary (1:13; 5:5-6; 8:1-2)

- the different genealogical background of Christ as high priest (7:1-28)

- the permanent nature of Christ's priesthood and sacrifice (7:23-28)

Hebrews 8:1-13

The author sets the stage by making brief but pointed comments on the earthly tabernacle, the locus of the "old" and now *obsolete* covenant (8:13). The true sanctuary is not the earthly tabernacle, but the *heavenly sanctuary*. The earthly tabernacle was only *a sketch and shadow* (8:5) of the true sanctuary in heaven. Having established the impermanent, unfinished nature of the old covenant and having reiterated Jesus' *more excellent ministry* (8:6), a transition occurs in 8:8. There the author announces *a new covenant*. Not surprisingly, this new covenant is promised in Scripture itself, in the prophetic words of Jeremiah (31:31-34). The new covenant, not taught or learned, is written directly into the heart and mind. Once this proof is laid out, the author can continue in chapters 9 and 10 to explain how the new covenant transforms the old.

OUTLINE

Summary, 8:1-6
Prophetic Announcement of the New Covenant, 8:7-13

EXPLANATORY NOTES

Summary 8:1-6

The author begins the summary with a review: *Now the main point in what we are saying is this . . .* (8:1). The Greek word used here means "head," but when used in this way it reminds the audience of the main point (*we have such a high priest* in the heavenly sanctuary) before moving on to the next topic. The author cleverly uses an *inclusio* created with two forms of the Greek word *leitourgos* in 8:2 and 6, a term that describes a servant, someone who performs a service, in the context of a ritual. The English word *liturgy* derives from it. In the LXX, this word describes the priests serving in the tabernacle (Num 16:9). In the broader Greco-Roman religious context, it describes the visible work done by priests. As L. Johnson points out, this work was often done with the priest's own resources and money (198).

Knowing how *leitourgos* was used in a broader context adds meaning to the description of Jesus as *leitourgos* (*minister*) in verse 2 and reminds readers of Jesus' significance as high priest. The work or ministry of the high priests is to *offer gifts and sacrifices* in the earthly sanctuary (8:3). Jesus has also offered a gift and a sacrifice: himself. Thinking about the offering that Jesus made in terms of a ritual event adds an interesting nuance and comparison to the sacrifices and offerings made by the Levitical priests in the sanctuary

144   Hebrews 8:1-13

and tabernacle, which was *a sketch and a shadow* (8:5) of the heavenly tabernacle. Jesus performed this service in the heavenly tabernacle. In the same way that the Levitical priests were facilitating or mediating the terms of the covenant, Jesus did the same. The difference is stressed: Jesus' ministry is as *the mediator of a better covenant* (8:6).

As the ministry of Jesus is different, so is the tabernacle, the locus of the ministry. Although the full elaboration on the distinctions between the earthly and heavenly sanctuaries does not occur until 9:1-22, the homilist introduces that distinction now. It follows that if there are distinctions between the priests (see Heb 7), the author would also understand their place of ministry to be different. Here in chapter 8 the author begins to emphasize those distinctions.

The homilist thinks of the earthly tabernacle or sanctuary as a *sketch and shadow of the heavenly one* (8:5). This language recalls a passage in Exodus 25:9-40: God shows Moses a *sketch/pattern* of the holy sanctuary to guide him in building the earthly tabernacle. The sanctuary itself and the items in it can be built to specifications given by God, but it was constructed by humans, from a pattern, and with earthly materials. For our author, the only possible outcome can be that the earthly tabernacle is reminiscent of God's design. It is not the heavenly sanctuary itself. This is not a new understanding. Other ancient Jews also comment in this way. (See TBC, "Earthly and Heavenly Sanctuaries.")

Hebrews offers a different context for this understanding and its consequences. With the word *but* in verse 6, the homilist moves from what we might consider a traditional Jewish understanding to something else. A change has occurred in the relationship between God and humans, marked not just by a different priesthood and sacrifice, but also by a new covenant. We are no longer merely talking about an earthly, temporal likeness of a heavenly structure, or a different order of priests. We are not just talking about a new (or second) covenant rather than a first (or old) one. We are now talking about a *better covenant* (Gk. *kreittōn*). In this context, the existence of an earthly tabernacle (let alone an earthly temple) no longer becomes necessary for the work of Jesus as high priest to take place.

Our author says as much already in 8:2. Jesus is the minister (Gk. *leitourgos*) *in the sanctuary and the true tent*. Although the phrase is translated in the NRSV as *sanctuary and true tent*, commentators are divided about whether the Greek phrase refers to the "holy of holies and the true tent" or "the sanctuary, that is, the true tent." In either

Hebrews 8:1-13

case, the meaning is clear enough: the true place of worship is the *heavenly* sanctuary, not the earthly one.

Now the author is ready to move on to the new and better covenant itself.

Prophetic Announcement of the New Covenant 8:7-13

Read with an assumption of Christian superiority, the words and phrases of this passage—*better covenant, better promises* (8:6)—are supersessionist, promoting the replacement of Judaism by Christianity. Most Christians, from antiquity to the present, have interpreted it this way [*Supersessionist and Anti-Jewish Interpretations of Hebrews, p. 257*]. Can we find a way of reading this passage, and Hebrews in general, that better honors the original intent and meaning of the text? Yes . . . with some qualifications.

Let us look at the passage closely without reading into the text what is not there. First, Hebrews never sets up a dichotomy between Christianity and Judaism. It focuses on how believers in Christ are to worship. Christ has created a new path to fullness (or perfection). Therefore, the author of Hebrews argues that the new path replaces the old.

Second, regardless of whether Hebrews was written before or after the destruction of the Jerusalem temple in 70 CE, the very categories of Christianity and Judaism are anachronistic [*The Parting of the Ways, p. 243*]. Neither the audience nor the author thought about religious practice in such sharply divided categories. At best, we see the Gentile/Jew distinction in Paul's writings, but even for Paul, it is not a distinction between Christian and Jew, but between Gentile and Jew. The recipients of Hebrews are deeply connected to Jewish thought and practice. Without that, they would not have understood the many references to Jewish Scripture. Hebrews uses the language of covenant, sacrifice, and priesthood because the audience understands those concepts. The same audience is also committed to following the way of Christ. That commitment has led them (and the author) to a new understanding of covenant and to new practices.

Third, if we allow for the possibility that Hebrews was written after 70 CE, when the temple was no longer standing, the real break with past practice (and old covenant) has come at the hands of an external source: the Romans. Jews and "God-fearing" Gentiles (Acts 10:22) who worship alongside them need to find new ways to worship and express their understanding of covenant.

With the historical context outlined earlier, Hebrews 8:7 and 13, bookends to the long quotation from Jeremiah 31, may not seem as

146 Hebrews 8:1-13

definitive as they might otherwise appear. However, the author is indeed announcing a true break from past practices and covenants. For our author, the Christ event is so significant that it has necessitated a reordering of thinking. Regardless of the status of the temple in Jerusalem, there is a new and better covenant, a better kind of priesthood, and better promises.

If we think about the historical context of the audience—separated from their wider religious traditions, either by time or geography or both—it is not surprising that the author finds scriptural proof in Jeremiah 31:31-34. It, too, was written as a promise of hope when exile loomed and Jerusalem was under siege from the Babylonians in the sixth century BCE. In this oracle, God promises that *the days are surely coming* (Heb 8:8//Jer 31:31) when a *new covenant* will be put into place. Unlike the previous covenant with those led out of Egypt, it will already be written *in their minds* and *on their hearts* (Heb 8:10//Jer 31:33). It will not need to be taught; the people will already know the Lord (Heb 8:11//Jer 31:34).

The oracle is part of a larger Book of Consolation in Jeremiah, containing oracles that give promise and judgment to the ancient Israelites. With many of the oracles beginning "in those days" or "on that day," the people of Israel are promised that Jerusalem will be rebuilt, the scattered ones will be brought back together, agriculture will restart, and there will be dancing in the streets again. In this context, the promise of a new covenant, especially one written on their hearts, is more about how people keep the covenant than about the content of the covenant. Jeremiah spoke about a new covenant to a group of exiled (or soon-to-be exiled) Judahites in the sixth century BCE. Their city, Jerusalem, had been overrun, and they were experiencing great hardship, uncertainty, and destruction. When the temple was destroyed in 587 BCE, their center of worship was gone. Amid all that, Jeremiah speaks these words of comfort from God: "Even though my covenant was broken, I will continue to be their God; they will know me, and I will be merciful toward them" (Jer 31:33-34 summarized).

In Hebrews, this passage speaks to the author's own time in somewhat similar circumstances (especially if we assume a post-70 CE dating, after the temple had been destroyed). Later in the text (10:32-33), the author comments about the persecutions and other travails that members of the audience have suffered. The prompt for the homily was, in some sense, an encouragement *not . . . [to] abandon that confidence of yours* (10:35) during a period of trauma and uncertainty.

Hebrews 8:1-13   147

Richard Hays sees chapter 8 standing firmly in a Jewish context of "realized eschatology" (161), meaning that Hebrews employs a "nowness" to the new covenant that is not present in Jeremiah. In other words, for the audience of Hebrews, Jeremiah's words are realized *now* (8:6), in Christ. So instead of erasing or replacing Judaism, the new covenant preached by our author is forging a new path within Judaism. This new covenant inaugurated by Jesus requires a new priesthood, a new sanctuary, and a new concept of sacrifice.

Our author's use of Jeremiah 31 is significant in another way. Hays notes that the Jeremiah oracle speaks to all the inhabitants of the lands of Israel and Judah. Hebrews does nothing to extend the prophecy to Gentiles (161), to make the text more relevant to an audience of mixed religious backgrounds (in contrast to Paul, who goes to great lengths to preach the gospel to Gentiles). We seem to be witnessing an "insider's" conversation about the nature of sacrifice and covenant. We have already noticed and will observe again in chapter 9 that Hebrews focuses on only certain aspects of the religious tradition, specifically the sacrificial cult: the priesthood and the sacrifices. These aspects of ancient Judaism characterize the "old covenant."

With these things in mind, we must now tackle the interpretative framework of the long quotation from Jeremiah 31: both the introduction (8:8b, *God finds fault with them when he says*) and the conclusion (8:13, *In speaking of "a new covenant," he has made the first one obsolete. And what is obsolete and growing old will soon disappear*). The introduction to the Jeremiah passage suggests that the people are at fault. The covenant needs to be updated because they are unable to keep it. The words of Jeremiah repeated in Hebrews 8:9b, *for they did not continue in my covenant*, confirm that. This indicates that it is not the covenant itself but the inability of the people to keep it that needs a new approach. The Jewish Scriptures are filled with attempts by God to renew the covenant with the wayward people of Israel, who keep breaking it. In this context, Jesus as high priest, the sacrificer and the sacrificed, is the next (and final, according to our author) attempt by God to restore relationship with God's people.

Since Jesus represents God's final and once-for-all attempt at covenant, the previous covenant(s) *will soon disappear* (8:13). Translators have faced several difficulties in translating 8:13, which sums up the passage and prepares the reader for what comes next. The word that the NRSV translates as *made . . . obsolete* can merely mean to "make old," so some commentators (e.g., L. Johnson: 209;

148   Hebrews 8:1-13

Hays: 161) choose to replace "obsolete" with "make old": the passage would read, *In speaking of "a new covenant," he has made the first one old.* The author of Hebrews believes that the old covenant needs updating, and the establishment of Jesus Christ as the new high priest is part of the update.

Jesper Svartvik suggests that we read this in an eschatological sense: "Is not the most plausible interpretation that the author here, too, articulates the belief that one day this world will 'grow old' and only God will remain? If so, this verse is an expression of an intense eschatological longing for the future, for a complete and perfected world" (2021: 35). In this sense, whether we use "old" or "obsolete," the framework is intended to establish the validity of the new approach to covenant: Jesus' once-for-all sacrifice. The scriptural support is the new-covenant language in Jeremiah.

In conclusion, one can hardly avoid seeing this text as supersessionist at one level: the new covenant, with Jesus at the center, does indeed replace the old, or obsolete, covenant. *However, where later Christian readers and theologians read this as a break with Judaism, our author does not.* We might think about the new covenant of Hebrews as being on a continuum of covenantal relationships that God establishes with God's people. For our homilist, there is no break between the Israelites in the wilderness and the homilist's congregation; they are merely the most recent generation in a long, unbroken line of people of God. In that sense, the author of Hebrews is not thinking of the new covenant as a break with the past, but as the fulfillment of all that has been promised through multiple covenants.

THE TEXT IN BIBLICAL CONTEXT

Covenants

Covenant is basic to the biblical understanding of humanity's relationship with God. A covenant is a formal relationship between two parties in which each assumes certain obligations. Biblical covenants are initiated by God's gracious care. In response, God's people are to remain faithful. The new covenant of Jeremiah 31 is one of several biblical covenants, all of which have a slightly different emphasis. A different sign accompanies each covenant.

- Noah: God made a covenant with Noah when he and his family entered the ark (Gen 6:18), and again after the floodwaters receded, promising that never again would every living thing be destroyed by the waters of a flood. The sign of this covenant is a rainbow (9:8-17).

- Abraham: Abram was called by God with the promise that he would become a great nation, that he would be blessed, and that through him all the families of the earth would be blessed (Gen 12:1-3). The covenant ceremony is told in Genesis 15. God's promise is so life-changing that Abram's name is changed to Abraham. The sign of the covenant is circumcision (17:1-14) for every male.

- Moses: The Sinai covenant in Exodus 19–24 identifies God's saving acts for Israel and stipulates instructions for their relationship to God and with other members of the community. God made this covenant with all of Israel. Moses relayed the stipulations of the covenant to the people. The sign of this covenant is the book of the covenant (Exod 20:22–23:33) and, more broadly speaking, the Torah, with the practices that it stipulates.

- David: God's covenant with David assures a permanent dynasty (2 Sam 7:14). Like the covenant with Abraham, it promises descendants. The covenant itself came to Nathan, the prophet, who delivered the message to David. The sign of this covenant is the establishment of David's throne forever (2 Sam 7:16).

- The prophets: The prophets criticized the people for not keeping the covenant with God when they veered off course by worshiping idols, robbing the poor, and not caring for the sick, the orphaned, and the widowed. Hosea uses the imagery of infidelity in marriage (Hos 2) to express the adulterous relationship the Israelites had with God. They broke the covenant with their disobedience (e.g., 4:1-3). Isaiah reminds them that they are to act as a faithful servant who rescues prisoners and is a light to the nations (42:5-8). Ezekiel dreams of repentance and forgiveness that will restore God's people to life (Ezek 36–37). Jeremiah promises a new covenant that will be written on the heart (31:31).

- Qumran: Covenant is an important theme running through several texts of the Dead Sea Scrolls. However, the covenant is no longer available to the entirety of Israel, but only to the remnant (the Sons of Light; i.e., the Essenes themselves) who remain steadfast. Covenant is the main theme of the Damascus Document, itself a covenant between members who promise to adhere to the group's strict interpretation of Torah. In it, the "new covenant" (without referencing Jeremiah) demands that the remnant live in exile (presumably in Damascus), away from the temple, observing the Sabbath and other festivals, and upholding the covenant made at Sinai. The covenant is renewed annually, probably on Shavuot (Gk. = Pentecost), the late spring/early summer wheat harvest festival that follows fifty days after Passover.

- The New Testament: In Luke's account of the Last Supper, the wine is identified as the blood of the new covenant (Luke 22:20), although the texts of the two synoptic parallels to this (Mark 14:24//Matt 26:28) do not contain the word "new." (Some textual variants do include it.) Paul speaks of Christ's death as sealing the "new covenant" (1 Cor 11:23-25) and later calls members of the Corinthian community "to be ministers of a new covenant, not of letter but of spirit" (2 Cor 3:6). The author of Hebrews places the greatest emphasis on the new covenant of any writer in the New Testament. Hebrews alone in the New Testament calls the previous covenant *obsolete*. Other New Testament writers did not understand the new covenant to invalidate the first covenant given to Israel (cf. Luke 1:72; Acts 3:25; Gal 3:17; see also L. Johnson: 203–15).

Earthly and Heavenly Sanctuaries

The notion that the earthly tabernacle is only a *sketch* or *shadow* of the true heavenly tabernacle is not new to Hebrews. The author of Hebrews is just expounding something already apparent in Exodus 25, where Moses receives plans for the earthly tabernacle that are based on the actual, real, heavenly one. Throughout the Jewish Scriptures, psalmists and prophets restated the obvious notion that God's real and everlasting home is in heaven (e.g., see Ps 11:5). They also speak of God's throne as "on high" (see Ps 47:8; Isa 6:1). In Isaiah 66:1, God says, "Heaven is my throne." The ancient Jews' understanding of the tabernacle, and later of the temple, was broad enough that they could accept the earthly temple or tabernacle as a representation of the heavenly one.

Another first-century Jew, Philo, writes of the tabernacle in much the same language as our author of Hebrews [*Philo, Neoplatonism, and Hebrews, p. 245*]. Philo writes that while Moses was still on the mountain, he was instructed by God to "build the holy edifice" and construct the furniture so "that it might be an imitation perceptible by the outward senses of an archetypal sketch and pattern" (*Life of Moses* 2.74). Philo claims that the form of the tabernacle and its contents had been imprinted in the mind of Moses so that he could make accurate material representations of them.

Hebrews 8:1-13 151

In the same book, Philo describes the tabernacle in great detail. He occasionally adds a bit of nuance by suggesting that the tabernacle was also a symbol of the universe (not merely a representation of the heavenly sanctuary of God). When describing the cherubim in the holy of holies, he claims that they are "the symbols of the two hemispheres, . . . for the whole heaven is endowed with wings" (2.98). The priest's garb is a "copy and representation of the world; and the parts are a representation of the separate parts of the world" (2.117). In another text, Philo is even more direct: the world is the real temple, "the highest and truest temple of God." It has stars as ornaments and angels for priests. The temple made with human hands represents the one made by God (*On the Special Laws* 1.66). The human-made temple gave sense to the reality of God's presence as an actual place.

For Hebrews, the structure of the earthly tabernacle signifies its inadequacy (Attridge: 240). This brief survey of the Jewish Scriptures and Philo shows that Hebrews is not alone in understanding the earthly tabernacle as a copy, not the real thing. The conclusion our homilist draws from that understanding differs from contemporaries' explanations, but not the idea itself.

THE TEXT IN THE LIFE OF THE CHURCH

Hebrews in the Revised Common Lectionary

Chapter 8 is not in the cycle of lectionary readings. However, Jeremiah 31:31-34 is paired with Hebrews 5:5-10 on the fifth Sunday of Lent in Year B. They are rounded out with readings from John 12:20-33 and Psalm 51:1-12. It is significant that the reading occurs during Lent because all these readings center on obedience toward God. Psalm 51:10 contains the famous verse "Create in me a clean heart, O God, and put a new and right spirit within me." This maps closely onto Jeremiah's prophetic announcement that the new covenant will be written on people's hearts. The psalmist inherently knew that if *our hearts* are changed and renewed, *we* will be changed and renewed. The New Testament readings focus on the obedience and subsequent glorification of Jesus. Hebrews 5:5-10 confirms Jesus' role as high priest and Son and emphasizes his obedience. Because he reverently submitted to God, he is now the source of salvation. It works well with John's passage, which focuses on Jesus' emphatic statement "You must lose your life in order to gain it" (cf. John 12:25). To serve, to be obedient, one must follow. John's passage shows why Hebrews considers Jesus to be

152   Hebrews 8:1-13

the pioneer in obedience. He is in touch with God in ways that no other humans have been or can be. Our response should be to follow him.

The New Covenant and Supersessionist Readings of Scripture

The NRSV of Hebrews 8:13 states that God made the *first* covenant *obsolete* by speaking of *a new* one. It is *growing old* and *will soon disappear*. Many Christian interpreters have brought their assumptions about Christian triumphalism to this text and have used it to assert that Judaism has been rejected by God and replaced by Christianity [*Supersessionist and Anti-Jewish Interpretations of Hebrews, p. 257*]. Kinzer argues that "Christians have brought assumptions about the abolishment of Jewish law to the reading of Hebrews" (93). As we have learned, the author of Hebrews is suggesting that Jesus is the replacement sacrifice. This passage and Hebrews more generally focus on the replacement of the Levitical priesthood and the sacrificial system by the sacrifice of Jesus. It reflects an understanding of the sacrificial system and the role of Jesus that would not have been shared by most Jews. What scholars might debate is whether Hebrews reflects the prevailing wisdom about Jesus *within* the movement of Jesus followers who were a mix of Jews and Gentiles. But this replacement for sacrifice and the priority of the new covenant does *not* mean that "Christianity" (not at that time a discrete entity in the understanding of our author and audience) has replaced Judaism itself.

Svartvik suggests that, with the heavy reliance on passages such as Hebrews 8:13, Christians betray their willingness to "pick and choose" passages that meet their polemical needs (2016: 336). As far back as Bede in the eighth century, Christians have used Hebrews 8 polemically. But the second theme in Hebrews, that of the wandering pilgrim people, is of equal concern to the author of Hebrews. In chapter 4, our author raises the example of the wayward Israelites who lost faith as wandering pilgrims looking for their home. Later in the text, our author spends an entire chapter discussing the faithful Israelites of the past who did not have a homeland but kept their faith in God despite difficult odds. Our author even praises the audience of this text for their previous attempts to remain faithful (e.g., see 6:10). Why, Svartvik asks, do commentators, exegetes, and theologians—both modern and those throughout Christian history—not focus on the theme of faithful pilgrimage from chapters 11 and 13 as often or intensely as they focus on chapter 8?

Hebrews 8:1-13   **153**

A broader Greco-Roman philosophical tradition in antiquity known as "Middle Platonism" *[Philo, Neoplatonism, and Hebrews, p. 245]* contributed to our author's approach to the material world and to what was considered "shadow" and "reality." Middle Platonist philosophers theorized about the world as divided into two principles: the pure, infinite, transcendent God; and the finite, material world, which some Middle Platonists considered corrupted, even evil. God's world exists "in timeless eternity, . . . while the perceptible world is subject to constant becoming. . . . The latter is subject to change and never remains in the same state" (Thompson 2011b: 33). Svartvik says, "To a middle Platonist such as the author of Hebrews, heaven always trumps earth. The metaphorical discourse of Hebrews is directed toward the future, not the past. The comparison is not between the new covenant, 'Christianity,' and the old covenant, 'Judaism,' but rather between the future and the present, between heaven and earth" (2016: 336). In other words, if we do not interpret the passage within the broad historical context in which it was written, we miss key elements. And if we bring a framework of polemics into our reading, that is what we will find in the text.

Hebrews 8 is not the only text mistakenly seen as supporting Christian triumphalism, the supersessionist belief that Christianity, as the superior and victorious religion, replaces Judaism and that Christians replace the Jews as the chosen people of God. In difficult passages such as Matthew's crucifixion scene, the crowd shouts to Pilate, "His blood be on us and on our children" (27:25). Many Christians have understood this passage as a confession of guilt and an eternal self-curse on all Jews, further proof that Christianity is the superior religion. Christians have blamed Jews as a whole people for the crucifixion of Jesus and have tragically persecuted the Jews for "their" sins. For centuries, Christian interpreters were comfortable with readings that rejected Judaism and the people who practiced it. In late antiquity there was evidence of Christian violence against Jews on the island of Minorca (Kraemer 2020). The Crusades in the Middle Ages and the pogroms in Eastern Europe in the nineteenth century are but two other examples. After the Holocaust in the twentieth century, Christian theologians began grappling with the complacency and arrogance of much Christian theology. These events of history have led Christian interpreters to reexamine how Christian triumphalism has distorted the nature of Christianity itself (L. Johnson: 203; see also Bader-Saye: 52–69).

This reexamination has led to important corrections regarding our relationship with other religions and with underrepresented

154   Hebrews 8:1-13

groups among us. It is important for Christians to remember the danger that is present when we maintain a sense of superiority that rejects or excludes people on the basis of their racial, religious, gender, or any other identity. The results never conform to the spirit of Christ. Modern history has demonstrated that Christian exclusion or condemnation of any group of people can result in unexpected or unintended acts of brutality that our "righteous" words may never anticipate.

Hebrews was written to people intimately connected to the Jewish Scriptures. Whether they are Greek adherents to the idea of Jesus as Christ or ethnically Jewish, the group clearly knows and aligns their worldview with the (Jewish) Scriptures. The writer of Hebrews in no way intends to reject Judaism. In fact, essentially all the pastor's arguments are based on the covenants and promises within the Jewish Scriptures. The author considers Jesus to be the enactor of a new covenant that replaces the "old" covenant. But we must see this within the context of the author's and the congregation's deep connection to the Jewish Scriptures.

The Term "New Testament" in the Early Church

The use of the Latin term *testamentum* (= Gk. *diathēkē*) signifies a will or a covenant. In the first several centuries, Christians typically used it to refer to the new salvation offered through Christ, not to a set of texts. It was a theological idea, not a literary canon. We don't have manuscript evidence that labels the texts themselves as the "New Testament" prior to the fourth century. Both Wolfram Kinzig (543–44) and Harry Gamble (19–22) have noted that it took centuries for "new testament" to become common parlance for the collection of writings that we now call the New Testament.

Around 200 CE, Marcion, a Christian leader born in Sinope (Pontus, Asia Minor) and living in Rome, denied the validity of the Jewish Scriptures and the God depicted in them. Kinzig thinks Marcion probably started to use the term "New Testament" to describe what he considered to be the canon of Christian Scriptures *[The Role and Use of the Jewish Scriptures by Early Christians, p. 251]*. Marcion's canon included a version of the Gospel of Luke edited by Marcion himself and ten letters of Paul, but excluded quotations of Jewish Scriptures and other writings now in what we now call the New Testament, such as Hebrews and the additional letters of Paul, John, and James, and the other gospels. But by this time, the four gospels were in heavy use, and most Jesus followers accepted all four. In fact, Marcion was considered a heretic by many leading

Hebrews 8:1-13

theologians of the day, including Tertullian, a North African Latin-speaking Christian author, who wrote a scathing treatise against Marcion; and Irenaeus, a Greek-speaking Christian bishop in Lyon, in what is now southern France. Contrary to Marcion, Tertullian and Irenaeus argued that the true Christian Scriptures were the Old Testament and Christian writings already in circulation and accepted by most Christians, which included the four gospels, along with the Pauline letters and other texts. For at least the first two centuries, "covenant" (*testamentum* in Latin) was only a theological term, not a term that indicated a set of writings. Only after the second century did Christians gradually begin referring to a specific set of Christian Scriptures as the "New Testament." The terminology was not regularly used until the fourth century and beyond.

Hebrews 9:1–10:18

The Two Covenants

PREVIEW

Sacrifice, blood (i.e., death), covenant, tabernacle, atonement, the high priest: all these elements from the old are in the new. But they have a new mediator, Christ, and a new purpose, perfection. Hebrews 9–10 blends the new and the old, repeating earlier themes of the text to solidify and hammer home the shift in the underlying foundation of the new covenant. Having already established in 8:5 that the earthly tabernacle is but *a sketch and a shadow*, the homilist now extends that metaphor to the priests and contents of the earthly tabernacle. They become a "parable," or illustration, for the present time of the new covenant (9:15).

In the same way that the old furnishings were purified with blood, the *heavenly things* (9:23) have been purified by Christ's blood. The difference is that Christ's sacrifice is *once for all* (9:12; 10:10). This is the only sacrifice that can cleanse and perfect people's consciences forever. The repetitive nature of the earthly sanctuary cannot permanently remove sins. Only Christ, *who offered for all time a single sacrifice for sins* (10:12), can do that. This is the new covenant for the author of Hebrews: the promise that sins will be forgiven and removed through Christ's once-for-all sacrifice for the (one) people of God.

Chapter 8 closes with *And what is obsolete and growing old will soon disappear*. Immediately thereafter, we read the description of the earthly tabernacle and its liturgical work in chapter 9 as one of impermanence, obsolescence, and inadequacy. This entire passage supports such a reading. But it does so through analogy and comparison, not outright dismissal of "the old." Chapter 8, with its emphasis on the new covenant, is the "thesis" for this section, which contains evidence for the argument. The last three verses (10:16-18) of this unit close with a restatement from Jeremiah 31. As the "heart and soul" of Hebrews, in this section the author argues that the purpose of this new and better sacrificial system is to *perfect the conscience of the worshiper* (9:9). The conscience is the "better," nonmaterial aspect of one's being. It is for this perfecting that Christ made his once-for-all sacrifice. This message is not a diatribe against one religion in order to promote another, but a statement of the best means to attain perfection through sacrifice.

This is another section that some Christians have used to support a triumphalist stance, understanding the tabernacle and Christ as stand-ins for Judaism and Christianity. It is easy to read this portion of Hebrews through supersessionist eyes, but doing so is dangerously anachronistic and unfair to the author, let alone to the millions of Jews who have died over the centuries as a result of this wrong reading. Here we must learn to read against the grain of our history in order to read with the grain of the text of Hebrews itself. Our author is updating the notion of sacrifice, not replacing an entire religious tradition.

OUTLINE

Sacrifice in the First Covenant, 9:1-10
Christ as the Sacrifice in the New Covenant, 9:11-28
Restatement of Themes, 10:1-18
    10:1-10   The Law Is Only a Shadow
    10:11-18   Christ Is the Perfect Sacrifice, Once for All

EXPLANATORY NOTES

Sacrifice in the First Covenant 9:1-10

The description of the physical tabernacle begins a lengthy section in which the author describes the workings of the *first covenant* in comparing it with the *new covenant* (9:15). It is helpful to see the entire structure of chapter 9 to understand where the homilist wants to take the audience (modified from C. Koester 2001: 424):

- 9:1-10: *Regulations* of the earthly/*first covenant* are to attain atonement.

- 9:11-14: Christ brings a new method for consciences to attain perfection/purification.

158   Hebrews 9:1–10:18

- Christ has come as the *high priest of the good things to come* (9:11 mg.).

- The *sacrifice* is *once for all* (9:12, 26).

- The sacrifice has taken place in the *heavenly sanctuary* (9:12, 24).

- Jesus himself is the sacrifice, using his own *blood* (9:13-14, 26).

- His sacrifice is to *purify* the *conscience from dead works to worship the living God* (9:14).

- 9:15-17: The will (covenant) of both systems cannot be enacted without a death.

  - Jesus is the mediator of the new covenant, offering his blood and death (9:15).

- 9:18-22: Rituals in the first covenant emphasize the importance and meaning of blood.

- 9:23-26: The high priest replicated what Moses had done; Christ, the new high priest, has become the onetime sacrifice *at the end of the age, to remove sin* (9:26).

- 9:27-28: In the new age, Christ will return *to save those who are eagerly waiting for him* (9:28).

The word *regulations* creates an *inclusio*. It occurs in 9:1 and 9:10, giving us a clue to what the author is trying to do. The tabernacle is a metaphor or symbol (Gk. *parabolē*) for the present time (9:9), when regulations such as food and baptism are an imperfect means to order the body until the time comes to set things right (9:10). The tabernacle is also a means of instruction that illustrates how regulations (superficial, earthly ways of doing things) are not the real avenue to perfection. In other words, people who operate under the *regulations* (9:1) of the old covenant cannot also participate in the new. The first tent, which refers to the daily operations and furnishings of the old way of thinking and doing, is in the way.

Drawing on the elaborate description of the tabernacle in Exodus 25–31 and 36–40, the author describes some of the contents and regulations. Using Scripture, not personal experience of the Jerusalem temple, the author roughly and quickly describes the design and furnishings of the biblical tabernacle. The crowning glory was the *hilastērion [Atonement, p. 231]*, which covered the ark holding the tablets, *the place of atonement* (9:5 mg.). On either side of

Hebrews 9:1–10:18

the *hilastērion* were two cherubim, overshadowing the *hilastērion* and representing God's glory. The discussion ends crisply with the statement: *Of these things we cannot speak now in detail* (9:5). One look at the detailed description in Exodus 25–31 explains why our author makes that comment! The homilist has more pressing matters to discuss: the daily work of the priests and the yearly work of the high priest; and most importantly, to explain what it all means for the contemporary audience.

Why does the author spend this effort in describing the physical layout and workings of the tabernacle, even with these rough brushstrokes? Hebrews 9:8-10 gives insight into how the homilist wants the congregation to think about the tabernacle, what sort of sacrifice "works," and the purpose of the sacrifice. The first tent is just a symbol of the sacrificial system, a system that *cannot perfect the conscience of the worshiper* (9:9). After the exodus, the tabernacle was the place designated "to cultivate and maintain the relationship between God and Israel, to assure the continuity of the Divine Presence" (Polen: 216). We saw this in Hebrews 7. But now, Christ is "the place" where that happens. His once-for-all sacrifice, first mentioned in 7:27 and again in 9:12, 26, alleviates the yearly need for the Levitical high priest to make a sacrifice for himself and for others. As with the tabernacle itself, the high priest's sacrifices concern only outward regulations for the body, on things like food and drink and baptisms, regulations in place only until Christ has come (9:10). In other words, the entire sacrificial system is *a sketch and shadow* (8:5): the regulations of the tabernacle, not just the tabernacle itself, are only symbols for the new covenant.

The homilist is therefore asking the congregation to make a paradigm shift in thinking about sacrifice. In the old covenant, sacrifice was designed to atone for *the sins committed unintentionally by the people* (9:7). Sacrifice in the new covenant is for the perfection of the people. Perfection cannot be achieved in the same way. It requires a new, different, and once-for-all sacrifice. The goal of the sacrificial system is now the attainment of perfection (9:9). Now that Christ has initiated the new covenant, sacrifice has a completely different purpose and meaning.

A new purpose for sacrifice requires a new method. In this sense, then, the old system has become obsolete. The Scriptures are there not to lay out the law, but to point to the new covenant and sacrifice. They, too, are a sketch and a shadow [*Philo, Neoplatonism, and Hebrews, p. 245*].

Christ as the Sacrifice in the New Covenant 9:11-28

The entire homily has been leading up to this point. Using the foundational language of the old/first covenant, the author of Hebrews shapes a new paradigm. Hebrews 9:1-10 repeats what has already been said in chapter 7 and earlier. The word *but* in 9:11 signals a contrast with what has come before. As we move into verses 11-28, the author expounds on the goal of the new covenant: *to perfect* (9:9). The word for perfecting in Hebrews has the same root as "end, complete, fulfill" (Gk. *teleō*). With Christ, worshipers are now able to reach the end, or perfection *[Perfection in Greco-Roman and Jewish Thought, p. 244]*. They do this not through imperfect or earthly elements—a physical tabernacle and an imperfect high priest—but through Christ, who was *without blemish* (9:14) and in a perfect tent (9:11), in heaven. This is where we come face-to-face with the author's shift in worldview from the "old/first" to the "new."

If we suggest a key passage in Hebrews, it might be 9:15: And therefore *he is the mediator of a new covenant, so that* once *a death* took place for the redemption of *transgressions under the first covenant, those who are called may receive the promised eternal inheritance* (Attridge: 254). Two key characteristics about Christ's work emerge here in 9:15: (1) he *redeems . . . from . . . transgressions*; and (2) *those who are called . . . receive the promise of eternal inheritance* as a result. The passage summarizes what the author has already said regarding eternal inheritance (1:3-4; 4:1; 6:17), which "culminated in the promise of the new covenant (8:6)" (Attridge: 254).

This key verse (9:15) forms the thesis for the entire text: Christ himself (9:14-15), not another sacrifice, redeems transgressions. And those who are called receive the promise of the new covenant, *the promised eternal inheritance*. Hebrews repeats the wordplay from earlier, using the Greek word *diathēkē*, which can mean "covenant," yet also "will" or "testament" (9:16). Legally, a will takes effect only after the death of the person who made the will. The inheritance cannot be received as long as the person who made the will (or covenant or testament) is still alive. We can now receive God's inheritance: the new covenant (testament or will) promised in Jeremiah.

The rest of the text helps the audience understand how the new covenant works, using the familiar language of the old/first covenant. If 9:15 is the key verse, chapter 9 is the microcosm of the entire text of Hebrews. Without abandoning the language or even the underlying assumptions of the "old" system (e.g., the efficacy of sacrifice), the author shifts it into new territory by adapting "old" language and thought. Using the sacrificial system of the "old

Hebrews 9:1–10:18 161

covenant," our homilist makes sense of Jesus' sacrifice (Regev: 280). In the old system, the efficacy was in the repetitive nature of the sacrifice; its goal was to maintain a relationship with God. Now repetition is abandoned with a *once-for-all* approach. The concept of sacrifice, however, remains constant.

The writer continues to emphasize *blood* as a necessary aspect of sacrifice in 9:18-22. Just as the first covenant was inaugurated by Moses with the use of blood as a purifying ritual (the author uses material from Exod 24:3-8; 29:12; Lev 8:15), so too did Christ himself (as the sacrifice) enter the heavenly tabernacle. For our author, both covenants are purified by blood. The author is not just speaking of the old/first testament/covenant when he states that without the shedding of a victim's blood, there is no forgiveness of sins (9:22). This passage does not negate the efficacy of sacrifice itself, just the method and pattern. The *new covenant* is better because Christ *has appeared once for all at the end of the age to remove sin by the sacrifice of himself* (9:26)—instead of the repetitive sacrifices priests made under the old/first covenant.

Regev understands the author to be "highly attached to priestly ideas and the sacrificial cult. . . . In Hebrews, the priestly system continues in a new and better format when it serves as the key for understanding who Christ is and how he saves the world" (281). In this way, the author's Christology "may seem more appealing to a Jewish audience" because our author retains the emphasis on sacrifice and the priestly cult, "building on both the themes of high priesthood and atonement sacrifices[,] which purify sin" (281). In other words, our author uses the sacrificial system and the role of the high priest to explain Jesus as atoning sacrifice (Regev: 280) [*Atonement, p. 231*].

The passage as a microcosm continues. The author repeats the earlier comparison of earthly and heavenly realities (9:23-24). As we saw in chapter 8, the author understands the earthly tabernacle to be a copy of the heavenly sanctuary. Here the author restates that. We also have seen that this kind of understanding is not unique to our author. Hebrews 9 confirms what the author has been saying throughout the text: the offering Jesus brought was his own sanctified life (his blood). He brought it into the actual presence of God (the heavenly sanctuary). That offering and Jesus' presence open the way for those who are called to be eternal inheritors of the new covenant.

In one last microcosmic moment, verses 25-26 bring the audience back to the beginning of the text: the reference to the *end of the*

162   Hebrews 9:1–10:18

age (9:26) reflects the opening of Hebrews, which speaks of *these last days*, in which God is speaking through a Son (1:2). As the clearest reference in Hebrews to the second coming of Christ, verse 28 uses eschatological language of the second coming, to save those who are awaiting Christ. When he comes again, it will be for the salvation of those awaiting him.

Restatement of Themes 10:1-18

10:1-10 The Law Is Only a Shadow

Completing a long *synkrisis* (comparison) between the new and old sacrificial systems, chapter 10 opens with a statement that summarizes what the author has been saying throughout chapters 7–9: the law is only a *shadow*, not the *true form* of *the good things yet to come* (10:1). The law, represented by the Levitical priests offering their periodic sacrifices, cannot perfect the consciences of people. The author argues that if the law were anything other than a shadow, the sacrifices would have already stopped because they would have accomplished what they were intended to do (10:2). It is impossible, says the author of Hebrews, *for the blood of bulls and goats* (and actions of priests), the shadows of the good things to come, *to take away sins* (10:4).

Throughout this passage, the author frequently uses three key words or concepts: *offering* (Gk. *prosphora*): 10:5, 8, 10, 14, 18; *sacrifice* (*thysia*): 10:1, 5, 8, 11, 12; and *sin* (*hamartia*): 10:2, 3, 4, 6, 8, 11, 12, 17, 18. After using all three concepts throughout the text, the author now brings them together in this summary passage in a concentrated way. All three concepts are found in Psalm 40, quoted later in the passage. At the crux of the matter is the obedience of Jesus: *"I have come to do your will"* (Heb 10:9; from Ps 40:8). After Jesus' obedience to God's will, he was given a seat *at the right hand of God* (10:12). The Levitical priests, on the other hand, stand as they offer their repeated sacrifices (10:11).

A few aspects of this brief section deserve some comment. First, the author's presentation of this concluding summary of the ideas through chapters 7–9 is Platonic. That is, it reflects and reiterates Plato's ideas about items in the physical world reflecting imperfectly the perfect prototype, which exists only in the spiritual realm. In Platonic perspective, the Mosaic law (and consequently the priests, the sacrifices themselves, such as the bulls, and the regularity of the sacrifices) is not the true form, but only the phenomenon that humans experience.

Hebrews 9:1–10:18   163

Second, the author mixes this Platonic approach with an eschatological mindset: *the true form* of the Mosaic law is *the good things to come* (10:1). Thompson describes the author's approach here as "living between two worlds" (2008: 194). From the open statement, *In these last days . . .* (1:1), the author has made it clear to the audience that the once-for-all true sacrifice of Jesus has ushered in a new age, which is both present and future.

Finally, the perfection of the individual conscience is the target of the true sacrifice, not the ritual purification of bodies. The perfection of the conscience is made visible by its ability to live an obedient life. For our author, sacrifice provides access to the presence of God. To gain access, one needs a clear conscience. The problem with the previous system is that it was unable to *perfect the conscience of the worshiper* (9:9-10; cf. 7:11, 19). Through Jesus' obedience, however, people have access to his once-for-all sacrifice, which *does* perfect those who draw near. The author is adamant about the need for the blood of Jesus *to take away sins*, not *the blood of bulls and goats* (10:4). As the obedient Son of God, Jesus is the better sacrifice.

Lest we anachronistically think that this view of animal sacrifice is a "Christian" critique of "Jewish" sacrifice, we should remember that the Hebrew prophets also criticized the people for approaching the altar without properly aligning the rest of their lives toward God and their neighbors, and not because sacrifice was inherently bad. In Micah 6:6-8, the prophet asks, "With what shall I come before the LORD? . . . Shall I come . . . with burnt offerings, with calves a year old?" The implied answer from God is "No!" Instead, the people are told "to do justice and to love kindness and to walk humbly with your God." In Amos, the prophet makes it clear that anyone offering sacrifices without concern for the poor, the orphan, and the needy is offensive to God. Instead, they should "let justice roll down like waters, and righteousness like an ever-flowing stream" (Amos 5:24). Plato (*Laws* 4.716e–717a) expresses a similar sentiment as he suggests that a god cannot accept a gift from an impure person (Ullucci: 64). Other Greeks also debated the merits of sacrifices because they were material in nature (Thompson 2011b: 181; Rives: 188). For example, Porphyry, a Neoplatonist philosopher who lived in the latter half of the third century CE, said in his work *On Abstinence from Killing Animals*, "For there is nothing material which is not at once impure to the immaterial" (2.34). He claimed that the offering or sacrifice should be similar to how a person is sustained: a farmer should offer produce, and a philosopher "fine thoughts about them" (Clark: 69). In other words, throughout antiquity, there was a

164   Hebrews 9:1–10:18

healthy debate about the nature of sacrifice and what it meant. For our homilist, even though Jesus' body was material in nature, what distinguished his sacrifice was not only his own perfection but also his obedience. This is what made his sacrifice *once for all* and perfect in the eyes of our author.

By way of biblical proof, the author quotes yet another psalm, one that closely matches the pastor's point of view. The words of Psalm 39:7-9 (LXX; 40:6-8 MT) become the words of Christ:

> *Sacrifices and offerings you have not desired,*
> *but a body/ears [LXX/MT] you [God] have prepared for me;*
> *in burnt offerings and sin offerings*
> *you have taken no pleasure.*
> *Then I said, "See, God, I have come to do your will."* (Heb 10:5-7)

The psalm is not a critique of the sacrificial system. Rather, it expresses a desire to do what pleases God. This is one last restatement of the new covenant: Jesus has done what the Levitical sacrificial system could not do: *make perfect those who approach* (Heb 10:1). The repetition of the Levitical priestly ritual could *never take away sins* (10:11). In contrast, Christ's obedience to God's will *has perfected . . . those who are sanctified* (10:14).

Our author's critique of the old sacrificial system is not a critique of Judaism, but of practices that do not perfect the conscience or display obedience to God. L. Johnson states, "What God desires is faithful obedience. Hebrews therefore here stands within the tradition of the prophets who deny the efficacy of ritual when the deeper covenantal obligations are being neglected" (252–53).

With this quotation of Psalm 39/40 (LXX/MT), we see another example of the author's reliance on the Septuagint. The Hebrew text of Psalm 40:6 reads, "Sacrifice and offering you do not desire, but you have given me open ears." Most Greek manuscripts of Hebrews 10:5 read, *Sacrifices and offerings you have not desired, but a* <u>*body*</u> *you [God] have prepared for me* (emph. added). Our author uses the Septuagint version as a commentary on Jesus' obedience to God through his bodily sacrifice.

10:11-18 Christ Is the Perfect Sacrifice, Once for All

The author then returns to Psalm 110. After reminding the audience that the Levitical priests must continue to stand, Jesus, having made his sacrifice, *sat down at the right hand of God* and is *waiting until his enemies would be made a footstool for his feet* (10:12-13). This rhetorical flourish closes a long section, which begins in chapter 7

Hebrews 9:1–10:18

with the quotation of the same passage from Psalm 110. The pastor then includes one more reminder that they are living in new-covenant times by recalling the words of Jeremiah 31 from Hebrews 8: God's laws are written in our hearts and minds (Jer 31:33; Heb 8:10; 10:16). God will no longer remember sins (Jer 31:34; Heb 8:12; 10:17).

The author's final statement, *Where there is forgiveness of these [sins], there is no longer any offering for sin* (10:18), reminds the audience that another kind of sacrifice is no longer needed "because Christ's sacrifice has perfected the conscience through the cleansing that comes from the perfect obedience to God's will" (L. Johnson: 254). This sets the stage for the following exhortation to the audience regarding their own responsibility in the new-covenant world. It is not enough to imagine Jesus sitting at the right hand of God, having made his obedient sacrifice. They must also follow Jesus' example.

THE TEXT IN BIBLICAL CONTEXT

The Tabernacle/Temple

As we have noted, the author of Hebrews likely did not have first-hand knowledge of the temple in Jerusalem (and does not even use the word *temple*). Our author draws on descriptions of the tabernacle in the Jewish Scriptures, not personal familiarity with the Jerusalem temple in the first century. In the Septuagint, the tabernacle is often referred to as the "tent of witness" (Heb. = "tent of meeting"). It contained the "ark of the covenant" (Exod 25:22; LXX: "ark of witness"; it held the stone tablets inscribed with the covenant, 25:16), an altar of incense, a candelabra, possibly a container of manna, and other items, as recorded throughout Exodus 25–31. For our author, the importance of the tabernacle is that the place of sacrifice is at its entrance and priests are serving there. However, the tabernacle itself is a pattern for the real place of sacrifice and the real sacrifice. As proof, our author quotes God's instruction to Moses for the tabernacle's lampstand and utensils: *See that you make them according to the pattern that was shown you on the mountain* (Heb 8:5; from Exod 25:40).

Moses pitched a temporary (?) tent outside the camp, where he would consult the Lord and intercede for the people; it is also called the "tent of witness" (33:7-11 LXX). This tent needed to be pitched whenever Moses wanted to enter it. The people would stand outside their own tents and watch Moses enter this tent, after which the

166   Hebrews 9:1–10:18

pillar that guided them through the wilderness would hover over the tent while Moses was interceding for the people. In a touching detail, Exodus 33:11 says that "the LORD used to speak to Moses face to face, as one speaks to a friend." Berlin and Brettler suggest that this tent was where Moses went to receive oracles from God, instead of the actual tabernacle used for sacrifices (187).

Both tents are called the "tent of witness" (LXX). As we see later in Hebrews, our author urges the congregation to go *outside the camp* because *Jesus also suffered outside the city gate* (13:11-12). One wonders whether the revelatory experience described in Exodus 33:7-11 was not in the back of the author's mind too.

The Jewish Scriptures contain a description of the first temple, built by Solomon around 966 BCE (1 Kings 6–8; 2 Chron 2–4). Solomon also built an inner sanctuary for the ark of the covenant (1 Kings 6:19//2 Chron 3:8). Second Chronicles 5:3-8 describes taking the vessels from the holy tent and moving them into the newly built temple; the ark was placed there "underneath the wings of the cherubim." The Babylonians destroyed Solomon's temple in 587 BCE, after which the Babylonian captivity lasted till 537 BCE. (Some Judeans were taken earlier, in ca. 608 and 596; Jer 25:11-12 and 29:10 prophesy seventy years for this exile.) After the Persian king Cyrus released the captives (2 Chron 36:22-23), Jewish survivors started returning to Jerusalem in 536. One early returning group, led by the priest Ezra, began to build the second temple, as recounted in the books of Ezra and Nehemiah. This is the start of the Second Temple period, lasting until 70 CE, when the Romans destroyed the temple.

Around 20 BCE, Herod the Great began a remodeling and enlarging project that amounted to a dismantling and rebuilding of the temple. A description of this effort can be found in Josephus, *Jewish Antiquities* 15.380–402. Work on the temple itself may have been completed around 15 BCE, but work on the area around the temple (the Temple Mount) likely was not finished until the middle of the first century CE (cf. John 2:20), just a few years before the temple was destroyed by the Romans in 70 CE. The temple complex was a sprawling city-like set of structures that supported the complex array of activities needed to support the sacrificial system set up in the Torah.

This is the temple that Jesus and Paul knew and where they and other first-century Jews came to make sacrifices for the three yearly festivals commanded by God in the Torah, which called all Jews to come to the "place that [the LORD] will choose" (Deut 16:16-17).

Hebrews 9:1–10:18

Pesach/Passover occurred in the spring (with the barley harvest; Lev 23:4-8; Deut 16:1-8), Shavuot/Pentecost in the summer (with the wheat harvest; Lev 23:15-21; Deut 16:9-12), and Sukkot/Booths in the fall (with the grape harvest; Lev 23:33-36; Deut 16:13-15). The Gospels, Acts, and the epistles of Paul all bear witness to both Jesus and Paul attending one or more of these festivals.

The New Testament is an important source of information about temple practices. Luke 2 describes several ways in which the temple featured in the lives of first-century Jews. Luke 2:22-24 has Mary and Joseph bringing the baby Jesus to make an offering for "their purification." Mary and Joseph "offered a sacrifice according to what is stated in the law of the Lord, 'a pair of turtledoves or two young pigeons'" (2:24). The "law of the Lord" refers to Leviticus 12, which contains the ritual of purification for women after the birth of a child. (Although Luke says "their purification," the only person needing purification was Mary.) The two turtledoves indicate the family's socioeconomic status. For wealthy women, the sacrifice required is a lamb. But for less wealthy folks, two turtledoves would suffice.

Anna, a prophet, never left the temple, "but worshiped there with fasting and prayer night and day" (Luke 2:37). Later in the same chapter, the text states that Mary and Joseph came every year for Passover (2:41-51). This same passage relates the story of Jesus as a young boy staying in Jerusalem to discuss the law in the temple with teachers. These two passages illustrate various uses of the temple: for sacrifice, for prayer, and for teaching. We know from the Acts of the Apostles that the temple was a place to pray (3:1), to beg for alms (3:10), to teach (5:21), and to make purification (21:26-30). As is true for many places of worship, the temple served multiple functions for a variety of people (see Matt 21:14, 23; Mark 11:27).

Sacrifice

The importance of sacrifice in the Bible cannot be overstated. Its meaning and function within ancient Israel and Judaism up to 70 CE have often been misunderstood and misinterpreted (especially by Protestant biblical scholars). Even the question about whether expiation (atonement, the making of amends) is at the core of all sacrifices is a matter of debate.

All agree, however, that there was no single function of sacrifice. Even a cursory reading of Leviticus 1–7 suggests that there are different sacrifices for different situations, and a one-size-fits-all approach may not do justice to the situation. Yoder's clear and accessible commentary on Leviticus outlines the various sacrificial purposes and functions.

Overemphasis on the yearly ritual outlined in Leviticus 16 for the Day of Atonement, which involved the high priest in atoning for the sins of Israel, may skew the reading of sacrifice in general, especially among Christian interpreters, since Hebrews 8–10 emphasizes the sacrifices of the Day of Atonement. Sacrifice simply had different meanings, depending on what was brought to be offered and the situation. Because there were different kinds of impurity (ritual versus moral), it stands to reason that the sacrifices to deal with the impurity were different. Ritual impurity kept people away from the tabernacle. Ethical misdeeds, or moral impurities, did not keep people away from the tabernacle, but they still required sacrifices for forgiveness (Yoder: 114–15).

There was also a daily offering of two lambs, one in the morning and another in the evening. The primary function of the daily sacrifice was to maintain the presence of God among the people of Israel (Exod 29:42-46). Moral sin and impurity drive God away. Daily sacrifices function to keep God's presence in the sanctuary. Jonathan Klawans argues that we should think about the daily sacrifice as a way of keeping God's presence among the people of Israel, despite the moral sins that are committed (68–72). It may seem as though our author considers the daily (?) *gifts and sacrifices offered* in *the first tent* to be no longer useful, because they *cannot perfect the conscience of the worshiper* (9:8-10); yet the concept of regular sacrifice is still relevant. Later in the text, our homilist exhorts the congregation not to *neglect to do good and to share what you have, for such sacrifices are pleasing to God* (13:16).

The prophets were critical of sacrifices offered without thought. Sacrifice without obedience is a rejection of the word of the Lord: "To obey is better than sacrifice, and to heed than the fat of rams" (1 Sam 15:22-23). When God led the Israelites out of Egypt, God commanded not burnt offerings, but obedience. The command given was "Obey my voice . . . and walk only in the way that I command you" (Jer 7:21-23). Only then would the Israelites be God's people. Hosea, Amos, and Micah all call the people to love (Hos 6:6) and "let justice roll down like waters" (Amos 5:21-27). They call God's people "to do justice and . . . love kindness and . . . walk humbly with . . . God" (Mic 6:6-8). In a stirring poetic message at the beginning of Isaiah, God pleads with the people to "cease to do evil; learn to do good; seek justice; rescue the oppressed; defend the orphan; plead for the widow" (Isa 1:16-17). Sacrifices without

Hebrews 9:1–10:18

those actions are nothing to God, who says, "I have had enough of burnt offerings of rams" (1:11). Several psalmists speak of sacrifices of contrition and thanksgiving as more acceptable to God. All the bulls and the rams of the world are already God's. What God wants is a "sacrifice of thanksgiving." God wants to be called upon "in the day of trouble" (Ps 50:14-15). The prayer of Psalm 51 recognizes that God "has no delight in sacrifice." What delights God is a "broken spirit; a broken and contrite heart, O God, you will not despise" (51:16-17). "An open ear" and a "delight to do your will, O my God," not "sacrifice and offering," are what the psalmist (Ps 40) understands God wants. Finally, like the biblical prophets and psalmists, the apostle Paul knew that without love and sincere motives, displays of piety are like a "noisy gong or a clanging cymbal" (1 Cor 13:1).

In the New Testament, Hebrews provides the fullest discussion of sacrifice; yet it is mentioned regularly in other texts. The Gospels attest to sacrifice as an important aspect of religious life. Although they do not directly mention Jesus himself offering a sacrifice, they note his regular travel to Jerusalem to attend the three major feasts, all of which include a sacrifice at the temple. There is no reason to believe that Jesus did not engage in this. The Gospels mention that he taught in the temple court. He cared enough about the activity in the temple to cause a disturbance about certain dubious practices of the money changers. Only the author of Luke-Acts describes sacrificial acts. Luke 2:22-24 tells us that Jesus' parents made a sacrifice for Jesus when he was presented in the temple after his birth. Then 2:41-42 also speaks of a Passover visit to Jerusalem, when presumably a Passover lamb was sacrificed. Luke also records Jesus instructing his disciples to "prepare the Passover meal for us that we may eat it" (22:8). This would have required the disciples to go to the temple and have their lamb sacrificed. Elsewhere, Acts 21:26 tells us that the apostle Paul offered a sacrifice in the temple on the counsel of James to appease the elders in Jerusalem and moderate the criticism of his ministry to the Gentiles. Matthew, Mark, and Luke describe Jesus' last meal with his disciples as a Passover meal; John places it on the day before the Passover.

Sacrificial metaphors appear multiple times in the New Testament. Jesus is called "the Lamb of God" (John 1:29, 36; 1 Pet 1:18-19; Rev 5:6-10; 13:8). His blood is said to cleanse from sin (1 John 1:7). Christ is called our Passover lamb (1 Cor 5:6-8). Hebrews 9–10 compares him to the offerings on the Day of Atonement (Lev 16; 23:26-32; 25:9; Num 29:7-11).

THE TEXT IN THE LIFE OF THE CHURCH

Responding to Jesus' Once-for-All Sacrifice

Modern Christians agree with the author of Hebrews that Jesus is the fulfillment of Jeremiah's new covenant. But as Amy-Jill Levine and Marc Zvi Brettler write, "Neither Christians nor Jews, nor anyone else, has God's instructions written on their hearts; if they did, there would be little need for ongoing Bible study or sermons, since we would be living in that perfect eschatological age, with the wolf living beside the lamb" (2020: 418). Clark Williamson makes similar observations about the new covenant as he concludes his article "Anti-Judaism in Hebrews?" According to the author of Hebrews, the new covenant is better because it is based on Jesus' once-for-all sacrifice. Priests no longer need to offer daily and yearly sacrifices: Jesus did it all. However, as we have also seen (and will see again in the next section), our author still uses strategies of exhortation in motivating the congregation to continue on the path of faithfulness. Williamson asks: "Has the perfection promised in Hebrews been any more actualized in the community of those who worship through the sacrifice of Christ than in the old covenant?" (278).

The Hebrew prophets regularly critiqued the Israelites about their motivations and behaviors as the people of God, Williamson reminds us. The Israelites were not upholding the covenant that God had laid out for them. Williamson challenges contemporary Christians to become self-critical: "The church today, unless it has a case of ecclesiastical amnesia, also has a long history . . . full of sin, particularly and ironically *against* the Jews" (278). In other words, the new covenant is only as good as the people who try to keep it. It may bring us to(ward) perfection, but only if we remain faithful [*Supersessionist and Anti-Jewish Interpretations of Hebrews, p. 257*].

Part 4

A Call to Perseverance, Endurance, Faithfulness

Hebrews 10:19–12:2

OVERVIEW

The author now shifts gears. The lengthy exposition of doctrine (7:1–10:18) transitions to exhortation (10:19–12:2). The pastor is stern at times. Knowing the faithful response to previous abuse and persecution, the author challenges the audience's current weariness and lack of confidence.

Willful rejection of Jesus as the Son of God deserves a far greater punishment than violating the law of Moses. The pastor calls for a renewal of boldness and confidence, again quoting prophetic Scripture as justification: *My righteous one will live by faith* (Heb 10:38; from Hab 2:4).

The author knows how to inspire. The long catalog of faithful acts by biblical forebears, many of whom endured great difficulties, inspires hope (Heb 11). God affirms these people for their perseverance and faithfulness despite many obstacles, even when they did not see the fulfillment of God's promises. The author calls these people *so great a cloud of witnesses* (12:1) and challenges the audience to *lay aside every weight and the sin that clings so closely, . . . [to] run with perseverance the race that is set before us* (12:1-2).

OUTLINE

Perseverance Is Essential, 10:19-31
What Faithfulness Looks Like, 10:32–12:2

Hebrews 10:19-31

Perseverance Is Essential

PREVIEW

Pastors often use a sermon to exhort their congregation and spur them to right action. Should the pastor admonish the worshipers, warn them of future judgment, or remind them of the good works they have already done? The pastor/author of Hebrews does all the above. In this short but challenging passage, the writer combines exhortations and warnings of judgment to encourage the people to hold fast to their commitments. As a fully fleshed-out early Jewish-Christian homily, Hebrews contains all the hallmarks of that genre, including exhortations and warnings.

In this conclusion to the long doctrinal passage from 7:1–10:18, the author aims to make a high rhetorical impact by using warnings.

OUTLINE

Exhortations, 10:19-25
    10:19-22   Let Us Approach
    10:23   Let Us Hold Fast
    10:24-25   Let Us Consider How to Provoke One Another
Warning against Apostasy, 10:26-31

174   Hebrews 10:19-31

EXPLANATORY NOTES

Exhortations 10:19-25

Like any good homilist, our author (in 10:19-21) starts with a review of what has been said: *We have confidence* (4:16; 6:9) . . . *to enter the sanctuary* (6:19; 9:12, 24) *by the new and living way that he opened for us through the curtain, . . . his flesh* (6:19; 9:8), . . . *since we have a great priest over the house of God* (cf. 3:5).

The sanctuary is not the earthly building, but the heavenly one described in chapter 9. Adding to the new-covenant motif from chapter 8, the author describes Jesus' sacrifice as *the new and living way, . . . opened for us through the curtain of his flesh* (10:20). The curtain, Jesus' (broken) flesh, opens the *living way*. The high priest opened the curtain to the holy of holies in the tabernacle, but Jesus' own body is the curtain to the real, heavenly tabernacle.

Through the brokenness of death comes life. The Greek word *enkainizō*, translated as "opened" in 10:20, also appears in 9:18, where it is translated "inaugurated" by the NRSV: *Not even the first covenant was inaugurated without blood.* Other translators use "consecrate" (Hart). This one word sums up what the author has been saying about Jesus: his broken body, through his once-for-all sacrifice, became the curtain and therefore the opening, the new and living way, to the heavenly tabernacle. Through that act, he also inaugurated, or consecrated, the new covenant [*Christology in Hebrews, p. 235*].

These are things that the congregation knows. The homilist then moves on to things they should do through a series of exhortations, all restating previous exhortations.

10:19-22 Let Us Approach

This exact exhortation, *Let us approach/draw near*, was also issued in 4:16. Here the homilist urges the hearers to *enter the sanctuary . . . in full assurance of faith* (10:19-22) because they have been washed with water and sprinkled with Jesus' blood. The homilist repeats the call for acting with boldness (or confidence) from 4:16 and picks up earlier themes from other chapters as well. Here they can act with confidence because they have been washed and sprinkled. This recalls the earlier theme in chapter 9 of purification by blood. Just as God sprinkled the tent and the vessels with water and the blood of calves (9:19-21), the *people* of God are now sprinkled and washed through Jesus' once-for-all sacrifice. In Hebrews 8:2, the earthly tent or tabernacle is an imprecise replica of the heavenly tent. Here we

Hebrews 10:19-31

have another image. Instead of purifying the earthly temple and the instruments of the liturgy by using the blood of animals, here, Jesus' blood purifies people. Their hearts and bodies have been made pure and become the sanctuary and the instruments of liturgy.

What an important transition! Although Jesus may reside in the heavenly tabernacle, the people are now the earthly place where the sacrifice is evident. Jesus' actions are not only *once for all*; they also signify a new role for the people themselves. Jesus the pioneer has paved the way. Now the people must follow *with a true heart in full assurance of faith* (10:22). We should not be surprised that the theme of faith or faithfulness resurfaces here. As in chapter 4, faith is not a belief but a state of being that leads to practice.

Finally, this practice emphasizes the "we": *Let us approach* (emph. added). The homilist has been advocating group responsibility since at least chapter 3 with the call *Exhort one another every day* (3:13). The wilderness generation of ancient Israelites did not reach the Promised Land, *because they were not united by faith with those who listened* (4:2). Another exhortation in 4:11 encourages individuals to behave with a group mindset: *Let us therefore make every effort to enter that rest, so that no one may fall through such disobedience as theirs [the Israelites]*. While the homilist does not disregard individual responsibility, the exhortation encourages the congregation to think about their lives in relationship to the larger group. As we see in chapter 10, the group has already lived through a period of persecution. As we have been suggesting throughout the commentary, a minority group living in a broader culture perceived as hostile needs to maintain its group identity by solidifying its cohesion as a group. *Let us* is a small but powerful statement, signaling the collective thinking and action required of them.

10:23 Let Us Hold Fast

The homilist repeats the refrain *Let us* and restates 4:14: *Let us hold fast to [our] confession*. This may be the confession of faith taken at the time of baptism or some other confessional statement. Based on internal evidence to this specific text, it could be the confession that Jesus is *the apostle and high priest of our confession* (3:1). The word "confession" translates the Greek word *homologia*, which implies that the confession, or acknowledgment of the belief, is *public*. The community knows where an individual stands on something by a public confession. Once again, the author emphasizes the communal nature of this set of exhortations. By extension, since these exhortations summarize the entirety of the homily so far, we also

176   Hebrews 10:19-31

understand the communal nature of the entire text. Faithfulness, confession, boldness: each needs to be enacted by individuals and to be a characteristic of the people at large.

10:24-25 Let Us Consider How to Provoke One Another

Provoke one another, . . . meet together, . . . encouraging one another. If we had any doubt about the importance of community in living a faithful life, it should be erased after reading these two verses. The homilist is exhorting the people to think about how they can *provoke* each other to love and good deeds. The Greek word for "provoke" becomes the English word *paroxysm*, a sudden attack or violent outburst. Our homilist is urging them to have a violent outburst of love! Such love is not a gentle stirring of the pot, but is sudden, maybe even a little frightening. Second, they are to gather, perhaps to share their paroxysms of love. Imagine thinking of church as an accountability group where the goal is to encourage each other in how to love, with good deeds as the focus of the following week's activities! Incidentally, the Greek word for the phrase *meet together* in 10:25 is *episynagōgē*, which is related to the English word *synagogue*. Although we tend to think of synagogues and churches as places, both Greek words speak of meetings or gatherings, with the emphasis on the gathering of people, not the place where the gathering is held.

As if encouraging and provoking to love and good works were not enough, the homilist reminds the people that all this is more urgent because *the Day [is] approaching* (10:25). Here the homilist means the day of judgment, when Jesus returns. "The Day" is used as shorthand by many, including Paul in 1 Thessalonian 5:4: "That day" might "surprise you like a thief." Isaiah 2:12 and Joel 1:15 warn people to be ready for the destruction of those who are haughty or sidetracked by unimportant issues. Although neither Isaiah or Joel may be referring to the end times in the way that Paul or our homilist does, it is a biblical refrain that early Christians took up and modified for their own times and purposes. Here it provides an excellent segue into the next section, which cautions people about the consequences of separation from God.

Warning against Apostasy 10:26-31

This warning follows on the heels of several others in this text. In 2:1-4, the people are exhorted to *pay greater attention* so as not to fall away. The extended quotation of Psalm 95 in Hebrews 3:7-19 reminds hearers of the dangers of unfaithfulness, exemplified by

Hebrews 10:19-31

their ancestors in the wilderness. A third warning in 6:4-6 describes the perils of falling away from the gifts and powers of the Holy Spirit. Now we have a fourth warning, starting with the clause *if we willfully persist in sin* (10:26).

Dealing with this passage has not been easy for either ancient or modern commentators. On the surface, it seems to ignore the concept of forgiveness and even the long-standing relationship between God and the people of Israel: God consistently forgives the people time after time. So what should we make of this summary and restatement of earlier warnings?

This passage directly follows exhortations that encourage people, as a collective, to work together in mutual boldness, provoking each other to love, and approaching God. *Let us!* Therefore, the warning against apostasy must be read in that same context of mutuality and community. While sins of individuals might constitute apostasy, the issue here seems to be corporate: *if we willfully persist . . .* This is a matter for the community at large about how to be a people of God.

The end of the passage confirms this. The homilist quotes Deuteronomy 32:35-36: "Vengeance is mine, and recompense. . . . Indeed, the LORD will vindicate his people." God was claiming retribution for the people of Israel against their enemies. The notion of collective accountability is present in the object of God's vengeance and in God's defense of Israel.

We might also think about what "sin" means here and in the wider context of Hebrews. The word "sin" (Gk. *hamartia*) occurs in Hebrews 1:3; 3:13; 10:26; 11:25; 12:1; and other verses. It is difficult to derive a definitive understanding of what constitutes sin from these verses. The Son came to make *purification for sins* (1:3), which can be sins committed knowingly or unknowingly.

However, all these references confirm the basic meaning of sin: to deviate from or miss the mark. In 3:12-13, the warning is to not turn *away from the living God* and *be hardened by the deceitfulness of sin*. In 11:25, our homilist speaks about Moses turning toward the people of Israel and away from the *fleeting pleasures of sin*. Finally, in 12:1 the Hebrews are reminded to *lay aside . . . sin* and *run with perseverance* (stick to the racecourse). Sin is not a set of dos and don'ts, but a deviation from an approach to life that focuses on faithfulness toward God. To keep on this path, the homilist urges the Hebrews to intensify community: *Exhort one another* (3:13; cf. 10:25), follow Moses' example in turning toward his people (11:25), and remember the cloud of witnesses who did the same (12:1). In short,

178   Hebrews 10:19-31

the Hebrews are to stay on the path by working together as a community.

Here the homilist's goal is to remind the people that persisting in this sin denies the sacrifice made by Christ. The homilist has already made a similar argument in 6:6. There, Christ is crucified again when they go astray. Here, Christ's sacrificial blood is profaned (10:29). The homilist employs the rhetorical strategy of *synkrisis* to make his point: if the people of Israel receive a punishment of death by violating the law of Moses, how much greater will be the punishment for those who spurn the Son of God (10:28-29)! After the detailed and complex argument to prove the greater merits of Christ's sacrifice compared with those of the Levitical order, the homilist is keen to make sure the people acknowledge that truth in their lives.

Unlike other gods, the God of Israel, worshiped by the people of Hebrews, is living and actively involved: *It is a fearful thing to fall into the hands of the living God* (10:31). Congregants who take seriously Christ's sacrifice understand the irreparable breach caused by the lack of care in willfully persisting in sin.

THE TEXT IN BIBLICAL CONTEXT

Apostasy in the Bible

Several Greek words in the Bible function as synonyms for apostasy: to fall away, rebel. Regardless of the Greek word, the meaning implies a willfulness to the action. In the Hebrew Bible, the willful movement away from the God of Israel toward other gods is a public sin since it threatens the very fabric of society. Other sins that fit into this category are blasphemy, incest, and violation of the Sabbath. Deuteronomy 13:13-18 and 17:2-7 both give details about punishments for such sin (i.e., death). In Deuteronomy 13, worshiping other gods results in the burning of an entire town. The town essentially becomes a burnt sacrifice to keep the rest of the nation pure. An example of this appears in Joshua 22, when Phinehas, a priest, confronts several tribes of Israel and urges them to stop building an altar to other gods. Not just those tribes would be affected, but all of Israel: "If you rebel against the LORD today, he will be angry with the whole congregation of Israel tomorrow" (Josh 22:18). Those tribes deny the charge and claim that they have merely made a "copy of the altar of the LORD" (22:28) since "the LORD has made the Jordan a boundary between us and you" (22:25). Clearly, it was a serious matter among the ancient Israelites.

Although the day of judgment is not a central theme in Hebrews, chapter 10 does warn about the judgment that those who *willfully persist in sin* (10:26) will receive. The phrase *a fury of fire that will consume the adversaries* (10:27) stems from the Jewish Scriptures. In Deuteronomy 4:24, God is called "a devouring fire, a jealous God." Two passages in Isaiah (26:11; 66:15) speak about the consuming nature of fire and the punishment that God issues with those flames. Finally, Zephaniah 1:18 cautions people that "neither silver nor . . . gold will be able to save them on the day of the LORD's wrath: in the fire of his passion the whole earth shall be consumed."

Other parts of the New Testament express concern that people can be led astray by false messiahs, a straying that may be a necessary step along the way before the day of the Lord. First John 2:18 expresses great concern about how "so . . . many antichrists have come," revealed by how they went away from the group and denied Jesus. The writer exhorts the people to "abide in the Son and in the Father" (2:24), that is, not to fall away. Matthew 24 (sometimes considered a "little apocalypse"); 2 Thessalonians 2:3; and 2 Timothy 3:1-5 specifically mention the period of distress and rebellion that will come before the day of the Lord. Much like what we read in Hebrews, the people are exhorted not to be deceived (2 Thess 2:3), to avoid those who deny the power of godliness (2 Tim 3:5), and not to be duped into following a false messiah (Matt 24:23). In all these cases, rebellion from God is a driving concern; yet an underlying tension is the discord brought to the entire people of God and the ultimate breakdown of the group.

THE TEXT IN THE LIFE OF THE CHURCH

Apostasy as a Breaking of Fellowship

The biblical material reviewed earlier stresses that apostasy is more than a private matter between an individual sinner and God: it is a matter for the entire community. For example, early Anabaptists were considered apostates by the Roman Catholics and other Protestant groups when they formed during the Radical Reformation. They were called heretics! We who have followed in the path of those early Anabaptists disagree with both labels: apostates, heretics. They broke fellowship with existing groups because they felt the leading of God to be something different. We claim that the early Anabaptists were following the light of God and correctly interpreting the biblical message. Depending on where someone is in the controversies, they are considered a heretic, apostate, or reformer.

We may also want to reconsider our understanding of apostasy, especially as it relates to "the Beloved Community," a term used by Rev. Dr. Martin Luther King Jr. to describe how everyone is cared for. In such a community, poverty, racism, hunger, and hate are no longer acceptable. When white people deny the effects of racism on their Black and Brown neighbors, or when able-bodied folks fail to incorporate accessibility into building designs or websites, are we not turning our backs on each other and therefore on God? An unexamined life in this regard is a life lived away from God, the consequences of which are irreparable breaches and broken community.

Mutual Encouragement

Breaking fellowship in our contexts today should therefore give us pause. Mutual accountability has historically been an important aspect of Anabaptism. But how can we care for the life of the group without becoming like the early persecutors of the Anabaptists? How can we be open to varieties of practice and belief while maintaining group cohesion? And how can we be responsible toward everyone in the ways they need, and not turn our backs on them? The words of the homilist of Hebrews 10:24-25 (adapted) are a good place to start:

> *Let us consider how to provoke one another to love and good deeds.*
> *Let us not neglect to meet together.*
> *Let us encourage one another.*

How can we break fellowship if we have these three things in mind?

Hebrews 10:32–12:2

What Faithfulness Looks Like

PREVIEW

By faith. The homilist now exhorts the congregation to continue living *by faith.* And how are they to do so? To answer that question, our author offers a magisterial catalog of the *cloud of witnesses* (12:1)— past heroes who lived *by faith,* thereby witnessing to their faith. This journey of faith first begins with memories of hardships they endured *by faith,* followed by a brief definition of faith (10:32–11:1). Instead of merely enduring suffering, the homilist exhorts the congregation to *run . . . the race* (12:2), reframing the image of jeering crowds into a vision of cheering crowds at an athletic competition. As if in a relay race, they are finishing what the *cloud of witnesses* have started, knowing what reward lies before them. Because Jesus is the *pioneer and perfecter* of their faith (12:2), these hearers are recipients of the gifts that the cloud of witnesses were only *promised* (11:39). It is their job to finish the race begun by those who have gone before.

The homilist continues to dazzle with rhetorical skill that surely sounds compelling to the audience. Like a refrain, the phrase *by faith* occurs nineteen times in 11:2–12:2. This rhetorical device is called *anaphora,* the repetition of a word or phrase at the beginning of clauses. If there were any doubt that this text was originally spoken, the use of anaphora should remove it. Rev. Dr. Martin Luther King Jr. skillfully used anaphora in his "I Have a Dream" speech. This is

182   Hebrews 10:32–12:2

similar. It creates excitement. It helps people remember. It causes hearers to take notice.

OUTLINE

Remember Your Own Faithfulness, 10:32-39
Remember the Faithfulness of Past Witnesses, 11:1-38
    11:1-3 The Character of Faith
    11:4-38   By Faith . . .

Abel, Enoch, and Noah	11:4-7
Abraham, Sarah, Isaac, Jacob, and Joseph	11:8-22
Moses and the Israelites	11:23-28
Rahab and the Fugitives from Egypt	11:29-31
Judges, Kings, Prophets, and Martyrs	11:32-38

They Wait for Us, 11:39-40
Look to Jesus, Who Endured the Cross, 12:1-2

EXPLANATORY NOTES

Remember Your Own Faithfulness 10:32-39

Memory is an important aspect of group identity. We make valuable meaning by repeating stories about who we are. Telling stories is especially important for marginalized groups since they are not part of the dominant culture. In contrast to the warnings that the homilist has just issued, the "Hebrews" are now invited to recall their conversion (or enlightening) experience when they first heard the message of Jesus and the personal experiences of suffering that they have endured. Through words and phrases such as *endured a hard struggle with sufferings* (10:32), *accepted the plundering of your possessions* (10:34), and *do not . . . abandon that confidence of yours* (10:35), the homilist emphasizes their previous acts of faithfulness. The homilist is now encouraging them to hold on to the faith and confidence they have manifested in the past.

True to form, the homilist uses a biblical quotation to reaffirm the message of this section. The introductory phrase, *in a very little while* (10:37), comes from Isaiah 26:20 and is eschatological language about a time of God's intervention. The prophet is instructing the people of God to hide "for a little while until the wrath is past." The remainder of the quotation is from the LXX version of Habakkuk 2:3-4. The prophet proclaims a "vision for an appointed time" (NETS), for which the people of God need to wait, regardless of when it arrives. Our homilist uses these passages to encourage the Hebrews to keep working by reminding them that God takes no pleasure in *anyone who shrinks back* (10:38), especially given that the

Hebrews 10:32–12:2

day of God's judgment is close. With that reminder, the homilist presents a working definition of faith/faithfulness.

Remember the Faithfulness of Past Witnesses 11:1-38

11:1-3 The Character of Faith

Our homilist starts the catalog with a whopper of a statement. The Greek is difficult, and translating it into English has proved challenging for many, since the meaning is opaque! Comparing the following two versions gives some sense of the difficulties in translating this passage—the versions are quite different:

Now <u>faithfulness</u> [*pistis*] is the <u>substance</u> [*hypostasis*] of things hoped for, <u>evidence</u> [*elenchos*] of things not seen. For by this, the ancients <u>were attested</u> [*martyreō*]. By faith, we understand that the ages were fashioned by God's word, so that what we see comes from what we do not see. (*L. Johnson: 276, slightly modified*)	Now <u>faith</u> [*pistis*] is the <u>assurance</u> [*hypostasis*] of things hoped for, the <u>conviction</u> [*elenchos*] of things not seen. Indeed, by faith our ancestors <u>received approval</u> [*martyreō*]. By faith we understand that the worlds were prepared by the word of God, so that what is seen was made from things that are not visible. (*NRSV*)

Although all translations can only approximate the original meaning, some things are clear. First, it recalls earlier statements from the text: in 3:6 (*Christ, however, was faithful over God's house as a son*), Christ's faithfulness is confirmed and the people's hope and confidence in that knowledge will keep them within the household of God. Second, the homilist has used the Greek word *pistis* in chapters 3–4 to describe the unfaithful behavior of some people of Israel. In the catalog of those belonging to the cloud of witnesses, we encounter the positive behavior of other people of Israel.

Third, the pastor reuses the word *hypostasis*—essence, reality, substance—from 1:3, where it describes the Son as the exact imprint of God's very being, or substance. Although many translations use the word "assurance" in 11:1, some scholars prefer a translation that resembles the meaning in 1:3, using "substance" instead, so that faithfulness itself has substance, a real thing that you can see. Fourth, the statement about the "ancestors" or "ancients" in 11:2 is puzzling. The homilist uses the verb *martyreō*, which usually means "to bear witness." In time, "martyr" came to identify someone who bears (the ultimate) witness in sacrificing their life. However, in this verse the homilist uses the passive form, which can often mean "be well spoken of" or "be approved." Should we read this verse as "In this [faithfulness] the ancestors were attested" (L. Johnson: 276), or "In this, the ancestors received approval"

184   **Hebrews 10:32–12:2**

(NRSV)? Although the two statements have similar meanings, since the verb is passive, we must assume that *God* favorably attests them, which is why they made it into this roll call of faithful ancestors.

11:4-38 By Faith ...

First, our author discusses each person or group in roughly canonical order, meaning that they appear in Hebrews 11 much as they appear in the Scriptures. Second, the examples named are not other Jesus followers but scriptural figures, all of whom are considered ancestors of the current audience. This should remind us that the homilist and the Hebrews are closely connected to the biblical narrative, both as a text and as a lived experience. The homilist does not reject the traditions but claims them and reinterprets them to guide the Hebrews in living faithfully in the present.

Except for David, a king, the people on the list are ordinary people—farmers, carpenters, shepherds, and enslaved people who make bricks. Many unnamed people also made big sacrifices to follow the leading of God's word. The homilist prizes offering things to God. Words used elsewhere in the text—*offer* (5:1-3; 7:27; 8:3-5; 9:9, 25, 28; 10:1-2, 8-14), *approach* (4:16; 7:19, 25; 10:1, 22; 11:6), and *obey/obedience* (5:8-9)—appear here to emphasize the connection between the "theory" of chapters 7–10 and the chapters that follow, which focus more on practice.

Person/ group	What we know about them	Sign of faithfulness	Biblical source	Verses in Hebrews
The audience/witnesses for the Hebrews	Early followers of Jesus	Were publicly exposed to abuse and persecution; showed compassion to those in prison; understand that the worlds were made from God's word	Gen 1:1-3	10:32-34; 11:3
Abel	Practiced husbandry	Offered a more pleasing sacrifice	Gen 4:1-16	11:4
Enoch	Walked with God	Pleased God	Gen 5:24	11:5-6
Noah	Carpenter (?), shipbuilder, farmer	Respected (was reverent about) God's warning, built an ark	Gen 6:9–9:28	11:7
Abraham and Sarah	Nomads	Obeyed, stayed, received the power of procreation, willing to offer Isaac	Gen 12:1-9; 18:9-15; 21:1-8	11:8-12, (13-16), 17-19
Isaac	Had flocks and herds	Invoked blessings	Gen 27:1-40	11:20

Hebrews 10:32–12:2   185

Jacob	A quiet man who lived in tents	Blessed each of the sons of Joseph	Gen 48:8-22	11:21
Joseph	Dreamer, slave, Pharaoh's chief of staff	Foresaw the exodus	Gen 50:24-25	11:22
Moses	Adopted son of Egyptian princess	Hidden by his parents, refused his elite status, left Egypt, kept the Passover	Exod 2:1-15; 12:1–13:10	11:23-28
The people	Enslaved people who were brick-makers, wet nurses, and mid-wives	Passed through the Red Sea	Exod 14–15	11:29
Israel	Israelites marched around Jericho, blowing trumpets	Walls fell after the Israelites heeded God's call to encir-cle Jericho for seven days	Josh 6	11:30
Rahab	Innkeeper/prosti-tute, dealer in flax	Received the spies in peace	Josh 2:1-21	11:31
Gideon, Barak, Samson, Jephthah, David, Samuel, prophets, [Daniel]	Judges; David, a shepherd (later a king); prophets	Conquered kingdoms, administered justice, obtained promises, shut the mouths of lions, quenched raging fire, escaped the sword, won strength, became mighty in war, put foreign armies to flight	Judg 4–8; 11–16; 1–2 Samuel; Judg 14:6; Dan 3; 6:19-23	11:32-34
Women		Received their dead by resurrection	1 Kings 17:17-24; 2 Kings 4:18-37	11:35
Others		Were tortured	(?) 2 Macc 6:18–7:42 (Eleazar, mother and seven sons)	11:35b
Others		Suffered mocking, flog-ging, chains, were stoned to death, sawn in two, killed by the sword, went about in skins, were desti-tute, persecuted, torment-ed, wandered in deserts	1 Kings 17:1-7; 19:3-9, 13, 19; 2 Kings 2:25; 21:16; 2 Chron 24:21 (stoning); 2 Macc 5–10	11:36-38

186   Hebrews 10:32–12:2

Abel, Enoch, and Noah, 11:4-7. Offered . . . approached . . . respected.
These three verbs indicate what landed Abel, Enoch, and Noah in
this catalog of faith, picking up themes the pastor has been stressing
throughout the sermon. Of course, Jesus has offered himself and
reverently submitted to God (5:7). The pastor has urged the audience to *approach [God's] throne of grace* (4:16). Abel, Enoch, and Noah
embody these actions.

Outside the story recorded in Genesis, Abel receives little mention in Jewish Scriptures, so it may have taken the audience by surprise when the homilist begins the catalog with him. Abel has a few
mentions in the pseudepigraphical literature of the Second Temple
period *[Jewish Literature in Antiquity, p. 238]*, such as 1 Enoch 22:7 and
the Testament of Abraham 13:2-3. Philo addresses Cain and Abel's
sacrifices in three different treatises (*On the Sacrifices of Cain and Abel,
That the Worse Attacks the Better,* and *On the Posterity of Cain*), treating
them as aspects of the soul.

The Hebrews homilist is clearly taken with Abel as well. In 11:2,
the ancestors, in general, *received approval.* Here the author proclaims that Abel specifically received God's approval by his offering
of *gifts* (11:4). The homilist closes this brief mention of Abel by
claiming that *through his faith [Abel] still speaks* (11:4). Perhaps the
spilling of Abel's blood is the connection for our author. According
to L. Johnson, this statement is reminiscent of Genesis 4:10, where
Abel's blood "cries out" to God because of Cain's actions (281). Abel's
actions are not only a true *witness* (Heb 11:4 KJV) that he was righteous before God; he is also a sign or symbol of the price Jesus paid
through his blood. Abel is therefore a fitting start to the catalog (cf.
Matt 23:35//Luke 11:52).

In contrast to the case with Abel, Jews in antiquity made a great
deal of Enoch, our next hero in the catalog, despite his brief appearance in Genesis 5:22-24. "Enoch walked with God; then he was no
more, because God took him" (5:24). This statement about Enoch
varies from the basic pattern of how Genesis records how people
lived and died. Most often the text simply states that the person
lived so many years, then died. When describing Enoch, the phrase
"he was no more" replaces the word "he died." The LXX adds that
Enoch "pleased God," which our homilist uses as well. Reflecting this
same tradition, Sirach 44:16 says, "Enoch was well pleasing to God"
(NETS). By the time Hebrews was written, extensive extrabiblical
traditions surrounded this figure. The lengthy apocalyptic text we
know as 1 Enoch is actually a library of five different writings written over a period of 250 years or so. Enoch is the main figure in

Hebrews 10:32–12:2   187

1 Enoch and 2 Enoch. He is listed in Luke's genealogy of Joseph and quoted as a prophet of judgment in Jude 14-15. These traditions likely inspired Hebrews' inclusion of Enoch in the list.

In the tradition of commenting on biblical passages, our homilist may have used "walked with God" to allude to Enoch's faithfulness, leading him to comment in 11:6, *Without faith it is impossible to please God*. Enoch could approach God because of that faith.

The commentary on Noah emphasizes the *unseen* aspect of the definition of faith in 11:1. Noah's warning from God was about events to take place in the future. As with Jesus, who in Hebrews is the Savior of his people, Noah's response to God's call saved his household. Our homilist comments that in this action Noah *condemned the world*. While this statement confirms the demise of those who did not heed Noah, the phrase may have additional meaning. Throughout Hebrews, the homilist contends that the people of God must maintain a certain set-apartness to remain faithful. Being set apart must, in some way, mean that one turns their back toward the world in order to turn toward God. In condemning the world, Noah became *an heir to the righteousness that is in accordance with faith* (11:7; cf. 2 Pet 2:5). Inheritance is an important theme in Hebrews. Recall that "Son" and "heir" occur together at the beginning of the text in 1:2 and in the discussion on a will in chapter 9. Here the homilist connects the dots between those discussions, the covenant that God gave Noah in Genesis 9, and his understanding of Noah as a righteous and faithful person.

Abraham, Sarah, Isaac, Jacob, and Joseph, 11:8-22. Obeyed ... dwelled ... offered ... blessed. The story of Abraham's sojourn is an obvious place to emphasize the theme of obedience in the face of the unknown. This is not the first mention of Abraham, who plays an important role in the story our homilist is telling. In chapter 7, Abraham the patriarch is recognized and blessed; he offered a tithe of his spoils to Melchizedek, thereby establishing Melchizedek's priestly role in the story. In chapter 6, the audience is reminded of the promise made to Abraham. Now we see the faithful actions that began Abraham's story. Because of Abraham's obedience when God first called him, God promised an inheritance to Abraham: offspring, land, and a blessing for everyone. For our homilist, living a life of faith is existing as a stranger, an outsider. Like Noah, Abraham and his family differed in some way from the majority culture. They lived as immigrants, where they may have been unwelcome, seen as different from those around them, with different customs, religious traditions, and language. Recalling the earlier discussion of the heavenly

188   Hebrews 10:32–12:2

home, where Jesus now resides, the homilist, in his own reinterpretation of the Genesis story, goes beyond the biblical narrative when he says that Abraham was looking for a *city* designed and constructed by God. The homilist continues using this metaphor to refer to a permanent heavenly dwelling place with God in 11:10, 16; 12:22; and 13:14, a city to which the faithful, beginning with Abraham, aspire.

In the middle of Abraham's story of obedience, the homilist offers some words about what makes the story of Abraham and the others distinctive: they died before they received the promises, but they kept looking forward. They did not look back. They understood that their real home was elsewhere. They were mere *strangers and foreigners* (11:13) wherever they were living. This is a compelling message and could hint at the Hebrews' own situation. If we had any doubt about the focus of this long catalog of people of faith, the commentary in 11:13-16 clears it up: they are sojourners in this transitory world, looking forward to the heavenly city, which is their real home. The homilist interprets everything through this lens. The recounting of the Akedah (the binding, or sacrifice, of Isaac) underscores the difficulty of this way of life. The language of sacrifice—*Abraham, when put to the test, offered up Isaac* (11:17)—is the same language the homilist used in the earlier discussion about sacrifice.

The homilist uses the Greek word *parabolē* to describe the function of this story. It is a parable, a symbol or metaphor, for resurrection (11:19), one that Abraham understood from the outset. *He considered the fact that God is able even to raise someone from the dead* (11:19). In a way, Abraham's faith gave him the capacity to know the end of the story and enabled him to offer his son to God. The author presents us with an interesting twist. Would it really have been a sacrifice if Abraham had known that Isaac would be resurrected?

Abraham faced a difficult problem: despite God's promise of many descendants, his wife Sarah was past her childbearing years. Faith was required to overcome this major hurdle. But whose faith? Reading the NRSV makes us believe that it was Abraham's faith: *By faith he received power of procreation, even though he was too old—and Sarah herself was barren* (11:11). However, many of the earliest manuscripts of the Greek text have a reading that can be translated *By faith Sarah herself, though barren, received power to conceive, even when she was too old.* The manuscript evidence here is so diverse that the committee working on the critical edition of the Greek text could not be confident about which reading was original. They decided to mark the reading used in the NRSV as "doubtful." In other words, it remains unclear whether the text should read "and Sarah was

Hebrews 10:32–12:2   189

barren" or "by faith, Sarah herself, though barren, received power" (Metzger: 672–73).

Of the sixteen people mentioned by name in chapter 11, Sarah is one of the only two women named. Despite manuscript difficulties, the homilist must have recognized the faith required of a woman much older than fifty who takes on the responsibility of rearing a child!

Moses and the Israelites, 11:23-28. After a perfunctory nod to the other patriarchs, Isaac, Jacob, and Joseph, who all acted on faith in their respective situations, the author moves on to the story of Moses, which brings together several of the homilist's themes: living as a foreigner, faithful action as a result of seeing the invisible, perseverance, sacrifice. The homilist also recognizes that the faithful actions of one person often require the support of an entire network. In the case of Moses, it started with his mother, whose faithful actions not only shaped Moses' life but also saved it (11:23). Living as an enslaved woman in a foreign land, at the mercy of her captors, Moses' mother committed an act of civil disobedience, choosing life for her child at great peril to herself. Moses himself, adopted into a life of wealth and luxury, decided to identify not only as a foreigner, but also as an enslaved person, *choosing rather to share ill-treatment with the people of God than to enjoy the fleeting pleasures of sin* (11:25). As the homilist has been counseling the Hebrews to do, Moses *persevered* (11:27), having seen the invisible (perhaps through the burning bush?), a direct reference to the definition of faith laid out in 11:1. And Moses, along with Abraham and Abel, manifested his faith by making a sacrifice.

In verse 26 our author emphasizes the abuse shared by all who follow God. *He considered abuse suffered for the Christ to be greater wealth than the treasures of Egypt.* Moses is a precursor to Christ. The homilist is suggesting that Moses identified with Christ and his life of sacrifice, choosing the same reproach or abuse as Christ chose, instead of worldly pleasures. Moses anticipated Christ and therefore imitated him. In the same way, the Hebrews congregation should choose world-renouncing actions.

Our author is not alone in reading the Moses story as one about living life as an outsider. The homilist uses some traditions about Moses that the first-century author Philo also uses [*Philo, Neoplatonism, and Hebrews, p. 245*]. For Philo, who as a Jew experienced the same lack of hospitality in Alexandria, Egypt, this was a motivating factor in Moses' decision to leave his adoptive family and return to the Israelites. Philo spends considerable time commenting on how host

190   Hebrews 10:32–12:2

countries should treat their foreign guests, something that the Egyptians failed to do, choosing instead to enslave them (*On the Life of Moses* 1.33–36). Our homilist puts a slightly different twist on it: Egypt is a hotbed of sin, from which one should disassociate. Later in Hebrews, the homilist counsels the people to live as though they are strangers, *outside the camp* (13:11). For both Philo and our homilist, their own condition informs the meanings they place on Moses and his actions. How stories are told almost always reflects the contemporary conditions of the storytellers and historymakers.

Rahab and the Fugitives from Egypt, 11:29-31. Why would early Jesus followers adopt Rahab, a prostitute, as a pillar of faith? Not only is she mentioned by our homilist, but she is also listed in the Gospel of Matthew's genealogy of Jesus (1:5). James 2:25 also notes her "works of faith," despite her infelicities. She was an outsider, a Gentile, much as many in the early Jewish-Christian communities were. But she decided to accept and welcome those in need. What we know about Rahab comes from Joshua 2:1-21 and 6:15-25. She was a businesswoman whose activities included prostitution, innkeeping (Josephus, *Jewish Antiquities* 5.1.2; Targum Jonathan [Aramaic interpretation]), and working with flax. She relied on good relationships with her neighbors.

However, she also was willing to independently assess the situation with the Israelite spies and act on her own. She and her family were later saved during the destruction of Jericho. Our homilist says that she *received the spies in peace.* The homilist uses language that emphasizes hospitality. Welcoming strangers in a dangerous and risky situation takes faith and courage. Our homilist makes sure to highlight Rahab's actions as an example.

Judges, Kings, Prophets, and Martyrs, 11:32-38. Almost as if the homilist knew the congregation's stomachs would be starting to rumble as they worried about their Sabbath dinner, the preacher stops the analysis to take a different approach. He quickly names such men as Gideon and Barak, who exemplified faith through their deeds of conquering kingdoms and administrating justice. Ruth Hoppin (1997: 47) makes an interesting observation about these men: behind each is a powerful woman, without whom the deed of the man would not have been known *[Priscilla as Author, p. 245].* But the homilist leaves it to the congregation to fill in these details. After this quick list of named folks, the catalog becomes a list of deeds, ways in which faith became action. Here again the homilist assumes knowledge of the biblical stories, leaving it to the congregation to assign names to the deeds:

Deed	Unnamed reference
Shut the mouths of lions	Daniel (Dan 6:19-23)
Quenched raging fire	Three Jews (Dan 3)
Escaped the edge of the sword	Esther (Esther 4:11)
Won strength out of weakness, became mighty in war, put foreign armies to flight	Judith (Judith in the Apocrypha)
Women received their dead by resurrection	Widow of Zarephath (1 Kings 17:8-24) Shunammite woman (2 Kings 4:18-37)

The words "persecuted" and "tormented" in describing suffering may apply to the circumstances of the readers as well as the ancient heroes of faith. The writer comments that the world is not worthy of such persons. This affirmative language encourages the audience to stay the course. The faithful heroes wandered, perhaps as the homilist's people are doing now. The world is often not hospitable for those who live by faith.

They Wait for Us 11:39-40

The end of the catalog is just the beginning: the message to the hearers is that *something better* (11:40) now allows them to complete the story started by their ancestors. The final verses of chapter 11 echo the start of the section in 10:32-39, where the author reminds the Hebrews that they *possessed something better and more lasting* (10:34).

They have Jesus, their pioneer, who *perfected for all time those who are sanctified* (10:14) and is the *mediator of a better covenant, . . . enacted through better promises* (8:6). These Hebrews are central to God's plan. The implied relay-race metaphor suggests that it now is the audience's turn to take the baton and finish the race. The story is not over. The Hebrews are to see themselves in the long line of God's people. It now is their responsibility to finish the race.

Look to Jesus, Who Endured the Cross 12:1-2

Hebrews 12:1-2 moves us into the imagery of an athletic stadium. We can think about the excitement of a relay race and the ease (or difficulty!) with which the athletes pass the baton to each other. The heroes of faith from Israel's history have passed the baton to the Hebrews and have become the spectators of the games. They are the expectant *cloud of witnesses*, the spectators waiting and cheering as the Hebrews now have their turn at the race.

192   Hebrews 10:32–12:2

In Greek, one who gives "witness" is a *martys* (10:28; 12:1), and the testimony itself is *martyrion* (3:5), from which comes the English term *martyr*. A martyr is anyone who provides testimony, proof, or even approval of something. To be a martyr means that one has *witnessed* for one's faith. This is how the catalog starts: with God as a witness to Abel's faith. The homilist uses the verbal form of the word frequently at the beginning of chapter 11 (vv. 2, 4, 5, 39) to describe the approval the ancestors have received for their faith. Now the ancestors are the witnesses to the faith of the Hebrews themselves. These ancestors were only a lead-up to Jesus, the real pacesetter, the *pioneer and perfecter of our faith* (12:2). The word translated as *pioneer* (Gk. *archēgos*, as in 2:10), may also be translated "leader, founder, forerunner, or initiator." It is paired with *perfecter* (*teleiōtēs*), which can mean "finisher or completer." This pairing may suggest that our homilist intends the juxtaposition of beginner and ender in a manner comparable to "the Alpha and the Omega" of Revelation (1:8, e.g.). Jesus is both the beginning and the end of faith. His faithfulness now sets the standard for what faithfulness looks like.

Jesus endured *for the sake of [Gk. anti] the joy that was set before him* (12:2). The preposition *anti* can also be translated "instead of." However, most translators have preferred "for the sake of" in the context of the athletic metaphor, where endurance is the quality that leads to the goal and the reward. The reward in 12:2 is taking his seat at the right hand of the throne of God (Ps 110:1). Here we have the final use of this psalm, applied five times to Jesus in Hebrews (see also 1:3, 13; 8:1; 10:12). In three of these uses the phrase is associated with Jesus' priestly functions. As high priest, Jesus makes purification for sins (1:3), mediates a better covenant (8:1), and offers a once-for-all sacrifice for sins (10:12). In all these, Jesus is seated, already enthroned. This is the final reminder to the Hebrews that they, too, have access to that throne and to the presence of God. The challenge is set by the homilist: if Jesus *for the sake of the joy that was set before him endured the cross* (12:2), the Hebrews also should be able to set aside whatever burdens them to run the race with perseverance.

The chiastic structure of these two verses helps us focus on Jesus as pioneer:

A *Since we are surrounded by so great a cloud of witnesses* (12:1a),
  B *let us lay aside every weight and the sin that clings . . .* (12:1b)
    C *Let us run with perseverance the race that is set before us* (12:1c).

Hebrews 10:32–12:2 193

> D keeping our eyes on _Jesus, the pioneer and perfecter of faith_ (12:2a),
> D' _who for the sake of the joy that was set before him_ (12:2b)
> C' _endured the cross_ (12:2c),
> B' _disregarding its shame_ (12:2c),
> A' and is _seated_ at the right hand of the throne of God (12:2d).

We can read this "poem" two different ways. If we read it from top to bottom, we see that the Hebrews, aware of the cloud of witnesses around them (A), are called to set aside sin (B) and run with perseverance (C) by setting their eyes on Jesus (D), who serves as the example. He recognized the goal (D'), endured the cross (C') and the shame (B'), and came to sit at God's right hand (A').

We can also read the corresponding lettered lines together, connecting an action or characteristic that the Hebrews are called to do with a corresponding action or characteristic already done by Jesus:

- A and A' describe those who watch over the audience: the cloud of witnesses and Jesus, sitting at the right hand of God.

- B and B' emphasize the need to ignore the human elements of sin and shame that prevent action.

- C and C' demand the characteristics of perseverance and endurance required to run the race.

- D and D' name Jesus as the focus and pioneer.

What a brilliant finish to the race!

THE TEXT IN BIBLICAL CONTEXT

Exhortations throughout the Bible

The exhortations of Hebrews 10:19-31 follow other sections of exhortation interspersed throughout this message. Hebrews 2:1-4 is a warning to pay attention. Then 3:7-19 is a scriptural example of the perils of unfaithfulness. In 5:11–6:12, the audience is cautioned about the danger of falling away. Here in 12:1-2, the hearers are called to persevere. Then in 12:3-12 they are challenged to be courageous. In 12:14-29, they are warned of the dangers of rejecting God's grace. Finally, chapter 13 reminds them of ways they can manifest faithfulness in the practices of daily living and their community life.

Exhortation is central to most letters in the New Testament. We could think of the entire letter of 1 Corinthians as an exhortation to a "more excellent way" of love (1 Cor 12:31). Even after the difficult

194   Hebrews 10:32–12:2

discussion in the early chapters of Galatians regarding the law and faith, Paul closes with exhortations to "bear one another's burdens" (6:2) and "sow to the Spirit" (6:8).

Timothy is exhorted to "pursue righteousness, godliness, faith, love, endurance, gentleness" (1 Tim 6:11). The exiles of the dispersion are urged, "as aliens and exiles, . . . [to] conduct yourselves honorably" (1 Pet 2:11-12).

Summaries of Faithful People

Our homilist is not the first to produce a list of heroes. The catalog of faithful people in Hebrews does not exist in a vacuum. Hebrews is organized around the theme of faithful perseverance in the face of adversity. Our homilist uses the feats of heroes to tease out important aspects of faithfulness emphasized throughout the text: obedience, the ability to approach God, and offering sacrifice. As gathered, the cloud of witnesses recognizes the outsider status of many who have gone before: Abraham, Moses, Rahab, and those killed by the sword. They were *strangers and foreigners on the earth* (11:13) who looked toward *a better country* (11:16). Other catalogs or lists focus on other themes unique to their literary contexts. Throughout biblical and extrabiblical literature, the focus is repeatedly on the saving hand or grace of God.

Nehemiah 9:6-38

Upon returning to Jerusalem after the Babylonian exile, Nehemiah led the people in rebuilding the walls of the city. Afterward, they celebrated the Festival of Booths (Sukkot) by living in temporary shelters outside the city walls for a week (Neh 8:13-18). At the conclusion of the festival, the people of Israel gathered, confessed their sins, and heard the priest Ezra memorialize their national history through a prayer of confession. Ezra's prayer to God remembers the many ways that God rescued Abraham, the Israelites fleeing from Egypt, and Moses, even though the Israelites had "stiffened their necks" (Neh 9:16). Even so, God had mercy on them and kept the covenant that was established between God and the people of Israel. Ezra pleads for God's rescue in their current distress. In this passage, God is the actor, and the people of Israel are the recipients of both God's favor and displeasure.

Psalms 105-106

These companion psalms remember the many instances of God's faithfulness through "wonderful works" (105:2). Psalm 105 praises

Hebrews 10:32–12:2 195

God in recounting of the covenant with Abraham, Joseph's release from slavery and subsequent rule in Egypt, and Moses and Aaron's leadership as God delivered the Israelites from slavery in Egypt. Psalm 106 repeats some of the same events, but through the lens of confession for the unfaithfulness displayed in situations like the rebellion at the Red Sea (or Sea of Reeds; Exod 14:11-12), the Israelites worshiping a golden calf (Exod 32), and the worship of Baal (Num 25). The psalmist acknowledges God's great forgiveness, even though God was angered by their unfaithfulness. God showed the people of Israel mercy and compassion by remembering the covenant with Abraham.

Psalms 135–136

As with the previous psalms, these mention God's goodness at specific times in the history of the people of Israel, especially their captivity in Egypt and their struggle to claim the Promised Land. Psalm 135 closes with a call for the houses of Israel to "praise the LORD!" (135:19-21). Psalm 136 was probably designed to be sung in a liturgical setting. The text begins and ends with giving thanks to God, "for his steadfast love endures forever" (136:1, 26). It, too, recounts the great work God has done by bringing the people out of Egypt, defeating "great kings," and giving "their land as a heritage" (136:17, 21).

Ezekiel 20

This could be the antithesis of Hebrews 11 because it is a detailed account of the many times the nation of Israel rebelled against the Lord, refused to listen, and failed to forsake the idols of Egypt (20:8). In this passage, a group of elders come to consult with Ezekiel. What results is a revelation from God about Israel's rebellion against God during their time in the wilderness. The focus on the time in the wilderness is on target because this and other visions in Ezekiel 1–20 were likely received and delivered during the Babylonian exile, another time of metaphorical wandering in the wilderness. But God is great. Despite the wrath that God could wage against them, God always chooses a response of mercy and love. "You shall know that I am the LORD, when I deal with you for my name's sake, not according to your evil ways, or corrupt deeds" (20:44).

Sirach 44:1–49:16

Many of the same figures featured in Hebrews 11—Enoch, Abraham, Isaac, Moses, the judges—also appear in Sirach/Ecclesiasticus, an apocryphal book of wisdom. This catalog is more similar to Hebrews than some of those already mentioned that focus on God's greatness and faithfulness toward the people. The Sirach "encomium," or eulogy of praise, focuses on the piety and faith of each person and how that helped the people of Israel. Sirach also recognizes that "there is no memory" (44:9) of many others—those who were just as faithful as the persons mentioned in the encomium. Instead, they live on in the lives of their descendants (44:11-15).

Wisdom of Solomon 10:1-21

An interesting variation occurs in the Wisdom of Solomon as the deeds of seven righteous men are recounted (Adam, Abel, Noah, Abraham, Lot, Jacob, and Joseph), none of whom are mentioned by name. Wisdom herself is praised for recognizing those who were righteous who served "her" (10:9) and were "holy" people and "blameless" (10:15).

4 Maccabees

Most likely, the Maccabean martyrs are the subject of Hebrews 11:35: *Others were tortured, refusing to accept release, in order to obtain a better resurrection.* The story of these martyrs also appears in 2 Maccabees 6:18–7:42. It is retold in 4 Maccabees, an extended encomium for the martyrs, Eleazar, the seven brothers, and their mother. That eulogy is wrapped up in a treatise on the importance of reason over emotion. In 4 Maccabees, the martyrs primarily displayed the virtue of reason. The text was written for the anniversary of the deaths of the martyrs (or for a festival of dedication; cf. 1 Macc 4:52-59; John 10:22) and is a product of the fusion between Greek and Jewish ideas. The Maccabean martyrs are also the subject of the fourth song in the *Ausbund*, the sixteenth-century Anabaptist hymnal still used by the Amish today: "Eine lobwürdig wunderthätige Historie" (A praiseworthy miraculous history; on 2 Macc 7).

Jesus as Example

Hebrews focuses on Jesus the *forerunner*, on whom we are to focus as we run our race of faith (see esp. 6:20). The idea is repeated in 12:2 with the notion of *looking to Jesus*, a phrase not used elsewhere in the New Testament even though Jesus as example is an important theme throughout. In the Gospels, Jesus' call to the disciples is "Follow me." At the Last Supper, after washing the disciples' feet, Jesus tells them, "For I have set you an example, that you also should do as I have done to you" (John 13:15). Paul admonishes the Philippians, "Let this mind be in you that was in Christ Jesus" (Phil 2:5). First Peter 2:21 is perhaps the most familiar call to follow Jesus:

Hebrews 10:32–12:2

"Christ also suffered for you, leaving you an example, so that you should follow in his steps."

Other Biblical and Extrabiblical Connections

When we compare how different authors use the same sources, we can see each author's emphasis more clearly. A case in point is the use of Habakkuk 2:3-4 at the beginning of this section in Hebrews 10:37-38: *The one who is coming will come and will not delay; but my righteous one will live by faith. My soul takes no pleasure in anyone who shrinks back.* Hebrews emphasizes perseverance in faithfulness during a time of duress, making the paraphrase at 10:37-38 the perfect introduction to the catalog of faithful ancestors that follows. Paul has a different emphasis in using Habakkuk in Galatians 3:11 and Romans 1:17. Paul's concern is the contrast between (1) doing the works of the law as the basis for God's affirmation and (2) having faith in Jesus.

As a third example, a commentary on Habakkuk found at Qumran poses some similarities to Hebrews (Attridge: 303). The commentary prizes faithfulness, setting up a strong polemic between those who follow the Teacher of Righteousness (or Righteous Teacher, likely the founder of the Qumran community) and those who have turned to "the Liar" (possibly the non-Zadokite high priest in Jerusalem). The unfaithful have abandoned the Teacher, broken the "New Covenant," and profaned God's name. The faithful are those who "observe the Law in the House of Judah, whom God will deliver from the House of Judgment because of their suffering and because of their faith in the Teacher of Righteousness" (8.1–4; Vermès: 482). Faithfulness and loyalty to the covenant of the group and to the Teacher are themes that appear in both texts.

Another theme that Hebrews has in common with other early Jewish literature is the athletic metaphor. Eleazar is described as a "noble athlete" in 4 Maccabees 6:10. Later in the text, all the martyrs are described as having been participants in a divine contest (17:11). Philo also uses the metaphor of an athletic contest to consider which contests are worth fighting and which are not. For Philo, the only contest worth fighting is for the "acquisition of the divine, and Olympian, and genuine virtues" (*On Agriculture* 112, 119). Paul often uses the image of running or participating in an athletic contest. He frequently refers to the Christian life as a struggle (*agōn*) or race in which he and his readers are participating (1 Cor 9:24-27; Gal 2:2; 5:7; Phil 1:30; 2:16; 3:12-14; 2 Tim 4:7).

The final use of Psalm 110 in Hebrews (12:2) reminds us of its importance in New Testament literature. Although our author uses both 110:1 and 110:4 throughout the text, other New Testament authors exclusively use Psalm 110:1. The synoptic gospels (Matt 22:41-46//Mark 12:35-37//Luke 20:41-44) record a conversation between Jesus and the Pharisees in which Jesus quotes Psalm 110:1 to claim the superiority of the Messiah (himself) over David. When Jesus is before the high priest at his trial, he quotes the same verse in combination with Daniel 7:13-14. "From now on you will see the Son of Man seated at the right hand of Power and coming on the clouds of heaven" is a statement about where the Messiah (himself) will be "seated at the right hand of [God]" (Matt 26:64), at the "right hand of Power" (Mark 14:62), at the "right hand of the power of God" (Luke 22:69). In Acts 2:32-36, Peter quotes Psalm 110:1 and declares that David did not ascend to the heavens, but his son, the Messiah, did so. In summary, these and other New Testament texts use Psalm 110:1 as a prooftext for Jesus as the Messiah who reigns in heaven "at the right hand" of God (Hay: 45–46).

THE TEXT IN THE LIFE OF THE CHURCH

The Faith of Our Fathers and Mothers

Hebrews and earlier biblical examples inform us that people of faith have been creating "catalogs" of heroes for thousands of years. Another New Testament text, the Acts of the Apostles, catalogs early activities of the Jesus movement. Peter, Stephen, Paul, and Silas come alive and give us words and actions to live by. Later generations of Christians continued writing stories about faithful people, developing an entire genre of "apocryphal acts" and martyrdom accounts that recount the wonders and faithful actions of people such as Thecla, Andrew, Perpetua, Felicitas, Thomas, and John. When we are in doubt, we can pull the catalog off the shelf and remember (see collections edited by Elliott and Musurillo). It allows us to go forward with a renewed sense of self, both as an individual and as a group, giving us a clearer sense of a faithful response to a current situation.

Countries like the United States also valorize catalogs of heroes: for example, the Founding Fathers, most of whom were enslavers and signed the US Declaration of Independence (1776), which addressed only the independence of white men in the ruling class. The nation still struggles with honesty about the history of the enslavement of Africans and the genocide of Indigenous peoples, whose legacies include structural racism in education, healthcare, housing, and cultural institutions.

Some in the historic peace churches and others have recognized these national sins. Similarly, we may also have difficulties with the valorization of such biblical military heroes as Gideon, Barak, Samson, Jephthah, and David. According to Scripture (and the homilist of Hebrews), they were called by God to lead the Israelites in battles and faithfully followed that call. We may never be able to come to terms with how these figures used violence to carry out what they considered to be God's will. However, we recognize that developing a catalog of heroes, founders, and exemplary people is what helps to strengthen a group or nation.

Anabaptists have tried to resist these cruel features of the dominant narrative by developing alternatives. The Church of the Brethren is shaping identity by recalling the works of its forebears: John Klein (1797–1864), peacemaker during the Civil War, assassinated; Dan West (1894–1971), founder of Heifer International (1944); Anna Mow (1893–1985), missionary to India (1923–40), preacher, and author; and Ted Studebaker (1945–71), peace activist in Vietnam, executed.

Brethren composers have written songs about them. Authors have written children's books. Their names and faithful actions have been regularly invoked at annual conferences and other meetings. As a result, there is no doubt about what it means to be Brethren and how to participate in the *cloud of witnesses*.

Our earliest Anabaptist forebears remembered their faithful ones as well. In 1660, Thieleman J. van Braght published (in Dutch) a long compilation of confessions of faith and accounts of individual Anabaptist martyrs called *Martyrs Mirror*. Later editions/translations include dramatic etchings by Jan Luyken. In statements, prayers, and confessions from the martyrs, biblical (canonical and noncanonical) figures are cited as examples of faith. In a letter to "Beloved companions in the Lord," Michael Sattler (1490–1527), imprisoned in the Tower of Binsdorf (in Baden-Württemberg), urges the "brethren and sisters" to "hold fast" (like Heb 4:14; 10:23) to what he presents in his letter (Braght: 346–49).

Earlier martyrs were on the mind of Adrian Corneliss, a glassblower, as shown in a (1552) prayer preserved in the same collection. He asks God to guide his steps just as God guided the steps of Shadrach, Meshach, Abednego, Tobit, Sarah, Joseph, and Eleazar the Maccabean martyr. Echoing Hebrews, Corneliss states, "We now go with thee, without the camp, bearing thy reproach" (Braght: 453). Other entries contain testimony from the martyrs' trials, as for Weynken (daughter of Claes), a widow burned at the stake in The

Hague in 1527. At her trial, Weynken firmly voiced her Anabaptist beliefs despite threats and pleas from church officials and friends (350–351). Maeyken Wens had her tongue clamped so she could not testify as she was burned at the stake in 1573 (891–892). In all, over eight hundred martyrs are mentioned. After numerous translations and printings, the collection remains in print to this day.

Today, we have virtual catalogs such as blogs and websites. The Bearing Witness Stories Project (MartyrStories.org) is one such catalog. It contains dozens of stories, including that of Lois Mary Gunden Clemens (1915–2005), a French teacher from Goshen (Ind.) College who traveled to France during World War II and rescued Jewish children from the Nazis.

We should also remember the "others" of Hebrews—those unnamed people who *suffered mocking and flogging* (11:36). These are the ordinary folks whose faithful lives go unmentioned and unremembered: yet they formed the foundation for those who are remembered. These unsung and unknown heroes surround us just as much as those we can name.

These catalogs are meant to inspire, encourage, and yes, maybe just a little, shame us, when needed. When we get too comfortable, self-satisfied, or unsure about what being faithful is all about, we can read about Ted Studebaker and Lois Mary Gunden Clemens to remind us. Hebrews and the Bearing Witness project invite us to join in the communion of saints. The great cloud of witnesses and the assembly of the firstborn enrolled in heaven are inspiring metaphors for the faithful people of God who preceded us: we can learn and be motivated by the stories told about them to "go and do likewise" (Luke 10:37), to "run with perseverance" (Heb 12:1).

The faith of our forebears brings focus to the "communion of saints" (the holy ones) as a symbolic assertion of the continuity of the fellowship of believers beyond geographical boundaries, beyond time, beyond the grave, and beyond confessional differences. All persons touched by God, all who have suffered unjustly, and all who have dedicated their lives to making the world a better place are our companions on the journey. They are a source of strength, inspiration, and support. We are not alone (cf. E. Johnson: 7–9).

Part 5

A Call to Service

Hebrews 12:3–13:19

OVERVIEW

Lentils were ubiquitous in the ancient world. Esau, Jacob's brother, would have been able to find a meal of them almost anytime he was hungry. Roman soldiers ate them regularly; Egyptians loved them. In other words, they were a dietary staple. Today, many people enjoy their nutty flavor and nutritional benefits for a low cost. That is why, probably for both the ancient and modern audiences, selling a bowl of lentils for a birthright seems unimaginable. But that is what Esau did: for a quick fix, he sold his birthright for lentil stew. His lack of discipline and his inability to endure even the small trial of a missed meal should be a cautionary tale to the Hebrews. Will the Hebrews be like Esau and the wandering Israelites, or will they belong to the *kingdom that cannot be shaken* (12:28)? This is the central question of the closing section.

The Hebrews are now enveloped in the cloud of witnesses: Enoch, Abraham, Rahab, and those they might have known earlier in their life who have gone before. They have been reminded that they are part of something bigger and better. Now, as the homilist draws the sermon to a close, they are exhorted to live a faithful life as sojourners like Abraham. Whether they are refugees living away from their native lands or living as though foreigners in the land of their birth, they are reminded that their real home is with Christ and the cloud of witnesses. They live in the context of a new covenant that includes Jesus as the once-for-all sacrifice. But with great gifts come responsibility and a need for gratitude. Living on or outside the margins—as the pastor says, *outside the camp* (13:11, 13)—is a permanent condition of faithful living. Will they fail to endure, like Esau, or will they rise to the challenge, like the cloud of witnesses? The homilist leaves them with blessings, trusting that they will do the will of Jesus Christ.

Hebrews 12:3–13:19

OUTLINE

Recapitulation of Argument, 12:3-29
Exhortation for Service Pleasing to God, 13:1-19

Hebrews 12:3-29

Recapitulation of Argument

PREVIEW

Having just heard the amazing acts of faithfulness done by the cloud of witnesses, the congregation may be asking, What can we do? We are no Abraham, Moses, or Rahab!

What can our small congregation do? We are not the Israelites passing through the Red Sea or present while God brings down the walls of Jericho! But with one word, *consider* (12:3), the homilist refocuses the Hebrews' attention on their own activities. The congregation needs to consider the following:

- how Jesus, the pioneer, endured hostility (12:3)
- the merits of discipline itself and the consequences of an undisciplined life (12:7)
- how to pursue peace with everyone (12:14)
- how not to refuse the one speaking (12:25)
- how to give thanks, which is acceptable worship (12:28)

In Hebrews, living a faithful life is simple yet also multilayered and complex. It is ironic: the long conclusion starts with a one-word rhetorical device that refocuses the audience's attention. Familiar rhetorical devices also return. Instead of athletics, the homilist now uses parenting as a metaphor. One last use of *synkrisis*, or comparison, reminds the Hebrews about the benefits they enjoy in their spiritual journey that previous generations did not have. We also observe an *inclusio* beginning at 12:18 with the words *a blazing fire* and ending at 12:29 with *God is a consuming fire*, a final reminder that the kingdom is attainable only through sacrifice.

OUTLINE
Exhortation: Endure Discipline, 12:3-13
Warning: Do Not Be like Esau, 12:14-17
Synkrisis: You Have Come to the Heavenly Jerusalem, 12:18-24
Shaken, Not Stirred, 12:25-29

EXPLANATORY NOTES

Exhortation: Endure Discipline 12:3-13

In closing, the homilist provides some strategies for how the Hebrews can grow in maturity and wisdom. As so often happens in this text, our homilist begins a new section by quoting Scripture. Proverbs 3:11-12 (LXX) supplies our homilist with the imperative to *endure . . . discipline* (Heb 12:7a): *My child, do not regard lightly the discipline of the Lord, or lose heart when you are punished by him; for the Lord disciplines those whom he loves* (12:5b-6a). Enduring discipline, then, is a command to experience love.

The NRSV's *Endure trials for the sake of discipline* (12:7a) is more interpretation than translation. The Greek says only *endure discipline*. The Greek word for discipline, *paideia*, means not only discipline but also comprehensive instruction in what is needed to become a responsible adult. In a sense, the Hebrews should consider themselves to be children receiving discipline and instruction from a parent. Our homilist says as much: *We had human parents to discipline us, and we respected them. Should we not be even more willing to be subject to the Father of spirits and live?* (12:9).

Comprehensive discipline or instruction requires training. At the end of the paragraph, in verse 11, our homilist acknowledges this and impresses on the Hebrews the importance of training and education in their growth toward spiritual maturity. For those who have been trained, discipline *yields the peaceful fruit of righteousness* (12:11). By combining the imagery of athletics and parenting, the homilist hammers home the importance of endurance and discipline.

The quotation from Proverbs also includes the concept of punishment: *Do not . . . lose heart when you are punished by him* (12:5). The

206　　　　　　　　　　　　　　　　　　　　　　　　Hebrews 12:3-29

homilist has warned the Hebrews about the consequences of unfaithfulness earlier in the sermon (3:16-19; 6:4-8; 10:38-39). At this point, the homilist focuses on discipline and the acceptance of that discipline by the congregation. A disciple is a person who learns. Therefore, the Hebrews should consider whatever they are experiencing as instruction and not confuse it with punishment from God. This is a learning opportunity and a sign that they are loved. Through this, they will produce *righteousness* (12:11). This is not a new idea: the homilist states that God has made Jesus, *the pioneer of their salvation[,] perfect through sufferings* (2:10); and observes that the *Son . . . learned obedience through what he suffered* (5:8). Since suffering was part of the process that made Jesus perfect, complete, or mature, so should it be for the Hebrews.

According to form, the homilist wraps up this section the same way it started—with an allusion to a biblical passage wrapped in an exhortation: *Therefore lift your drooping hands and strengthen your weak knees* (12:12; cf. Isa 35:3: "Strengthen the weak hands, and make firm the feeble knees"). The context of this passage in Isaiah is the hopeful return to the Jerusalem area after exile. It is not surprising that our homilist uses it here: just as the Israelites needed fortitude and discipline to finish so they could find themselves back in their homeland, so the Hebrews should do the same so they can find themselves in the presence of God.

Warning: Do Not Be like Esau 12:14-17

The Hebrews have just heard about many examples of faithful living to inspire them when the going gets rough. They have also heard that discipline produces the *peaceful fruit of righteousness* (12:11). In verse 14 is another exhortation to pursue peace and holiness. Now, using the example of Esau and the wilderness generation, the homilist warns the audience that those who fail to obtain the grace of God *become defiled* (12:15). This is reminiscent of the warning issued in 4:1, where the author urges the congregation not to fail in *entering [the] rest* that is open to them. Unlike the wilderness generation who did fail, the congregation—if united by faith—can obtain that promise. Allowing a *root of bitterness* to spring up *causes trouble* (12:15). Esau is the example.

The grace that had been provided for Esau as a birthright was lost because he did not value it, leading our homilist to describe Esau as *immoral* (Gk. *pornos*, which generally means *sexually* immoral) and godless (Gk. *bebēlos*, profane or unholy). Neither the Genesis story itself nor other ancient commentators include this

Hebrews 12:3-29

description. Genesis says that he "despised his birthright" (25:34) and married two Hittite women (26:34-35), despite his parents' disapproval. In both respects Esau rejected the covenant expectations.

Once Esau sold his birthright, he was unable to get it back. What is sold is sold. Genesis says that Esau "cried out with an exceedingly great and bitter cry" (27:34) when he learned this news. Bitterness is the fruit of both his faithlessness and his loss. The writer of Hebrews reminds the audience of this fact in 12:17. Esau could find no opportunity to repent, a reaffirmation of the writer's previous assertions about the impossibility of repentance for those who despise and reject God's blessing and grace (2:3; 4:1; 6:4-6; 10:26-31).

This negative example (after so many positive examples in ch. 11) reminds the Hebrews of some important themes. The Hebrews are tempted to turn away from their faith for immediate relief from situations facing them. It is easier to neglect, turn away, and reject their experiences of signs and wonders and blessings (2:4) than it is to face additional difficulties. This reminder to keep their eyes on God and Christ and not turn away is a theme throughout the text. In chapters 3-4, we saw the negative example of the wilderness generation rebelling in the wilderness, resulting in their inability to enter "rest," the Promised Land. In chapter 6, we find another reminder of the difficulties of coming back to repentance after falling away. Finally, here is Esau, who rejected God's grace in the form of his birthright in exchange for satisfying a fleeting appetite. The surrender of his birthright for a pot of lentil stew displays a lack of discipline: the homilist warns of dangers in what seems like the easy way out. Living in a foreign land as people of God can be beguiling: they may be tempted to sell their birthright, their identification within the people of God, for easier living.

Synkrisis: You Have Come to the Heavenly Jerusalem 12:18-24

We now come to another moment in the text when the homilist uses *synkrisis* (comparison) to help the Hebrews remember what they are working for: access to God's throne. The comparison is between the earthly Mount Sinai and the heavenly Mount Zion (the heavenly Jerusalem). This comparison sums up all that the homilist has been trying to say about the nature of the new covenant: not the "sketch and shadow" version of Mount Sinai (8:5; 10:1), but the true covenant that the earthly version is based on, Mount Zion (paraphrased text in the chart).

Mount Sinai	Mount Zion (heavenly Jerusalem)
12:18: You have not come to something (the heavenly Sinai) that can be touched (so despite the warning in Deuteronomy not to touch Mount Sinai, the earthly mountain *can* be touched),	12:22: You have come to Mount Zion, the city where the living God resides, the invisible Jerusalem,
12:19: in order to hear God speak words that the hearers begged not to hear.	12:23: where there are a myriad of angels and the assembly (*ekklēsia*) of the firstborn.
12:20-21: When they heard the words "If an animal touches the mountain, it is as good as dead," they were afraid to move. Even Moses was afraid.	12:24: You have come to Jesus, who presents us with a new covenant, a fresh charter from God. He is the mediator of this covenant. The murder of Jesus, unlike Abel's—a homicide that cried out for vengeance—has become a proclamation of grace.

The way the comparison is constructed is interesting. The homilist is working from Exodus 19, where Moses and the Israelites encounter God at Mount Sinai. The mountain exudes fire, smoke, thunder, and lightning. There are loud trumpet blasts. The people of Israel must have been awestruck. God instructs Moses to prepare the Israelites to see God with instructions to wash themselves and "be careful not to go up the mountain or to touch the edge of it" (19:12). If they do touch it, "they shall be stoned or shot with arrows" (19:12-13). Our Hebrews homilist, however, ironically says that Mount Sinai, in all its awesome splendor, *can* be touched. In other words, it is still the "sketch and shadow" version. So, as awesome as the Mount Sinai experience was for Moses and the Israelites, who trembled (Heb 12:21; Exod 19:16; cf. Deut 9:19), it is nothing like the experience the Hebrews will have in the heavenly Jerusalem. There, the people will be drawn together with the *angels* (perhaps referring to the *cloud of witnesses* from Heb 12:1), *the assembly of the firstborn, . . . God, and Jesus* (12:22-23). In this mountain, they are surrounded by those awaiting them.

Shaken, Not Stirred 12:25-29

The Hebrews and other Jews in the first century CE had plenty of experience living in difficult circumstances. This passage may serve not only as a warning to the Hebrews but also as a reminder that the difficulties they are experiencing (possible exile, isolation, living as a minority group in a foreign land) will pass. They—*that is, created things* (12:27)—will be *shaken* and removed, and only the true, lasting *kingdom* will *remain.*

The homilist returns to the example of the wilderness generation with a warning similar to the one used in 3:12 (*Take care that none of you . . . turns away from the living God*): *See that you do not refuse the one who is speaking; for if they did not escape when they refused the one who warned them on earth, how much less will we escape if we reject the one who warns from heaven!* (12:25). Here the readers are invited to see themselves in the light of that same generation, who, because of fear, did not want to hear the commands of God from the mountain. God's voice thundered, the lightning flashed, the mountain smoked (Exod 20:18-21). The same question posed in Hebrews 2:3 is repeated: *How can we escape?* The implied answer is clear: they cannot (12:25).

Exodus 19:18 reports that "the whole mountain shook violently" in an earthquake; in Hebrews 12:26-27 the homilist smoothly combines the natural wonders of the blazing fire, darkness, gloom, and shaking mountain of the Sinai experience with an allusion to the prophecy of Haggai 2:6, 21, in which the kingdoms on earth are shaken. We can imagine God's voice being so thunderous that it shakes the earth, so it is not difficult to imagine how the two images are associated. In Haggai, the prophet is encouraging the returning exiles to finish rebuilding the temple. He reminds them of the promise that God's presence will be with them to provide the resources they need. God "will shake the heavens and the earth" (2:6) and overthrow the kingdoms of the nations. Hebrews uses Haggai to speak about what God will do in the future: God *will shake not only the earth but also the heaven* (12:26).

Only created things will be removed. The contrast here is not the Platonic dichotomy between the material and the spiritual, but rather between what cannot be shaken and what can be. A similar contrast is made in 12:10 between discipline that endures *for a short time* and participating in God's *holiness,* which is to become a permanent state of living with God. The Hebrews *are receiving* an unshakable *kingdom* (12:28), the kingdom of God, into which Jesus invites his followers to enter.

The final phrase, *for indeed our God is a consuming fire* (12:29), is an adaptation of Deuteronomy 4:24, "Your God is a devouring fire, a jealous God," where Moses speaks of God's anger toward him (4:21) and exhorts the Israelites to remember their covenant with God (4:23). Fire is a symbol of judgment that the homilist has used previously (Heb 6:8). Some commentators see this as a final judgment at the end of time (Cockerill: 664–72). Others see it as a refining or

210   Hebrews 12:3-29

transforming process in the life of the faithful (Attridge: 379–83; DeSilva: 477; Thompson 2008: 268–70; L. Johnson: 334–38). If we read it in the context of the preceding clauses, *Let us give thanks, by which we offer to God an acceptable worship with reverence and awe* (12:28), we remember the emphasis on sacrifice, discipline, and faithfulness that the pastor has been making throughout the sermon. This statement conjures images of sacrificial fires that the hearers would see throughout the Greco-Roman world. Fire is both judgment and refinement or cleansing: judgment of the hostile earthly kingdom and refinement of the people of God.

THE TEXT IN BIBLICAL CONTEXT

Esau, the Notorious Bad Boy

In the Genesis story, Esau and Jacob eventually come to an uneasy truce. Esau and his clan live on Mount Seir, a region south of the Dead Sea; Jacob and his family live in Canaan. Esau had plenty of possessions and did not seem to suffer much from relinquishing his birthright. However, later biblical texts cast the Edomites, Esau and his descendants, as enemies that deserve destruction, most likely because they helped sack Jerusalem and handed Jewish captives over to the Babylonians (Obad 10-14).

Our homilist is calling on this understanding of Esau as Edom with the comment about Esau as *an immoral and godless person* (12:16). For example, Psalm 137 is a lament about the Babylonian exile in the history of Israel: "By the rivers of Babylon—there we sat down, and there we wept when we remembered Zion. . . . Remember, O LORD, against the Edomites the day of Jerusalem's fall, how they said, 'Tear it down! Tear it down!'" (137:1, 7). An example of prophetic vindictiveness against Esau, or Edom, appears in Obadiah, a short prophetic text that rails against the Edomites "for the slaughter and violence done to your brother Jacob" (Obad 10), again referring to the Babylonian conquest. For this, the Edomites will be justly rewarded on "the day of the LORD. . . . As you have done, it shall be done to you" (Obad 15). Israel, the righteous people, will eventually triumph. In a related passage, the prophet Jeremiah cries out: "[Edom] shall become an object of horror" (Jer 49:7-14). However, even though God has "stripped Esau bare" (49:10), the care for widows and orphans remains, even among the Edomites. Through the prophet, God says, "Leave your orphans; I will keep them alive, and let your widows trust in me" (49:11). The concern for "the least of these" overrides the ills of a nation (Matt 25:40).

Earthquakes in Biblical Literature

Biblical literature often signals the presence of God through nature. The story of the exodus is a primary example. Occurrences in the natural world warn Pharoah to release the Israelites from slavery. Earthquakes feature in three psalms as they comment on the experience. In Psalm 77:18, the redemption experienced by enslaved Israelites was accompanied by thunder, lightning, and the trembling of the earth. Exodus mentions an earthquake at Mount Sinai (19:18). Psalm 68:8 says that when God led the people through the wilderness, "the earth quaked, the heavens poured down rain."

Last, in response to freedom from enslavement, various natural occurrences signal God's presence. The psalmist says, "The mountains skipped like rams," and tells the earth, "Tremble . . . at the presence of the LORD, . . . the God of Jacob," who turns "the rock into . . . water" (Ps 114:4, 7-8). These psalms confirm the deep and powerful experience of the exodus; by including earthquakes, the poets of the psalms are identifying an experience that has left nations shaken.

Other passages use earthquakes to signal God's judgment. The Psalms use earthquakes to show God's displeasure toward those who unjustly treat individuals (18:7) and groups, such as the widowed and orphaned (82:3-5). Job claims that no one can be just before God, who "removes mountains, . . . shakes the earth out of its place, and its pillars tremble" (9:5-6). The prophet Amos uses the imagery of the earth rising and sinking like the Nile to describe the destructive power of the presence of God for those who are complacent (Amos 9:5-6). Sirach exclaims that when God judges the people of the earth, the "heaven, and the highest heaven, the abyss and the earth, tremble at his visitation!" (16:18). Isaiah's calling consists of a vision of the Lord "sitting on a throne," accompanied by seraphs calling to each other "Holy, holy, holy" so loudly that "the pivots on the thresholds shook at the voices." When God called, "Whom shall I send?" Isaiah responded, "Here am I; send me!" (6:1-8).

Earthquakes also announce the eschatological coming of the Lord. Haggai is only one example (2:21). The "little apocalypse" in the Gospel of Matthew makes vivid use of such dramatic scenes: the Son of Man will appear after "the stars fall from heaven, and the powers of heaven will be shaken" (24:29). The gospel writer calls on a vast store of images from the Prophets (such as Isa 13:10, 13; 34:4; Ezek 32:7-8; Joel 2:10). Finally, when the Lamb opens the sixth seal in Revelation 6, John witnesses, among other natural catastrophes, "a great earthquake" so terrible that everyone begs the mountains to

212   Hebrews 12:3-29

"fall on us and hide us from the face of the one seated on the throne and from the wrath of the Lamb" (6:12, 16).

Feeling the earth shake beneath our feet is a powerful reminder that God's presence is awesome.

God as Fire

A lot lies behind the final statement of Hebrews 12: *God is a consuming fire*. Without fire, life would be difficult. The control of fire for warmth and well-being has advanced human civilization. Humans have figured out how to use heat to cook, change the form of metals, and many other things. Its power is awesome (such as in wildfires made worse by the warming climate); many people fear the flames as they gaze or flee. Biblical writers have used humans' relationship with fire as a compelling narrative tool. In the exodus story, fire represents God.

God appears to Moses in the burning bush (Exod 3). Later, God returns as fire when the Israelites are escaping from enslavement in Egypt (13:21). The fleeing Israelites are reassured of God's presence with them on their dangerous journey by the appearance of a cloud by day and a pillar of fire at night. Elijah prays for fire from heaven to prove God's power during the reign of King Ahab (1 Kings 18:36-38). This prophet of the Lord orchestrates a contest with the prophets of Baal: the god who sends fire from heaven to consume the sacrifice is the true god, "the LORD."

Fire also represents the passionate spirit of God. Jeremiah experiences God's message as fire in his bones (Jer 20:9). The passion to preach God's message consumes his will and his energy. In the New Testament, the Holy Spirit is identified with fire in Luke 3:16, at Jesus' baptism; and in Acts 2:3, on the day of Pentecost. The believers gathered at Pentecost proclaim God's salvation in language understood by people from many nations: these speakers are filled with the presence of God in their midst, shown by tongues "as of fire" over their heads (2:6).

Fire is also a source of refinement, representing God's effort to make the people pure. In Malachi, the "sons of Levi" need to be purified to make an offering in righteousness. Fire offers a refinement that purifies them and purges them as gold and silver (3:3). G. F. Handel used this to great effect in the alto aria "But Who May Abide the Day of His Coming" in his *Messiah* oratorio. Isaiah is cleansed by a live coal so that he can speak for God as a prophet (Isa 6). Refinement by fire is also associated with testing. Paul says his mission and that of other leaders will be tested by fire (1 Cor 3:11-15).

Perhaps working from Malachi, Paul says that what is of value will remain like gold or silver. That which is not pure and true and good will pass away like straw that is tossed into the fire. First Peter 1:7 continues this theme. Things perishable are tested by fire. Genuine faith and faithfulness will survive and bring honor to God.

Finally, fire represents eschatological judgment. In Luke 12:49, Jesus proclaims that he came to bring "fire upon the earth." This fire refines the earth for the new age that God will usher in. Matthew 5:22 speaks of a "hell of fire" as punishment, and Revelation 20:14 names a "lake of fire" as the destination of Satan, Hades, and all whose names are not written in the book of life. In these passages, fire is full of dread and death.

However, Hebrews is probably not talking about a final eschatological judgment when the homilist declares that *God is a consuming fire*, although we cannot rule out whether the congregation made such an association. Based on the context of the statement, God's consuming fire does test and refine. What is good and faithful will remain and be purified. The rest will be burned away.

THE TEXT IN THE LIFE OF THE CHURCH

Trials as Divine Discipline?

Hebrews calls us to regard the trials and difficulties from living as faithful people of God as learning experiences provided by God for our good, a sign of God's love. The implication of this passage is that we are to think of the hardships faced by stepping out on behalf of the widow, homeless, migrant, immigrant, and the wrongly jailed as provided by God for our growth and benefit. A similar perspective is found in James 1:2-4: "Whenever you face trials of any kind, consider it nothing but joy, because you know that the testing of your faith produces endurance." Facing trials that we as individuals or as groups of individuals voluntarily choose on account of our faith should be considered a joy because such testing leads to maturity and perfection. We can always learn something from challenging experiences. Our faith can grow. However, passages like this should never be used to suggest that racist, misogynist, or other types of oppression are trials designed as "opportunities for learning" and spiritual growth for those experiencing the oppression.

A Willingness to Come with Reverence and Awe

This passage challenges our Protestant notions of worship as a quiet, ordered, one-hour event on Sunday mornings. Instead, it asks us to note the awesomeness of God and to respect that. The descriptions of the mountains Sinai and Zion show that we should worship God with a state of humility, willing to be awed by God's glory. Throughout the text, the homilist has urged the community to be faithful, to follow the example of Jesus, and to remember the cloud of witnesses and be inspired by them. Worship of God through liturgy, an act of justice, or a kindness done is not a form of entertainment to please ourselves, but an act of faithfulness toward God—an act that has its own power to awe and inspire. In a world built around consumerism, our relationship with God and with others must resist the commodification of worship as entertainment. Hebrews 12:28 confirms the awesomeness in true worship: *Since we are receiving a kingdom that cannot be shaken, let us give thanks [and] . . . offer to God an acceptable worship with reverence and awe.* Deep gratitude, filled with reverence and awe, is acceptable worship.

And that is enough.

Hebrews 13:1-19

Exhortation for Service Pleasing to God

PREVIEW

Philadelphia: "brotherly love." Thus begins the conclusion of Hebrews. The NRSV translates this as *Let mutual love continue*. Here we find the culmination of the homilist's argument and a final call to serve God, doing good and offering *sacrifices . . . pleasing to God* (13:16). The homilist makes a final push to encourage the group to "exist as a collectivity rather than a scattering of individuals" (Tölölyan: 29) *[Diaspora, p. 237]*. The author asks the Hebrews to take a place *outside the camp* (13:13)—a place set apart, based on these practices of faithfulness, the totality of which create social and political identity; this is a social identity created out of practices that have *philadelphia*, mutual (sibling) love, at the center. This metaphorical meeting with Jesus, where he suffered outside the camp, makes them outsiders, too. But this meeting place is where connection with Jesus as high priest, as the altar, and as the sacrifice also creates a strong identity between one another and marginalized people: mutual love.

The writing concludes with requesting prayer for the author.

OUTLINE

Exhortations, 13:1-9
Excursus on Jesus' Sacrifice, 13:10-15
Resumption of Exhortations, 13:16-19

215

216   Hebrews 13:1-19

EXPLANATORY NOTES

Exhortations 13:1-9

The *acceptable worship* of God (12:28) finds expression in how the Hebrews live their lives in community. The moral exhortations here come in four pairs and consist of general maxims that can be applied to appropriate ethical living across religious affiliations. In this set of recommendations, the homilist is not telling the Hebrews to do anything outlandish or radical. All these could be found as core values in the wider Greco-Roman world (Dunning: 60–61).

For example, the first set concerns the love that individuals should show those around them. Love of one's friends and family was a basic virtue expounded all over the Mediterranean world. The use of the Greek word *philadelphia* (sibling love), however, was not common. Paul has adopted this term, and other letter writers use it as well. In exhortations it expresses mutual love for one another in several letters (Rom 12:10; 1 Thess 4:9; 1 Pet 1:22; 2 Pet 1:7). The Hebrews homilist urges the congregation to continue their mutual love for one another (*philadelphia*), but also not to neglect hospitality to strangers (*philoxenia*; lit. *love for strangers*). Both words imply action, not merely emotion—action expressed in sharing possessions and activities. What for Paul was somewhat of a novelty, using *philadelphia* to speak of mutual love between believers not biologically related to each other, has by the writing of Hebrews become a standard term for the early followers of Jesus.

Hospitality was another basic virtue in ancient Mediterranean cultures. It extends the same concerns of mutual love to outsiders. In the itinerant culture of the early church, it was especially important to welcome unknown persons from other communities (Rom 12:13; 1 Tim 3:2; Titus 1:8; 1 Pet 4:9). The homilist supports the admonition for hospitality with the observation that some have *entertained angels* unknowingly (13:2). Several biblical stories describe such an experience. Abraham and Sarah show generous hospitality to three men, later understood to be angels (Gen 18), who announce the birth of Isaac. Lot shows hospitality to the angels who visit Sodom when the other men of the city want to refuse them hospitality (19:1-14). A visit from an angel commissions Gideon, and an angel announces the birth of Samson (Judg 6:11-14; 13:2-25).

The instruction to welcome strangers may have been threatening to a community whose very existence might have been in doubt. The natural inclination might have been to close their doors to persons they were not positive they could trust. The homilist encourages them to risk being friendly.

The second pair of exhortations is to remember those who are in prison and those who are being tortured. This admonition recalls their previous experience of befriending those who suffer abuse and persecution and those who are in prison (10:32-34). Prison is a common experience for those who preach the gospel (Acts 5:18-22; 8:3; 12:4-7; 16:24-27; 28:16-17). The readers are called to empathize as if they themselves are experiencing imprisonment, as if *their* bodies are being tortured. This recalls Paul's discussion of the body of Christ (1 Cor 12:14-26). Although the concept may not be identical, the final verse—"If one member suffers, all suffer together with it; if one member is honored, all rejoice together with it"—appeals for the same kind of empathy and group solidarity. When any part of the body is in pain, the whole body suffers.

The homilist exhorts the Hebrews to beware of sexual misconduct and greed (Heb 13:4-5). This is common in ancient moral codes. Such Greco-Roman authors as Cicero, Epictetus, and Philo issue similar warnings (Attridge: 387nn45-46). The Holiness Code of Leviticus (chs. 17–26) places concerns for economic and sexual misconduct side by side (chs. 18–19). Both greed and adultery manifest excessive or disordered lust. The homilist has already identified Esau's gluttony as fornication and idolatry (Heb 12:16). In books of the Prophets and Psalms, marriage is a symbol of fidelity to Israel's covenant with God. Adultery is therefore a metaphor of idolatry and disloyalty (Isa 5:1, 4-8; 57:3; Jer 3:6-10; 13:27; Hos 3:1; 9:1; Ezek 16:38; 23:45; Ps 72:27). Paul makes the same connection between sexual immorality and idolatry: he asks the Corinthians not to associate with those among them who are "sexually immoral or greedy or an idolater, reviler, drunkard, or robber" (1 Cor 5:11). In Ephesians we read that "fornication and impurity of any kind, or greed, must not even be mentioned among you" (5:3-5). In both these passages, sexual immorality is associated with greed and idolatry. Hebrews displays the same association in the statement *for God will judge fornicators and adulterers* (13:4).

The love of money (*philargyria*) was a classic vice in Greco-Roman society (Attridge: 388nn62-63). The readers of Hebrews have had their possessions taken away by force (10:34). That experience may have inclined them to be anxious about the potential repetition of such loss. They are counseled to be content with what they have and to rest in the confidence that God will provide. In 13:5, our pastor quotes God as saying *I will never leave you or forsake you*. Although this assurance resembles several passages of Scripture, it is not identical

218 Hebrews 13:1-19

with any of them. In Jacob's dream at Bethel, God tells him, "I will not leave you until I have done what I have promised you" (Gen 28:15). When Joshua becomes Moses' successor, Moses tells Joshua, with all Israel present, "The LORD . . . will be with you; he will not fail you or forsake you" (Deut 31:7-8; cf. Josh 1:5). The Hebrews may be mindful of these divine assurances as the pastor issues this statement of comfort and assurance regarding their (lack of) worldly possessions.

The pastor follows by quoting Psalm 118:6: *The Lord is my helper; I will not be afraid. What can anyone do to me?* (Heb 13:6). This affirmation of God's faithfulness reiterates important earlier themes in the text. The recipients are reassured that they can draw near to God with boldness (3:6; 4:16; 10:19, 35). Fear of God and trust in the power of God overcomes fear of anything that humans can do. This was true for both Moses (11:27) and his parents (11:23). The readers are reminded that help comes from God. Help is to be found at *the throne of grace* (4:16). Jesus was tested in every way that other humans are so that he can help humanity (2:18). The Hebrews' trust in God enables them to be faithful and generous in their community life.

The final pair of exhortations calls the readers to remember or pay attention to their leaders and to imitate their faithful way of life. Leaders are mentioned three times in this final chapter (13:7, 17, 24). They are the ones *who spoke the word of God to you*; their *way of life* and *faith* should be considered and imitated (13:7). Just as the readers are to run the race *looking to Jesus* (12:1-2), so now they are asked to remember those who preached the gospel to them and set an example for them by their faithful way of life.

Excursus on Jesus' Sacrifice 13:10-15

For the last time, the homilist returns to the theme of sacrifice, placing it squarely in the context of the ethical call just issued and, even more important, linked with the call to follow Jesus. The focus of the argument is verse 13, *Let us then go to him outside the camp and bear the abuse he endured.* The Hebrews who have experienced and continue to experience rejection and abuse are reminded that Jesus chose to go to God *outside the camp*, where he was crucified, just as the sacrifice on Yom Kippur (the Day of Atonement) was burned outside the camp (see Lev 16:27; Num 19:2-3). The Hebrews are called to become or remain outsiders, bearing abuse as Jesus did.

Understanding that their life is on the margins brings the rest of this short passage into sharper focus. The homilist states, *We have an altar from which those who officiate in the tent have no right to eat* (13:10). Normally, priests who performed in the temple sacrifices shared in

Hebrews 13:1-19 219

eating the sacrificial offerings from the altar (1 Cor 9:13). For our homilist, remaining *in the tent* (i.e., inside the camp) does not allow the followers of Jesus to experience the full meaning of Jesus' sacrifice. The allusion to Golgotha (where *Jesus also suffered outside the city gate in order to sanctify the people by his own blood*, 13:12), "near the city" (John 19:17, 20), is tied to the Scripture concerning the Day of Atonement. Jesus' rejection and death outside the gate are an "entering into the heavenly sanctuary . . . and an eternal offering for the sanctification of the people" (L. Johnson: 349).

Many commentators understand *altar* in verse 10 to be a metaphor for something. Some propose the communion table, some the cross. Others find more meaning in the altar as a heavenly or spiritual reality (Attridge: 396). L. Johnson (348) proposes that the altar represents the "heart" that is to be renewed under the new covenant (8:10), on which God will inscribe the laws (8:10; 10:16). Such a heart is cleansed so people can approach God and worship God in praise and thanksgiving (12:28). Thompson suggests that the altar is a metaphor for the alternate reality of heaven (2008: 274–75). Or perhaps Jesus is the altar, as the pioneer and the Savior. He has offered himself in the presence of God (the heavenly sanctuary), dispensed God's grace (in contrast to food), which those who rejected Jesus refused to receive. However we may understand the altar, the homilist makes clear that one can fully experience it only by going out to the margins.

The Hebrews have no lasting (earthly) city; they are *looking for the city that is to come* (13:14). Like Abraham, who *looked forward to the city . . . whose architect and builder is God* (11:10), and like those heroes who died in faith while headed for a city that God has prepared for them (11:13-16), the destination is *the city of the living God* (12:22). The homilist calls the Hebrews to live outside the gates of the earthly cities, in preparation for the city to come.

Concluding this brief section, the homilist explains the sacrifices pleasing to God: *praise, . . . the fruit of lips that confess his name* (13:15). The sacrifice is not the confession itself but the *fruit* of that confession: acts of compassion and the other ethical injunctions named earlier. That is the calling of Jesus' followers. Jesus is the *high priest* of this confession (3:1; 4:14). And these acts become a confession of hope (10:23).

Resumption of Exhortations 13:16-19

Our homilist then returns to more exhortations. Like Micah, another biblical prophet, our homilist questions the validity of mindless sacrifices. Micah asks, "What does the LORD require of you but to do

220   Hebrews 13:1-19

justice and to love kindness and to walk humbly with your God?"
(Mic 6:6-8). Sacrifices that are pleasing to God are full of thanksgiving and the fruit of the confession. The homilist reminds the
Hebrews to make their work a sacrifice pleasing to God. Second, just
as the readers were admonished in verse 7 to remember and imitate
their leaders of the past, they are now reminded to obey and submit
to their current leaders, who guard and keep watch over them. The
verb used for "keep watch" is the same one used in Mark 13:33 (cf.
Luke 21:36): Jesus tells the disciples, "Keep alert; for you do not
know when the time will come." In Hebrews, the homilist is again
advocating a community approach to faithfulness that assigns the
leaders a certain job and asks the rest of the community to accept
that leadership with joy, not with sighs and groaning.

Finally, the homilist asks for prayers. Echoing 10:22, where the
homilist exhorts the Hebrews to approach the (true) sanctuary with
a *true heart, . . . clean from an evil conscience*, the homilist now claims a
clear conscience, desiring to act honorably in all things (13:18) and urges
the Hebrews to do likewise so the pastor *may be restored* to them
soon (13:19). The homilist knows and loves the congregation.

The author's final word is touching: *Grace be with all of you.*

THE TEXT IN BIBLICAL CONTEXT

Outside the Gate: Aliens and Exiles

The theme of the people of God living in exile as resident aliens
looms over the entire text. The context of Hebrews 13:9-16 is sacrificial; the passage is rooted in Leviticus 16:27, which stipulates that the
heifer for the Yom Kippur sacrifice be *burned outside the camp*. In
using the Leviticus passage, the homilist reinterprets the notion of
sacrifice to fit the audience's situation as aliens in a strange land.
Benjamin Dunning writes that this passage uses sacrifice to "work
out a certain notion of 'Christian-ness'—a conception . . . whose
accent falls on embracing outsider status, rather than a clear and
unambiguous stance on a certain type of Christian cultic practice"
(59). The author uses sacrifice and the location of that sacrifice (*outside the camp*) to spotlight the biblical themes of alienness and exile
in Exodus, the Prophets, Daniel, and many other Jewish texts used
earlier in the sermon. At various points the homilist has spoken
about how Abraham, the Israelites, and the heroes of faith have operated as aliens or strangers in their own land—or in a foreign land.

Exile is a mark of their faithful journey, as the homilist has illus-
trated in chapter 11. Like their ancestors, the Hebrews are living

Hebrews 13:1-19 221

outside the camp. They are resident aliens in an impermanent city (13:14). Outsider status is at the heart of their "Christian-ness," as Dunning suggests. The Hebrews are to take on the status of aliens and are *to do good and to share what you have, for such sacrifices are pleasing to God* (13:16).

The author has fully integrated the biblical past into the hearers' present. Jesus is the once-for-all sacrifice of the new covenant. He is the pioneer, the one who shows them how to live on the margins.

THE TEXT IN THE LIFE OF THE CHURCH

Community and Hospitality

Members of Anabaptist churches often show hospitality to strangers, starting such powerful ministries as Church World Service, the Heifer Project, Mennonite Central Committee, and SERRV (Sales Exchange for Refugee Rehabilitation and Vocation) in efforts to ensure that strangers have what they need to live good lives in their own and other countries. Many of us work daily to welcome immigrants and make them feel at home.

Jesus lived his own life as a marginalized person and found himself *outside the camp*, both literally and figuratively, before his death. The homilist of Hebrews requests that the congregation go outside the camp with Jesus. By doing so, they can access the power of his sacrifice and can build their identity as a people who create bonds with one another outside the space normally seen as acceptable. We can become outsiders, too, belonging together in a home that God created. This is a powerful message—both in the world of antiquity, when so many were outsiders, and in today's world, fractured as it is with division and superficiality.

Oddly enough, sharing outsider status with others fosters a sense of belonging. The challenge is how individuals, congregations, and denominations can share this message of belonging with others while remaining distinctive groups. The Hebrews were drawn together because of their understanding of Jesus. They were being challenged by the homilist to live faithful lives in response, not just as individuals but also as a group. We face the same challenge. What marks us as a group? How do we bring others into the group so they truly belong?

Prison Ministries

When Hebrews was written, some of the homilist's friends were in prison because of their faith (10:34; 13:3). We do not know the exact circumstances. Then as now, prison was a painful and shameful experience. But these people were willing to face it. The Gospels and Hebrews call us to visit and care for those who land in prison because of bad decision-making and terrible circumstances. But there is another kind of "prison ministry." Martin Luther King Jr., Dietrich Bonhoeffer, and Rosa Parks were all willing to risk a prison sentence for their acts of civil disobedience because of their faith."

Redefinition of Sacrifice

Hebrews follows a long line of biblical authors who challenge their listeners to do more than make the appropriate sacrifice. We hear the famous words of Micah 6:6-8, "What does the LORD require of you but to do justice and to love kindness and to walk humbly with your God?" That is only one of several calls in the Bible for right action beyond sacrifices. God exclaims in Isaiah 1:11-13, "I have had enough of burnt offerings of rams and the fat of fed beasts." Instead, God implores the people to "seek justice; rescue the oppressed; defend the orphan; plead for the widow" (1:17). The psalmist of Psalm 51 also asks God, "Create in me a clean heart" (51:10). The psalmist recognizes that God takes "no delight in sacrifice; if I were to give a burnt offering, you would not be pleased. The sacrifice acceptable to God is a broken spirit" (51:16-17).

In several instances in the Gospels, Jesus is at the temple, likely to offer a sacrifice. However, he also extends the requirements of the law (see esp. the Sermon on the Mount in Matt 5–7). Hebrews continues this approach. Jesus' sacrifice is lifegiving only because he has offered himself in total obedience to the will and spirit of God. In like manner, the readers of Hebrews are called to offer themselves in obedience to God. They are invited to *go to him outside the camp and bear the abuse he endured* (13:13). They are to offer sacrifices of praise to God and confession of his name in a time and place where such testimony may lead to mockery and abuse. Their sacrifice will be gratitude to God, showing compassion, doing good, and sharing what they have, *for such sacrifices are pleasing to God* (Heb 13:16).

Ethics—what we do and how we do it—are important in both Jewish and Christian perspectives. In the modern world, which highly values comfort and convenience, many of us have difficulty believing in the importance of sacrifice and its meaning. Conventional wisdom suggests that we should not have to sacrifice time, energy, money, or anything else. We have apps to warm our cars before we get into them on cold winter days. We have frozen food at the grocery store and microwave ovens to heat it up quickly. We buy vegetables already cut up. We have smart speakers that play music at our command without our lifting a finger.

Are we looking for comfort and convenience in our spiritual lives, too? Would our homilist suggest that the Hebrews congregation might be looking for an easy way out, if not for actual conveniences? Our pastor is suggesting that true, faithful living is a sacrificial offering. How can we incorporate offerings, or sacrifices, into our daily lives in ways that will daily reconnect us to God and to each other? How do we live *outside the camp* when the world is telling us through all sorts of media to come on in? "The world's camp is great!"

Hebrews 13:20-25

Epilogue
Benediction and Greetings

OUTLINE

Benediction, 13:20-21
Appeal and Greetings, 13:22-25

EXPLANATORY NOTES

Benediction 13:20-21

After requesting their prayers, the homilist prays for the readers. The blessing is replete with faith affirmations and biblical imagery.

First, God is *the God of peace*. This recalls earlier instances in the text: *Melchizedek, . . . "king of peace,"* is an archetype of Jesus (7:1-2). *Rahab* received Israel's spies in peace (11:31). Discipline produces the peaceful *fruit of righteousness* (12:11). Pursuing *peace* is a necessary step toward holiness (12:14).

Second, God brought *Jesus . . . back [up] from the dead* (13:20). The Greek verb used in this verse, *anagō* (lead or bring up), is not the usual New Testament verb for resurrecting (*egeirō*). It is a word that means to bring up from a low to a high place. In that sense, it is consistent with the frequent use of the Psalm 110, affirming that Jesus is now *high priest forever* and *seated at the right hand* of God in glory (1:3, 13; 2:9; 4:14-15; 5:5; 6:20; 7:17, 26; 8:1; 10:12-13; 12:2). Jesus has been exalted to sit at God's right hand. Jesus has become a heavenly high priest, like Melchizedek, and will exalt his followers in the

Hebrews 13:20-25   225

presence of God. The homilist uses a form of the same verb (*agō*) in Hebrews 2:10 to proclaim that God is *bringing [leading] many children to glory* through Jesus.

Third, Jesus is *the great shepherd of the sheep* (13:20). The shepherd watches over and protects God's people. The great shepherd may be a cognate for the great high priest elaborated earlier in Hebrews as intercessor for the people. If so, it smoothly connects to the next phrase, *by the blood of the eternal covenant,* of which Jesus is the mediator. This phrase also connects to other instances in the text where *salvation* (5:9), *judgment* (6:2), *redemption* (9:12), *Spirit* (9:14), and *inheritance* (9:15) are all described as *eternal*. All these may be understood as aspects of the eternal covenant.

As Jesus was perfected, so will the Hebrews. Jesus was made *perfect through sufferings* (2:10) to do God's will (10:7) and to work what is pleasing in his sight (11:5-6; 13:16). Likewise for the Hebrews. Believers are enabled to do these things *through Jesus Christ* (13:21), the *pioneer*, or leader (12:2), the high priest who sacrificed himself (9:26), the intercessor (7:25), the obedient one (10:7), the one who identifies with his brothers and sisters (2:12-13), the one who has been exalted by God because of his faithfulness (1:4-8).

The final word of the benediction is a doxology, a word of praise. Jesus is the one whom God has glorified. The homilist affirms both the glory that God has given Jesus and the glory of God's own self in closing the benediction.

Appeal and Greetings 13:22-25

The writer asks the readers to accept the message of exhortation, a word suggesting that the text was originally a sermon. Addressing them as brothers and sisters implies the familial relationship and feelings that they have for one another. The writer sends word that Timothy, Paul's companion in ministry mentioned in Acts and other Pauline letters, *has been set free*. The Greek word translated as "set free" can also be translated as "released" or "sent away," so it is not possible to make definitive conclusions about the circumstances of the sermon/letter or the relationship to Paul or the Pauline churches. However, we do see here a strong family-like network of people who keep in contact with each other. They share news, exhortations, teachings, concerns, and, most of all, love with each other. Who said social networking was a late twentieth-century invention?

The final sentiment? Grace. *Grace be with all of you.* The homilist has spoken several times about the impact of grace in their lives (2:9; 4:16; 10:29; 12:15; 13:9). It is a fitting ending to the text.

226   Hebrews 13:20-25

THE TEXT IN BIBLICAL CONTEXT

Jesus as the Great Shepherd

The benediction designates Jesus as *the great shepherd of the sheep* (13:20). This imagery is prevalent in the biblical tradition, which arises from a culture in which shepherding, one of the earliest occupations, was crucial. Large flocks were a sign of power. Keeping flocks well and safe was an important undertaking. Our homilist has already made extensive use of Jeremiah 31. Shepherd imagery there refers to God: "He who scattered Israel will gather him and will keep him as a shepherd does a flock" (Jer 31:10). God as shepherd also occurs in Psalm 23, "The LORD is my shepherd"; and in Isaiah 40:11, "[The Lord GOD] will feed his flock like a shepherd." Since the role of the shepherd is so crucial, biblical texts often use the title of shepherd as a designation for the leaders of Israel (Ps 80:1; Ezek 34:5, 8, 12, 23; 37:24; Zech 10:2; 11:16). In the ancient Near East, both gods and kings were often called shepherds.

King David was earlier a shepherd. Some expected a Davidic messiah who would shepherd his people. In Matthew and Luke, Jesus tells the parable of lost sheep (Matt 18:12-13//Luke 15:3-7); God is like the shepherd who searches high and low for even one sheep that goes astray. In John's Gospel, Jesus declares, "I am the good shepherd" (10:14). Finally, 1 Peter 2:25 and 5:4 refer to Jesus as "shepherd" and "chief shepherd," in a manner similar to that of Hebrews [*Christology in Hebrews, p. 235*].

Epistolary Conclusions

Despite the absence of elements present in most New Testament letters, the final words fit the usual pattern of letters. Similar endings may be found at the conclusion of all the New Testament letters. They may contain personal remarks, a request for prayer, benediction, doxology, travel plans, greetings, and almost always closing words of grace and peace to the recipients. Although most believe that Hebrews originated as a sermon, it most likely also circulated as a letter, hence the traditional epistolary form at the conclusion.

THE TEXT IN THE LIFE OF THE CHURCH

A Word of Hope

Hebrews is an intriguing blend of mystery and clear assurance. Its profound interaction with biblical literature in Greek translation gives us a clue to the background of the author. Whether the

Jerusalem temple still stood when the sermon was written is almost beside the point; the author and the Hebrews congregation understand themselves to be foreigners in a strange land, willingly or not, subject to earthly principalities that have treated them harshly.

In these tenuous circumstances, our author has a message of hope. Moving beyond the affirmation of Jesus as Son of God, Savior, Redeemer, Messiah, we find in Hebrews another designation for Jesus: the *great high priest* (4:14), like Melchizedek, an obscure priest-king in the story of Abraham. The homilist uses Psalm 110 (LXX 109) as a prooftext. This new priesthood requires a heavenly sanctuary and the new covenant promised by Jeremiah (31:31-34), where God's law is written on the heart. There is no more need for the earthly sacrificial system, since Jesus is the once-for-all sacrifice, sitting at God's right hand in the heavenly tabernacle.

For a triumphalist Christianity, the message of Hebrews appears to be supersessionist: Christianity is the new, better replacement religion for Judaism. *But*, while our author clearly argues for a replacement to the sacrificial system, the argument does not extend to a replacement of an entire religious tradition. We should remember that and read Hebrews with a heart grateful for the traditions handed down to us from Second Temple Judaism. We should let the text challenge our constructions of piety. Where might we need to have a new covenant and a new way of challenging previous beliefs and understandings?

The author urges the Hebrews to offer sacrifices of gratitude and praise. Seated at the right hand of God, Jesus intercedes for us and calls us to follow him in faithfulness to God's will and in ministry to one another, described so eloquently in chapter 13, which may be the clearest presentation of the priesthood of all believers in Scripture.

Like the *cloud of witnesses* that have gone before (12:1), the Hebrews are to lead exemplary lives, inspired by their faith—lives that may not conform to the ethics or norms in the broader world. We, too, are asked to live *outside the camp* with Jesus (13:13). Together, we are to live as people of God, aliens in an alienating world.

Therefore, hold fast to your faith!

Outline of Hebrews

**PROLOGUE: PROPHECY ABOUT THE SON
AND HIS PLACE NEXT TO GOD**   **1:1-4**

God Has Spoken by a Son   1:1-2a
Nature and Work of the Son   1:2b-3
The Son Is Exalted above the Angels   1:4

**PART 1: LISTEN TO WHAT IS SAID ABOUT JESUS
AND FOLLOW HIS EXAMPLE!**   **1:5–4:13**

The Son Is Greater than the Angels   **1:5–2:4**

Catena: The Son Is Exalted above the Angels   1:5-13
Summary: Angels as Servants   1:14
Pay Attention! We Must Not Neglect This Salvation   2:1-4

Jesus the Son Is a Human Being, like Us in All Things   **2:5-18**

Psalm 8 as a Witness to Jesus' Glory, Honor, and Humanity   2:5-8
Through His Suffering, Jesus Leads Us to Glory   2:9-10
By Sharing in Our Humanity, Jesus Destroys the Power
of Death   2:11-18

The Faithful Are to Enter into Rest   **3:1–4:13**

Jesus Compared to Moses   3:1-6
The Holy Spirit Is Speaking Today   3:7-11
Exhortation to the Audience   3:12-19

Outline of Hebrews

The Rewards of Faithfulness	4:1-11
Accountability to the Word of the Living God	4:12-13

PART 2: JESUS' HIGH PRIESTHOOD — 4:14–7:28

Jesus: Son and Great High Priest — 4:14–5:10

Approach the Throne of Grace with Boldness	4:14-16
The High Priesthood	5:1-10
Every High Priest	5:1-4
Jesus as High Priest	5:5-10

Grow Up! (A Message on Group Identity) — 5:11–6:20

Insult and Shame: Move On to Maturity	5:11–6:3
Warning: It Is Impossible to Restore Those Who Have Fallen Away	6:4-8
Exhortation: Persevere Because God Is Just	6:9-12
Teaching: God's Promises Are Sure	6:13-20

Jesus the Son Is Foreshadowed by the Priest-King Melchizedek — 7:1-28

When Melchizedek Met Abraham	7:1-10
Midrash on Melchizedek	7:1-3
Elaboration on Melchizedek's Greatness	7:4-10
Perfection Is Attainable through Jesus' Priesthood	7:11-19
An Oath Confirms Jesus' Everlasting, Holy, and Perfect Priesthood	7:20-28
Confirmed by an Oath	7:20-22
Eternal	7:23-25
Holy and Perfect	7:26-28

PART 3: JESUS' PRIESTLY MINISTRY IN A NEW COVENANT — 8:1–10:18

Christ Is High Priest and Minister of a New Covenant — 8:1-13

Summary	8:1-6
Prophetic Announcement of the New Covenant	8:7-13

The Two Covenants — 9:1–10:18

Sacrifice in the First Covenant	9:1-10
Christ as the Sacrifice in the New Covenant	9:11-28
Restatement of Themes	10:1-18
The Law Is Only a Shadow	10:1-10
Christ Is the Perfect Sacrifice, Once for All	10:11-18

230 Outline of Hebrews

PART 4: A CALL TO PERSEVERANCE, ENDURANCE, FAITHFULNESS — 10:19–12:2

Perseverance Is Essential — 10:19-31

Exhortations	10:19-25
Let Us Approach	10:19-22
Let Us Hold Fast	10:23
Let Us Consider How to Provoke One Another	10:24-25
Warning Against Apostasy	10:26-31

What Faithfulness Looks Like — 10:32–12:2

Remember Your Own Faithfulness	10:32-39
Remember the Faithfulness of Past Witnesses	11:1-38
The Character of Faith	11:1-3
By Faith . . .	11:4-38
Abel, Enoch, and Noah	11:4-7
Abraham, Sarah, Isaac, Jacob, and Joseph	11:8-22
Moses and the Israelites	11:23-28
Rahab and the Fugitives from Egypt	11:29-31
Judges, Kings, Prophets, and Martyrs	11:32-38
They Wait for Us	11:39-40
Look to Jesus, Who Endured the Cross	12:1-2

PART 5: A CALL TO SERVICE — 12:3–13:19

Recapitulation of Argument — 12:3-29

Exhortation: Endure Discipline	12:3-13
Warning: Do Not Be like Esau	12:14-17
Synkrisis: You Have Come to the Heavenly Jerusalem	12:18-24
Shaken, Not Stirred	12:25-29

Exhortation for Service Pleasing to God — 13:1-19

Exhortations	13:1-9
Excursus on Jesus' Sacrifice	13:10-15
Resumption of Exhortations	13:16-19

EPILOGUE: BENEDICTION AND GREETINGS — 13:20-25

Benediction	13:20-21
Appeal and Greetings	13:22-25

Essays

ATONEMENT In Hebrews, we see the development of thinking about Christ as the "once for all" sacrifice. The author of Hebrews largely bases this understanding on Leviticus 16, which instructs the people of Israel on the ritual for Yom Kippur (Day of Atonement). Hebrews 9 summarizes this ritual by describing the tabernacle, the holy of holies, and the *hilastērion*, the cover of the ark of the covenant, where the yearly sacrifice is offered. This yearly ritual cleanses the tabernacle (and later, the temple) and the people from impurities and sin. To do this, the priest must first cleanse himself by sacrificing a bull as purification. Then he is to sacrifice one pure goat to cleanse the people and use the blood from the bull and the goat to cleanse the altar.

To atone for the sins of the people, a second identical and pure goat, the scapegoat, is sent out to the wilderness, symbolically carrying the sins of the people. Although Hebrews 9 contains only a summary, our pastor and the audience are familiar with the details in Leviticus and other biblical texts.

The word *atonement* arises out of this ritual. William Tyndale used this term in his sixteenth-century English version of the Bible, translating several Greek words that relate to reconciliation, appeasement, making amends, and repentance. It became the defining term for the result of Christ's sacrifice: through this sacrifice, humans are made at one with God (at-one-ment). *Atonement* is thus a nonbiblical word distinctive to the English language that conveys a range of biblical ideas originally expressed with various Hebrew and Greek words. The word *atonement* occurs twice in the NRSV of the New Testament (Rom 3:25; Heb 2:17), and *atoning sacrifice* twice (1 John 2:2; 4:10; cf. 4 Macc 17:21-22; Heb 9:11-15; 1 Pet 1:19; 1 John 1:7). The Greek words used in these passages are these:

- *hilaskomai* (to propitiate, to expiate, to have mercy), in Luke 18:13 and Hebrews 2:17

232   Essays

- *hilastērion* (the means, or place, of expiation or atonement), in Romans 3:25 and Hebrews 9:5, where the NRSV has *mercy seat*
- *hilasmos* (the action in which God is propitiated and sin expiated; the act of setting aside sin), in 1 John 2:2 and 4:10, "atoning sacrifice"

These Greek words occur a total of only six times. In contrast, words with similar meanings appear over seventy times in the Old Testament. All the aforementioned passages relate closely to the act of sacrifice. First John 2:2 and 4:10 describe Jesus as the "atoning sacrifice," meaning that he made himself the sacrifice for us as a substitute. While Hebrews does not say this specifically, Hebrews 2:17 claims that Jesus became a high priest *to make a sacrifice of atonement for the sins of the people*. Hebrews emphasizes that Jesus is both the one who sacrifices *and* the one sacrificed, so in that sense Hebrews and the author of 1 John have similar understandings of Jesus' act.

Other words, such as the Greek words behind "reconciliation, to reconcile," appear in 2 Corinthians 5:18-20; Romans 5:10-11; Colossians 1:20, 22; and Ephesians 2:16. These also fit into the "atonement" category. For our purposes, we focus on the words that appear in Hebrews in relation to Leviticus 16 and Exodus 25-31, the instructions for building the tabernacle that God gave to Moses, which Hebrews summarizes in chapter 9. We then examine how Hebrews has been used and connects to broader Christian theologies of atonement.

Leviticus uses the Hebrew words *kippur* and *kapporet* (see Seely: 35-39, for a more thorough philological discussion). Both words are forms of the three-letter root *kpr*, which has several meanings: "to cover," "to appease," "to make amends," "to reconcile." The noun *kapporet* identifies the cover of the ark of the covenant, on which the high priest sprinkled the blood of the sacrifice on Yom Kippur (Day of Atonement). The Septuagint, the Greek version of the Hebrew Bible, translates both *kippur* and *kapporet* with forms of the verb *exilaskomai* (to propitiate, appease a god, have mercy on; cf. *hilaskomai* in Luke 18:13; Heb 2:17), a word closely related to the verb used in the New Testament and the related noun *hilastērion*. The translators probably chose these Greek words because they were already in use to describe non-Jewish Greek sacrificial practices (*TDNT* 3:310-12). Since Leviticus 16 describes a sacrificial ritual, it makes sense that the translators used corresponding Greek words with a similar connotation.

In the Latin Vulgate, translated by Jerome around 400 CE, the noun *kapporet/hilastērion* was translated as *propitiatorium*, meaning a "place of propitiation," or "appeasement." For *kippur/exhilaskomai*, the Vulgate used the verb *expiationum*. John Wycliffe's fourteenth-century English translation (of the Vulgate) followed the Latin translators by using the English cognate *propitiatory*, or "place of appeasement," for *kapporet/hilastērion*.

In his 1523 Reformation-era German translation of the Bible, Martin Luther (incorrectly) translated *kapporet/hilastērion* as *Gnadenstuhl* or *Gnadenthron*, which William Tyndale (1526-34) followed by using "mercy-seate" (the English meaning of *Gnadenstuhl*). The Authorized Version (King James) of 1611 followed Tyndale, as have most subsequent English translations, even though the *hilastērion/kapporet* was not a seat at all, but a *cover*

Essays   233

for the ark. God promised to meet Moses above that cover (Exod 25:22) and was said to be "enthroned on/above/upon the cherubim" (1 Sam 4:4; 2 Kings 19:15; Ps 80:1; Isa 37:16; cf. Heb 4:16: *throne of grace*). Semantic reasons in Hebrew connect the ritual act that occurred on Yom Kippur to mercy; yet *mercy seat* (Heb 9:5) fails to convey the meaning of the word. If we do not recognize this, we lose much impact of the comparison between the sacrifice by the high priest on behalf of the people and the sacrifice that Jesus made of himself on behalf of the people. "Place of atonement," or the older "propitiatory," should be used instead of "mercy seat."

But sacrifice, the focus of Hebrews, is just one of the lenses the New Testament authors use to explain the significance of Jesus' death and how his death works as atonement, or how humans are saved from their sins (Hershberger: 15–16). There are other models of atonement. Some interpreters see the cross as Christ's victory over the "powers" that hold humanity in bondage (Rom 8:18-39). A version of this idea may be found in Hebrews 2:14-15: Jesus shared our humanity *so that through death he might destroy the one who has the power of death, that is, the devil, and free those who all their lives were held in slavery by the fear of death*. This theory was first developed by Irenaeus in the third century (see Hershberger: 54); more recently by Gustaf Aulén in his book *Christus Victor* (1930, Swedish; 1931, English); and by Walter Wink in his trilogy on the Powers: *Naming the Powers* (1984); *Unmasking the Powers* (1986); *Engaging the Powers* (1992).

Jesus is recognized as the Redeemer (e.g., Luke 1:68; 24:21; Titus 2:14; Heb 9:15; Rev 14:3-4), who delivers people from death, slavery, sin, and the human condition. Jesus redeems people by giving himself as a ransom (e.g., Matt 20:28; Mark 10:45). Paul also considers Jesus Christ to be a redeemer (Rom 3:21-26), who made the atoning sacrifice.

In the New Testament, Jesus' death on the cross also reveals the depth of God's love for us. This is developed in the Gospel of John and is capsulized in the verse many of us learned as children, John 3:16. In John, Jesus is God's Logos, God's Word, God's purpose made flesh. God, too, was suffering in Jesus when he was on the cross. Paul says, "But God proves [God's] love for us in that while we were yet sinners Christ died for us" (Rom 5:8). "In Christ[,] God was reconciling the world to himself" (2 Cor 5:19). Hebrews reflects this perspective in the prologue: *[God] has spoken to us by a Son* (Heb 1:2).

Jesus' death reveals a way of life that transforms believers spiritually and psychologically. In Acts, they were known as followers of "the Way." Paul says, "I have been crucified with Christ; it is no longer I who live, but it is Christ who lives in me" (Gal 2:19-29). He has died to an old way of being and has been raised into a new way of being. Paul reminds the Corinthians that "in Christ there is a new creation; everything" has become "new" (2 Cor 5:17). Paul elaborates, telling the Romans that, having been "buried with [Christ] by baptism into death," we will "walk in newness of life" because "Christ was raised from the dead by the glory of the Father" (Rom 6:1-4). Hebrews 2:10-11 speaks of a powerful new sanctified life that transforms believers into children of God and siblings of Jesus, the Son of God.

Jesus' death and resurrection are a vindication over unjust religious and political authorities. The authorities rejected and killed Jesus, but God has vindicated Jesus by raising him to God's right hand. We find this view in Peter's sermon in Acts 2:31-36. Hebrews repeatedly emphasizes Jesus' enthronement at God's right hand (e.g., 1:3; 12:2). This negates the judgment of the forces that killed him. Throughout history, those who challenge the social structures of injustice and violence are frequently victims of that violence. In Hebrews, Jesus' life demonstrates perseverance in doing right regardless of the cost, even to the final limit of human life. Jesus is the pioneer and perfect example of faithfulness (Heb 12:1-2). Hebrews 6:20 calls Jesus *a forerunner on our behalf*. In this view, sometimes the emphasis is on the love of God for us manifest in Christ's willingness to identify with humanity, even to suffering and death on a cross (Phil 2:5-10; Heb 2:11-13).

In the Anabaptist tradition of nonviolence, we see a model in Hebrews. "Jesus' victory over evil is not only a cosmic battle but also a historical one—a battle with evil that begins in real time. . . . Jesus defeating the powers with nonviolent love provides the key for us to continue this real-life victory" (Hershberger: 63). According to Michele Hershberger, if we pay attention to what really happened on the cross, we will see that Jesus went there nonviolently. This act should wake "us up to our own acts of brutality" (66, quoting James Cone). For Hershberger, the sacrifice that Jesus made "once and for all" (Heb 9:23–10:18) was not a sacrifice "that appeases an angry God. It was a sacrifice of love" (67).

Briefly, there are multiple biblical ways of understanding the mystery of the saving act of Jesus, resulting in various models of atonement. Many of these models "favor a single biblical metaphor" (Hershberger: 54). Modern Protestant Christianity has focused primarily on the aspect of sacrifice and what is called substitutionary atonement theory. The innocent (and perfect) Jesus died on behalf of humans (the guilty and imperfect). He paid the price for the sins of all humans. Hebrews supports this theory: Jesus died once and for all. But if we fail to recognize that Hebrews originally made sense in a culture that had a mix of Greco-Roman and Jewish understandings of sacrifice, we may miss *why* Hebrews focuses on the issue of sacrifice. Hebrews speaks a language that the audience understands. Western culture prizes penal justice (a price must be paid for a crime). So the substitutionary atonement theory appeals to many Western Christians because its culture has developed a system that believes punishment for wrongdoing is more appropriate than restorative justice. Thus many of us in the West, and especially in the US, tend to read the New Testament in light of that understanding (Green and Baker: 28).

In the twenty-first century, many people no longer find the language of sacrifice helpful. We don't appreciate that it arose out of an ancient culture, where it was commonplace. At the same time, rather than challenging and correcting abusive behavior, the church has mistakenly encouraged women, children, and people of color to become surrogate sufferers for others. Christians have used the story of the crucifixion to commit violent acts of anti-Jewish behavior, often during Lent or on Good

Essays 235

Friday. When it is stripped of its cultural and religious context, some "critics find the cross-centered atonement faith of Christianity to be a toxic nexus of guilt, retribution, and violence, twisting everything it touches, from gender relations to legal systems" (Heim: 26).

For others, this theology is transformative. Poor and marginalized people are aware of their situation of bondage and weakness. In the message that Christ died for them, they hear the word that despite the rejection of a world that views them as worthless and insignificant, they are infinitely precious in God's sight (cf. Heim: 29–33). Christ is also available to those who are complicit in those systems that oppress the weak and the poor. As J. Denny Weaver states in *The Nonviolent Atonement*,

> The location of the oppressors is quite clear. . . . In the New Testament narrative, these are represented by the ultimate political authorities of Rome, the complicitous Jewish religious leadership, the rabble that howled for Jesus' death, the disciples who slept through his ordeal, Peter, who denied knowing him, and Judas, who betrayed him. Recognizing our complicity with these forces requires confession and repentance, and a change in sides, joining Jesus as a part of the host of witnesses that make visible the reign of God in contrast to the world. (221)

The author of Hebrews asks the congregation to go *outside the camp* (13:13) to resist the temptations of the world. At its best, an atonement theory needs to do what the pastor of Hebrews asks the congregation to do: step outside their comfort zone and persevere in acts of faithfulness so that both the oppressor and the oppressed receive the gifts offered by God through Christ. In this way atonement becomes a "liturgy—a form of worship—[in which] we realize we are *undergoing* atonement, not just understanding it" (Hershberger: 68, emph. in the original).

CHRISTOLOGY IN HEBREWS Christology is the study of the nature and work of Christ. As the Greek translation of the Hebrew word "messiah," "Christ" means "anointed one." Christology, therefore, becomes the study of who and what the anointed one is and what the anointed one did. The Gospels identify Jesus as the Christ, usually as the son of David (Matt 22:42; Mark 12:35); Son of God (Matt 3:16-17; Mark 1:1 [see mg.]; Luke 1:35; John 11:27); or even the anointed (Messiah) of God (Luke 9:20; 23:35). So what is his role as Christ? In Mark, Jesus is a healer and casts out demons. In Matthew, he is a prophet who reinterprets the Mosaic law. Paul emphasizes the salvific and sacrificial role Jesus Christ has played through his death and resurrection. Also, Paul stresses the humanity of Jesus Christ: he is the representative new Adam. As Adam died, all humans die. As Christ died and rose, we die and rise (1 Cor 15:20-28). This sacrifice has conquered death so all those united with him can conquer the "power/ fear of death" (Rom 6:5-8; Heb 2:14-15).

The Christology of Hebrews is a unique combination of ideas already in circulation: Jesus as Son (of God), Jesus as sacrifice, and Jesus as high

236   **Essays**

priest within Second Temple Judaism (Eisenbaum 2004: 129). As the author clearly states, *the main point in what we are saying is this: we have such a high priest, one who is seated at the right hand of the throne of the Majesty in the heavens, a minister in the sanctuary and the true tent that the Lord, and not any mortal, has set up* (Heb 8:1-2).

Our Hebrews author uses multiple christological traditions imprecisely. For example, the catena (chain of quotations) in Hebrews 1:5-13 establishes the primacy of Jesus as Son. Our author makes clear to the audience that Christ is better than the angels (1:4-14), Moses (3:16), and the previous words of the prophets (1:1-2). But our author leaves unclear exactly when that first moment of sonship happened. Was it at the creation of the world (1:10)? At the incarnation (1:5-6)? Or at the exaltation (1:3, 13)? The primary concern of this catena is to "establish the significance of Christ for the present and future of [the] addressees by indicating the superiority of the Son" (Attridge: 55).

In Hebrews, the Son is also high priest. For our author, two of the most important functions of Jesus as high priest are his intercessory role and self-sacrifice. Both concepts were already present in other New Testament texts. In Romans 8:31-39, Paul claims that Jesus is both sacrifice and intercessor; thus nothing separates "us from the love of God." First John 2:1-2 understands that Jesus is both an "advocate" and "the atoning sacrifice for our sins."

Independent of Hebrews, the tradition of Jesus as high priest appears in three different early Christian texts (Attridge: 100). Ignatius, bishop of Antioch in Syria, became a prisoner of the Romans and was forced to travel to Rome, where he was scheduled to be killed in the amphitheater (ca. 108 CE). He wrote letters to various churches in Asia Minor. In his letter *To the Philadelphians*, he claims that the high priest (Jesus) has been entrusted with the holy of holies (9.1). Polycarp, the bishop of Smyrna, was killed by the Romans (ca. 155 CE). In his letter *To the Philippians*, he calls Jesus the "eternal priest." According to the anonymous Martyrdom of Polycarp, written sometime after his death, Polycarp said a prayer to God at the point of his death in which he called Jesus the "heavenly high priest, . . . thy [God's] beloved child" (14.3).

Perhaps the most distinctive aspect of our author's argument is the use of Yom Kippur in Leviticus 16:1-17 as the background for understanding Jesus' sacrificial death. Our author also links the blood of Jesus' sacrifice to the new covenant itself: Hebrews 10:29 calls Jesus' blood *the blood of the covenant* and in 13:20 *the blood of the eternal covenant* (Eisenbaum 2004: 146). Jesus' sacrificial act has opened the doors of the heavenly sanctuary for the people of the new covenant to enter (10:19). Through his sacrifice and blood, Jesus not only was "entrusted with the holy of holies" (Ignatius, *To the Philadelphians* 9.1), but also made it available to all who are faithful.

In Hebrews, many see the "highest" Christology in the New Testament; yet the letter has the effect of leveling the playing field. As Attridge states, "Because it is an act of flesh and blood, an act of the Son who leads many . . . to glory, it is something that can be imitated by Christ's followers" (147). Jesus is the pioneer; the people of God need only to follow faithfully.

Essays

DIASPORA This Greek (now also English) word means "dispersion, scattering." The term appears in the Septuagint in Deuteronomy 28:25, "You shall be a dispersion in all kingdoms of the earth"; and Psalm 146:2 (LXX), "When the LORD builds Jerusalem he will also gather in the dispersions of Israel" (NETS). But in these cases, "diaspora" translates different Hebrew terms. So technically, the word "diaspora" is more an artifact of Greek translation than it is a Hebrew concept. The biblical concept it translates is the result of being exiled.

Traditionally, the Diaspora refers to the dispersion of Jews outside their homeland, those living in exile. Some living in the northern kingdom of Israel were sent into exile by the Assyrians in the eighth century BCE. They never returned (the ten lost tribes). Later, some inhabitants of Judah, the southern kingdom, were taken into exile in the Babylonian captivity of the sixth century BCE. After some decades, some Jews (mostly later generations) trickled back to Judah. The term then came to apply to any Jew living outside the land of Israel during any period in history. Some Jews lived in Egypt at Leontopolis, Elephantine, and Alexandria and eventually at many other places in the Mediterranean world (cf. Acts). In Hellenistic Egypt, the Hebrew Scriptures were translated into Greek (the Septuagint, or LXX) because many Jews who had been living there for generations could not read or understand Hebrew. This Greek version was often copied (by Christians) in Byzantium (Constantinople; Istanbul).

Despite the longings of the Hebrew prophets to return to the land of Israel, most Jews in Babylonia and Persia elected to stay there. Jewish communities thrived all over the ancient Mediterranean: in Alexandria, Rome, Antioch, Ephesus, and Corinth. It would be historically inaccurate for us to believe that they all thought of themselves as "exiled."

Today, "diaspora studies" is a branch of academic inquiry that studies the effects of forced exile on the cultural identity and behaviors (e.g., language and foodways) of minority groups and individuals living in a majority culture. If we read the Letter to the Hebrews through the lens of diaspora studies, we can see the author encouraging the group to retain their identity by reinterpreting their shared biblical past, or "homeland," and reshaping it into a set of behaviors that they can pursue in their current circumstances. Living "outside the camp" is living in a type of diaspora. The author is asking the group to embrace diasporic living as an act of faithfulness.

GNOSTICISM The term Gnosticism refers to a broad category of belief systems that arose out of rethinking the biblical creation stories through the lens of several Hellenistic philosophical movements between the second and fifth centuries CE. Gnosticism is derived from the word for "knowledge," *gnōsis*. Adherents claimed they had special or "hidden" knowledge regarding the relationship between the created world in which they lived and the divine, unknowable world of the true god. Most, but not all, Gnostics believed this world to be evil, the creation of a lesser, fallen god, named Yahweh. The "fall" was the god of the material world separating himself from the true, unknowable god of the divine world. Since they

238   Essays

were created matter, humans were considered defiled. Salvation was attainable only through knowing that at death the soul would be released back to the divine unknowable god.

Because humans were part of the created, corrupt world, most Gnostics could not accept the full humanity of Jesus. Hence, various theories arose to explain how Jesus was connected to his human body. For most Christians, Jesus' suffering and death were meaningful because Jesus was a real, fully human person. Since Christianity arose out of Judaism and relied so heavily on the Jewish Scriptures, it was ultimately impossible for most Christians to justify the gnostic approach to those Scriptures. The fundamental gnostic assumption (the material world is bad) was such a thorough rejection of the Jewish (and now Christian) Scriptures that the larger church rejected gnostic sects and deemed them heretical.

The relationship to the material world emphasized by gnostic groups affected the reading and transmission of the text of the New Testament. Examples of textual variants [Textual Variants, p. 260] that reflect different understandings of the nature of Jesus occur numerous places. For example, in Luke 3:21-22, on the baptism of Jesus, most manuscripts read "You are my Son, the Beloved; with you I am well pleased." However, an important early manuscript reads "You are my Son; today I have begotten you" (emph. added). This reading seems to support an "adoptionist" approach to Jesus: at the moment of baptism, the (divine?) soul of Jesus went into the (human) body. Jesus was human, born of a woman, but "adopted" as divine by God at his baptism, the start of his early ministry. Adoptionism held that Jesus participated in the material during his ministry only to reveal hidden knowledge about salvation to his followers.

JEWISH LITERATURE IN ANTIQUITY During the Second Temple period (516 BCE–70 CE) and the period immediately following, Jews in Palestine and the Diaspora produced a vast amount of literature in both Hebrew and Greek. The breadth and variety in this literature attest to the wide range of Jewish thought and practices across the Mediterranean world during this period. The literature includes many genres (apocalypse, poetry, history, testament, philosophy, biblical literature and commentary, and letters, to name a few). The texts circulated in various ways. Apart from the scriptural material written in Hebrew and the texts in the Dead Sea Scrolls, much of it was written in Greek and largely preserved by Christians.

Throughout our study of Hebrews, we have highlighted the connections between Hebrews and some Jewish literature and authors (e.g., Philo, the Dead Sea Scrolls, and biblical literature). This essay complements those connections and provides a brief introduction to the rich literary heritage on which our author was drawing. The essay proceeds in rough chronological order.

The Hebrew Bible and the Septuagint [The Septuagint in Hebrews, p. 252] contain a wide range of literary genres: history, law, poetry, prophecy, origin stories—plus wisdom literature, a broad category that many consider

Essays 239

to be reflections on the human condition: why things are the way they are and why bad things happen. In the canonical biblical literature, Ecclesiastes, Job, and Proverbs are considered wisdom literature. It is a difficult category to define because each book has its own character. Proverbs, for example, contains many pithy maxims; Job records a debate about the relationship of suffering and sin based on a story about a man who loses everything and therefore questions the meaning of life.

Some wisdom literature occurs outside the Hebrew biblical canon in a section that Protestant Christians now call the Apocrypha. The texts included in the Apocrypha were either written or translated into Greek by Jews between 250 BCE and 90 CE. Often designated as the "Old Testament Apocrypha," the collection is a set of thirteen or more texts in several genres: history (1–4 Maccabees [though technically, 3–4 Maccabees are not part of the LXX], Additions to Esther, 1 Esdras); wisdom, poetry, and psalms (Sirach, Wisdom of Solomon, Psalm 151, Prayer of Manasseh), novels and stories (Tobit, Judith, Additions to Daniel), and letters (Epistle of Jeremiah, Baruch). All these texts appear in one or more of the fourth-century CE Greek manuscripts that contain the Septuagint (Sinaiticus, Alexandrinus, Vaticanus). Except for the Hebrew (or some Aramaic) parts of Esther and Daniel, they are neither in the Jewish biblical canon nor the Masoretic Text.

Early Christians and Jews in the Second Temple period often used Sirach (sometimes called Ecclesiasticus or Ben Sira) and the Wisdom of Solomon. Hebrews alludes not only to Proverbs 8, but also to Sirach 24:1-12 and Wisdom of Solomon 7:12, 21; 8:4. All these give a voice to Wisdom (feminine); Hebrews and other early Christian texts like John 1 rework Wisdom into the Logos (Christ).

Despite the texts' inclusion in the great biblical manuscripts of the fourth century, their acceptance into the biblical canon has always been somewhat of an issue for Christians. When Jerome, the great biblical scholar of the late fourth century, translated the Jewish Scriptures into Latin, he based his translation on the Hebrew texts, not the Greek translation. The result was that he initially excluded the apocryphal texts from his Latin Bible (the Vulgate), even though earlier Latin translations of these texts continued to appear in other Latin Bibles. (Eventually, Jerome was pressured by Augustine of Hippo and others to add the apocryphal books, so he produced a new Latin translation of them as well from the Greek.) Throughout the Middle Ages, both the Latin West and the Greek East accepted the Apocrypha as canonical. During the Reformation, Martin Luther decided that the "Old Testament" canon should follow the canon set forth in the Hebrew Bible. Consequently, he collected the apocryphal material into one section, placed after the Old Testament in a section called "Apocrypha." (He did something similar with Hebrews, James, and Revelation in the New Testament.) Because the earliest Anabaptists used Bibles that contained the Apocrypha, early Anabaptist leaders quoted regularly from the Apocrypha and treated it as canonical. Not until the seventeenth century did most Anabaptists begin ignoring the Apocrypha.

240   Essays

Since then, most Bibles produced by Protestants do not contain the Apocrypha. Roman Catholics and Orthodox Christians still consider these texts to be canonical. Eastern Orthodox Christians have a slightly larger set of "deuterocanonical" books than Roman Catholics, and the Ethiopian Orthodox Tewahedo Church has an even larger set of canonical books than the Eastern Orthodox canon. A modern study Bible, like the one produced by the Society of Biblical Literature in conjunction with a publisher, such as HarperCollins or Oxford University Press, places the Apocrypha in a separate section between the Old and New Testaments. While ostensibly nondenominational, it reflects a non-Catholic, English speaking perspective.

Another group of texts written during roughly the same time as the Apocrypha is a set of materials called the Old Testament Pseudepigrapha. Technically, pseudepigrapha are texts written under false names, in the name of someone who did not write the text. In practical terms, however, "Old Testament pseudepigrapha" refers to any Jewish text written roughly between 300 BCE and 200 CE and not contained in the Hebrew Masoretic Text (equivalent to the Christian Old Testament), the Apocrypha, the Dead Sea Scrolls, or the writings of Josephus and Philo. Many of the texts are written in the name of such biblical characters as Enoch, Solomon, and Abraham; these texts are revelatory in some way, narrating revelatory visions (1 Enoch) and tours of heaven and hell. Other texts are considered "rewritten Bible," like Jubilees, which offers a different narrative of creation and the history of Israel from what is found in the Pentateuch. Another text, the Letter of Aristeas, purports to describe the origin of the Septuagint. Most of these texts were never considered canonical by Jews or Christians, with a few notable exceptions like 1 Enoch, which the Ethiopic Church includes in its canon. An important compilation of the Pseudepigrapha is the two-volume set edited by James Charlesworth, *The Old Testament Pseudepigrapha*, the first volume of which is made up entirely of apocalypses and a related genre, testaments. These texts are evidence of the central importance of the biblical text and Jews' constant engagement with it in antiquity.

For the most part, the literature of the Pseudepigrapha and the Apocrypha is anonymous or pseudepigraphical, written in the name of someone who didn't write the text. Yet clearly identified are texts from this period by Philo and Josephus, important authors who lived in the first century CE. Philo (ca. 20 BCE–ca. 50 CE) was from a prominent family in Alexandria, Egypt. Some sources suggest that both his brother, Gaius Julius Alexander, and his nephew Tiberius Julius Alexander were involved in politics and business in Alexandria and beyond.

In the 30s CE, Philo himself went to Rome to petition on behalf of the Alexandrian Jewish community, which was facing economic, social, and political difficulties imposed by Rome in its rule of Alexandria (see *On the Embassy to Gaius*). Philo is famous for describing a group of ascetics called the Therapeutae (see *On the Contemplative Life*). They lived in the Egyptian desert, spending six days of the week in solitude and the seventh in communal worship. Philo knew the Jewish Scriptures in Greek translation

Essays 241

extremely well; he likely did not know Hebrew or Aramaic. He is an important example of Jewish life in the Diaspora and provides access to the thriving (albeit sometimes threatened) Jewish life in Alexandria and elsewhere in Egypt. (For more on Philo and his relevance to Hebrews, see the essay *Philo, Neoplatonism, and Hebrews, p. 245*).

Unlike Philo, who lived in the Diaspora, Josephus was born in Jerusalem, eventually joined the Pharisees, was drawn into the struggle against Rome, and was sent as a commander to the Galilee area, which was ripe for revolt. Although Josephus served as a general for the Jews in their revolt against Rome in the 60s CE, he later became an advisor to the emperor Vespasian, and then to his son, Titus. After the war, Josephus lived in Rome and wrote several important works: *Jewish War*, *Antiquities of the Jews*, *Against Apion*, and an autobiographical account called *Vita* (*Life*). The first two works seek to explain the Jews to the Romans. They are invaluable evidence for Second Temple Judaism. Along with the New Testament, they are important historical sources for understanding such groups as the Pharisees, the Sadducees, and the Essenes. They also are incomparable resources for understanding what life was like for a typical Jew in Judea in the first century CE.

Until the middle of the twentieth century, the writings of Josephus, Philo, and Pliny the Elder (along with a handful of other lesser-known classical sources) were the only sources of information available about the group called the Essenes, an apocalyptic, separatist Jewish movement. Some of the Essenes lived at Qumran, near the Dead Sea, but the majority lived in small exclusive communities scattered throughout Israel.

In late 1946, a Bedouin shepherd boy discovered some ancient scrolls of biblical texts and other writings in a cave near Qumran, just northwest of the Dead Sea, scrolls that almost certainly were produced by the Essenes two millennia earlier. It was the beginning of one of the greatest archaeological finds of the twentieth century: its importance cannot be overestimated. Every Hebrew text of Jewish Scripture, with the possible exception of Esther, is represented in the Dead Sea Scrolls.

Prior to the discovery of the Qumran scrolls, the oldest manuscripts of the Hebrew Bible were tenth-century medieval productions. Suddenly, biblical scholars had manuscripts at least one thousand years older! The scrolls quickly became crucial for understanding variations in the biblical text in antiquity and aided in better understanding of the relationship between the Septuagint's Greek and the Hebrew text. In addition to the biblical texts, the Essenes also produced documents that give insight into their community, spiritual life, and theology. The Essene movement likely arose as a protest against the Maccabees in the second century BCE. The Essenes criticized the Maccabees (later known as the Hasmoneans) for desecrating the temple, rejecting the properly authorized high priest, essentially stealing the high priesthood from the Zadokites, and using a lunar calendar instead of a solar one. As a priestly protest movement, the Essenes rejected the politically motivated Maccabean seizure of the high priesthood.

Their literature reflects an apocalyptic mindset. Several documents narrate an imminent battle between the Sons of Light and the Sons of

242   Essays

Darkness. Important for the study of Hebrews, one text, 11Q13 (11QMelch), describes Melchizedek as a messiah who will deliver the sons of righteousness (probably the Essenes) from Belial (Satan) in the year of Jubilee.

Taken altogether, the literature produced by Jews in the ancient Mediterranean is vast, rich, and representative of multiple voices and concerns. The material is a reminder that Judaism was multifaceted and reflected engagement with the world based on the experience of people who were in the world, but not always of the world.

LOGOS Beginning in antiquity up through today, many books have been written about the concept of *logos*, a Greek word that has a variety of meanings. With some broad brushstrokes, this essay gives a sense of the multiplicity of meanings and how *logos* functions in Scripture. In antiquity, *logos* could refer to thought, word, account, and rationality, both human and cosmic. In Greek, it never refers to a single "word": other Greek terms, such as *rhēma*, were used for that. The meanings depend on the philosophical tradition. The Platonic notion of *logos* focuses on rational discourse; in Stoic thought, *logos* has more to do with the natural order of the universe. Middle Platonism, a thought system prevalent during the period when the New Testament was written, goes back to the Platonic idea of rational discourse, but some Middle Platonists did think of *logos* as the active force in the world.

This oversimplified summary provides a backdrop to the use of *logos* in the Septuagint [*The Septuagint in Hebrews, p. 252*]. The translators of the Hebrew Scriptures sometimes used *logos* as a translation for the Hebrew word *dābār* (word). For example, *logos* is used to translate *dābār* in the context of creation, where God's word was the impetus for creation (Ps 33:6; cf. "and God said" ten times in Gen 1). *Logos* is also used alongside "Wisdom" (Gk. *sophia*) in wisdom literature and the work of Hellenistic Jewish philosophers, such as Philo [*Philo, Neoplatonism, and Hebrews, p. 245*]. A simple example of how this works can be seen in the Wisdom of Solomon 9:1-2:

> O God of my ancestors and Lord of mercy,
>   who have made all things by your *word*
> and by your wisdom have formed humankind
>   to have dominion over the creatures you have made.
>   (emph. added)

Many of Philo's writings are philosophical (Middle Platonist) interpretations of the Pentateuch, in which *logos* features prominently. Like other Middle Platonists, Philo combined Platonic and Stoic notions of *logos*, understanding *logos* to contain both metaphorical and real aspects of the divine.

Although the New Testament does not reflect knowledge of Philo, we should read it with Philo's texts in mind. When we read the prologue to the Gospel of John or the opening verses of Hebrews, we cannot think of *Logos* as only "word" in its most simplistic aspect. We must have in

Essays 243

mind the various thought systems around *logos* that circulated in the ancient world.

THE PARTING OF THE WAYS The "parting of the ways" is a model that scholars have created to understand the development of what we now call Christianity and Judaism, both together and separately, in the first century through the fourth century CE. It is commonly understood that both religions grew out of religious practices of Jews in the land of Israel and the Diaspora when the Jerusalem temple was still standing. However, the destruction of the temple in 70 CE ended the sacrificial system and eventually led to a new form of Judaism, based in rabbinic commentary on the Torah. During this same period, Jesus followers, many also Jews, were developing their own set of texts and practices while also attracting non-Jews to their communities. At a certain point, according to the model, two distinct branches were formed and parted ways. What scholars try to explain is when, where, why, and how this happened.

Dating the separation may seem straightforward, but complications quickly arise. Did Christianity start with Jesus? With Paul? After the destruction of the temple? After the Bar Kochba Revolt in 135 CE, when Jews rebelled against the Romans founding their pagan city Aelia Capitolina on the ruins of Jerusalem, putting an altar to Jupiter over the ruins of the temple, and expelling Jews from the city? Or when Constantine legitimized Christianity in 313 CE?

Did the parting occur in Judea among the earliest Jesus followers? That may depend on how we read the Gospel according to John. Are "the Jews" in that gospel a group of Jews not following Jesus during his earthly ministry, or Jews completely distinct from the gospel writer's community? Perhaps the parting occurred in Antioch, where the word "Christian" first appears in Scripture (Acts 11:26). But was this term meant to signify Greeks who were Christ followers, a subset within the larger group of Jewish Jesus followers? Or all Christ followers? Or a different group of folks only loosely connected to the original group in Jerusalem and Judea? Did the parting occur in Asia Minor and Greece as Paul was evangelizing the Gentiles and then eventually spread throughout the Hellenized world? Was Paul aiming to create a new religious movement, or was he attempting to make space for Gentiles *within* first-century Jewish practice? Is the Letter to the Hebrews evidence of a split occurring elsewhere (perhaps at Rome) because of a different set of concerns, such as the destruction of the Jerusalem temple?

The aftereffects of the temple's destruction and accompanying violence to Jews in Judea looms large in this discussion. Perhaps the "parting of the ways" was motivated by external sources that affected Jews, causing them to splinter even more than what they might have already been (Goodman: 122), rather than by internal motives within splinter groups, such as Jesus followers themselves.

Both Christianity and Rabbinic Judaism arose out of a complicated world. Honoring our forebears requires us to pay attention to the world in which they lived while navigating on their terms, not ours. If either

244   Essays

religion is "taken to be meaningful only in some sort of direct relationship with what it became in its later classical forms, . . . then some aspects of the ancient evidence will be privileged over others" (Kraft 2007: 90). This means that if *modern* categories and assumptions about who is Jewish or who is Christian and when they diverged from one another are used, then the ancient practices and beliefs of these individuals and groups that are found in a wide range of sources will be missed because they aren't considered relevant.

In this essay, we have raised many questions and provided few answers. With some certainty, we can say that by the mid-fourth century, the ways had largely parted (Kraft 2007: 87). Even then, we should not conclude that the process was unilinear or universal or that the break was complete by the mid-fourth century. John Chrysostom (*Discourses against Judaizing Christians*, passim) appeals to his community in Antioch of Syria near the end of the fourth century to quit attending the synagogue and observing Jewish festivals (van der Horst). But how, why, and where are such questions still under discussion? The literature on the "parting of the ways" is vast. For an excellent introduction to the topic and many recent articles, see *The Ways That Never Parted*, edited by Adam Becker and Annette Yoshiko Reed.

PERFECTION IN GRECO-ROMAN AND JEWISH THOUGHT Behind the use of the term *perfect* and related words in Hebrews are several thought worlds that use the term in a variety of ways. Hebrews can serve as a lens to view these worlds. According to Aristotle, perfection is the "aggregate from which no component part is absent" (*Metaphysics* 4.16.1021b; quoted in Peterson: 21). The root of "to perfect" in Greek is *tel-*, whose basic meaning is "to complete" or "fulfill." So at its root, the group of words we translate as "perfect" or "perfection" suggest a finished state, a goal having been met. According to L. Johnson, the term was used in Greek philosophical discourse to describe those who completed the full set of initiation rituals into mystery religions (17). But since the term had such a range of meanings in Greek thought, scholars claim that the meaning can be determined only within its specific context. When an author uses it in conjunction with plants, animals, or even humans having reached "perfection," the author may be saying that they reached maturity: they have developed into what they were supposed to become.

The Septuagint (LXX) uses the term in a distinctive way to describe the consecration of priests. The phrase in Exodus 29:9 is to "fill [or perfect] the hands" (NETS: "validate"). The implication in using this word is that the priest is now as priestly as he can get. He has reached the full priestly status and is therefore qualified to be the priest. But that is not the only meaning in the LXX. It occurs in claiming the completion of the wall in Jerusalem (2 Esd 16:15-16 LXX = Neh 6:15-16), and in recounting the death of the martyrs in 4 Maccabees 7:13-15 (Thompson 2008: 66). The author of Hebrews may have had these meanings in mind.

One other ancient Jewish source contributes to our understanding of this word. Philo uses it in a moral sense to describe the ultimate human

Essays

ideal, Moses, who was full of virtue. Philo also believed that one's devotion to God can lead to perfection in a salvific way. Both meanings indicate that attaining an ideal status has larger-than-life benefits. But since Philo uses the term over four hundred times, we should be cautious about any generalization. Still, for Philo, the "goal of human existence . . . is to rise above the imperfection of this world to the immediate access to God" (Thompson 2008: 66; Philo, *Allegorical Interpretation* 3.44–45).

For many modern people, "perfection" is a state of unmatched excellence in one's morality. Even though, according to the *Oxford English Dictionary*, this meaning did not arise until the medieval period, it is now the meaning most of us attach to the word.

PHILO, NEOPLATONISM, AND HEBREWS Many of Philo's writings from the first century CE are philosophical interpretations of the Pentateuch. Philo's philosophical approach is called either Neoplatonism or Middle Platonism, which understood the material, perceptible world to always be changing and therefore fall short of the ideal. God, on the other hand, never changes. Philo considered God to be the one "transcendent deity" (Thompson 2011b: 35). God remains on a separate level of reality, unattainable by humans. Middle Platonism bridged the gap between the material world of humans and the transcendent world of God (2011b: 34). Philo uses *logos* to mean "thought," "word," "speech," or "reasoning" to bridge the gap between humans and the unknowable God (Thompson 2008: 25). "The *logos* of God" is the instrument by which the world was created (*On the Cherubim* 127) and the way in which each human is connected to God (*On the Creation of the World* 146).

Philo's comments about the "pattern of the tent" that Moses saw while on Mount Sinai (Exod 25:40) is a good example of his Neoplatonism at work. In *Allegorical Interpretation* 3, Philo praises Moses, who was eager to see God not through created works, but "in thee thyself, the true God" (3.101). Philo says God called Moses to the mountain so that Moses "might receive an idea of the appearance of God from the Creator himself" (3.102). Regarding the tabernacle, Moses "fashioned the archetypal forms" given to him by God when he was on the mountain. At this point Philo quotes Exodus 25:40 in exactly the same way as the author of Hebrews: "Thou shalt make everything according to the example which was shown thee in the Mount" (see Heb 8:5). In other words, Moses (and by extension Neoplatonism) is the bridge between the unknowable and ordinary humans.

In *Allegorical Interpretation* 3 and in other texts in which Philo quotes Exodus 25:40, Philo's goal is to praise Moses. Neoplatonism is the unremarkable accepted method by which Philo interprets the biblical message. Moses is the focus of the commentary. In other words, Philo was not doing anything strange by using Neoplatonism: it was the accepted hermeneutical method.

PRISCILLA AS AUTHOR Although most modern commentators do not spend much time speculating about the authorship of Hebrews, a lively

246 Essays

debate about this mystery has percolated for millennia. The text itself does not reveal its authorship. Its goals are to emphasize Jesus as priest, God's continuing revelation through Scripture, and faithfulness as a hallmark of Christian living (Kittredge: 450). Yet as early as the late second century, Hebrews was included in $\mathfrak{P}^{46}$, a papyrus manuscript of Paul's letters. Because the scribe(s) who compiled the manuscript arranged the texts in order by length, Hebrews appears between Romans and 1 Corinthians, with no indication that it was written by anyone other than Paul. We will probably never know whether that placement was a proactive move by the scribe to promote Paul as author or whether the scribe(s) simply assumed that Paul wrote Hebrews.

However, the idea that Paul wrote Hebrews did not go unchallenged. Tertullian, a theologian at Carthage, North Africa, in the second and third centuries, thought that Barnabas, one of Paul's traveling companions, might be the author. Origen, a third-century biblical scholar and Christian philosopher at Alexandria, Egypt, thought it impossible to know. Eusebius, a church historian of the third and fourth centuries who recorded Origen's comments about the text, countered with his own proposal: Luke. By the early Middle Ages, through the quiet assent of both Augustine and Jerome, Pauline authorship was accepted, even though issues of style, language, and content raised some doubts.

During the Reformation, new ideas began to surface. Martin Luther, for example, suggested that Apollos, a Jewish man converted by Aquila and Priscilla (Acts 18:24-28) at Ephesus, wrote Hebrews. Apollos was from Alexandria, which could explain the language and style of Hebrews being similar to the writings of Philo of Alexandria [Philo, Neoplatonism, and Hebrews, p. 245]. In Acts, Apollos is described as "eloquent" and (after being taught by Priscilla and Aquila) as "showing by the scriptures that the Messiah is Jesus" (18:24, 28), a strategy assumed by the author of Hebrews as well. Luther's ideas were taken up by several scholars in the early to mid-twentieth century. However, recent commentators (e.g., Attridge: 5; C. Koester 2001: 46; L. Johnson: 44; Thompson 2008: 4–6) either reject that idea or remain agnostic because we know so little about Apollos and therefore can only speculate about the likelihood of Apollos's authorship.

At the turn of the twentieth century, Adolf von Harnack, a German scholar of early Christianity, proposed a new idea, that Priscilla wrote Hebrews; she, along with her husband, Aquila, was a companion of Paul. In 1900 this idea was revolutionary. Harnack's basic research question was, Why would the author of Hebrews not be named? Harnack assumed that the author was in the "second generation" of apostles, but also within Paul's circle of close associates (Timothy is mentioned by name in Heb 13:23). Harnack reviewed the list of possibilities and concluded that the only reason the author would be unnamed was *because* the author was a woman. Already by the late first century, women were not free to speak with authority in the early church, so any writing by a woman would need to be done anonymously. In the case of Hebrews, Harnack believed that the person writing had been a close companion to Paul and could speak

Essays 247

on behalf of a close group of associates. The author was also well educated and connected with Rome (13:24).

The only known female candidate who qualifies is Priscilla.

To justify his case, Harnack looked closely at the personal pronouns used by the author: *I*, *you*, and *we*. He determined that the "we" statements fall into two categories: those indicating a close connection between the author and the readers (see 5:11–6:12), and those signifying that the author speaks for more than just self. That is, the author speaks for herself and her closest companions (see esp. 13:18-23). Harnack tackled the use of a masculine self-referential participle in 11:32 (*And what more should I say? For time would fail me to tell* . . . , where the author uses a participle with a masculine [= neuter] ending), claiming that the "I" is really a "communicative we" (Harnack: 401), meaning "I and you." So the masculine participle does not indicate a male author but rather is a more generic, literary way of saying "we/us": *What more should we say? For time would fail us to tell* . . . Harnack's theory was not popular: most think the use of the male participle provides strong evidence that the author of Hebrews was a man. But Harnack argued that the author, knowing that her authorship would be frowned upon because she was a woman, wrote an anonymous text.

In his concluding arguments, Harnack provided manuscript evidence that Priscilla's name was erased by later scribes in some manuscripts of other texts, such as the Acts of the Apostles. The author anticipated erasures like this by writing an anonymous letter.

Harnack was a towering giant in biblical studies in the early twentieth century. His scholarly output was enormous. Whatever he wrote was published and commented on. Even today, several of his books and articles are seminal reading. Such is the case with his relatively brief article on Priscilla. Not surprisingly, that article has been used and reexamined since the late 1960s as scholars attempt to recover women leaders in early Christianity. Ruth Hoppin, a freelance author who has read extensively about Priscilla and early Christianity, has published several works on Priscilla as the author of Hebrews (1997; 2004).

Hoppin follows Harnack's premise that Hebrews is anonymous *because* it was written by a woman. She adds several dimensions to Harnack's discussion. First, she contributes additional evidence to his original discussion regarding the use of the male participle in Hebrews 11:32. She notes that women's names have been changed in the manuscript history of two other texts: Romans 16:7 and Colossians 4:15. Both of those texts originally used female names, Junia and Nympha, respectively; but manuscript copyists changed them to the male names Junias and Nymphas. This manuscript evidence was not available to Harnack when he wrote his article.

Second, Hoppin conjectures that Priscilla, because of her status as an "intellectual aristocrat" from Rome (1997: 105) and her marriage to a Jewish man, had an unusual number of acquaintances that allowed her to develop ideas from Philo and other Jews, such as the Essenes. According to Hoppin, the result of these possible conversations was a letter that

248 Essays

shares themes—such as angels, the Day of Atonement, the new covenant, and the notion of a priestly messiah—with the Dead Sea Scrolls, and has a philosophical approach similar to that of Philo. Although others have also noted these similarities, Hoppin believes Priscilla was in the right place at the right time (primarily Rome and Ephesus) to connect with people who were generating or collecting ideas.

Hoppin further proposes that the text reflects a "feminine style and outlook" (1997: 33). Compassion, sympathy, empathy, emphasis on parental discipline, and education are features of the text that, for Hoppin, hint at a feminine mind. Even the author's style, which other commentators have suggested indicates a well-trained rhetorician, is "dainty" (29), and the entire text is full of "gentle tact and diplomacy" (32). The author of Hebrews also identifies with women, notable in the numerous references to women in Hebrews 11, the catalog of faithful heroes. In addition to the named women (Sarah and Rahab), Hoppin examines several statements in 11:32-35 that probably refer to episodes in the Jewish Scriptures involving women. For example, the *women who received their dead by resurrection* in 11:35 are allusions to the widow of Zarephath (1 Kings 17:8-24) and the Shunammite woman (2 Kings 4:18-37). Hoppin states, "If a man were telling this story, it would be reasonable to expect" that the focus would be on Elijah and Elisha (1997: 35), the prophets who brought their sons back to life. Instead, Hebrews features (unnamed) women. Hoppin compares this reference to Sirach 48:4-5, 12-13, which specifically mention Elijah and Elisha without mentioning the mothers of the sons.

Another example comes in Hebrews 11:34 with the phrase *put foreign armies to flight*. Following James Rendel Harris (169–74), Hoppin believes Judith is the referent (1997: 39). The statement in 11:34, *escaped the edge of the sword*, is similar to the statement in Esther 4:11 that describes the peril faced by anyone who goes to King Artaxerxes unbidden.

Hoppin's extended discussion about the women of Hebrews 11 allows modern readers to experience the text more fully. Teasing out the unnamed women brings life and nuance to the text that we might miss. It is the faith of the named *and* the unnamed that comprises the *cloud of witnesses*. Hoppin's point of view as a woman allows modern readers of Hebrews, perhaps especially female readers, to find complexity and nuance in the text and to connect more fully with it.

Hoppin's interests arose during a period in the late twentieth century when uncovering women's history became an importantly scholarly endeavor. There was a deep desire to know what role women played in early Christianity and what women's lives were like. However, women scholars themselves began to question what can be known and how we know what we know, especially when limited evidence is available. This is especially true in determining the gender of an author based on internal characteristics of a text when we know so little about female authors in antiquity and their outlook (Kittredge: 450; Kraemer 1991: 233). As Ross Kraemer notes, the methodological problems are enormous. For proof, we need only examine some modern examples, such as Phyllis Schlafly, who campaigned against the Equal Rights Amendment in the 1970s and promoted

Essays 249

traditional roles for women. Kraemer asks, "Two-thousand years from now, will some scholars of late twentieth-century American culture argue that Schlafly must have been a man writing under a woman's name, because no women would write such things?" (1991: 233).

Already in the third century, Origen admitted that "God only knows" who wrote Hebrews. His sentiment is affirmed by Cynthia Briggs Kittredge: "The author does not emphasize her or his identity but rather stresses God's continuing speech in scripture, the perfection made possible through Jesus in human life, and the undergirding of hope with faith in God" (450). Regardless of who wrote Hebrews, we know that God is still speaking.

RHETORICAL HABITS OF THE AUTHOR Rhetoric is the study of how an author or orator crafts speech to persuade an audience. The author of Hebrews uses many of the classical principles of Greek rhetoric. These include arguments from example (e.g., 4:7-11; ch. 11); from comparison, known in ancient rhetoric as *synkrisis* (e.g., 3:1-6; ch. 8); and for exhortation (e.g., 6:1-12; ch. 13). *Synkrisis* was a heavily used rhetorical strategy in antiquity, taught to young people (all boys, of course) in school. It was used by rhetoricians to evaluate and compare "good with good, . . . bad with bad, . . . good with bad" (Thompson 2008: 13). Our author uses it most often when comparing Jesus with the prophets (1:1-3), angels (1:4–2:18), and Moses (3:1–4:13). Last, the author lays out a structured argument that appeals to the audience based on the author's knowledge or understanding of their situation. They are (or were) experiencing difficulties of various sorts and are flagging in their faith. A device like this creates connection between the homilist and the congregation, encouraging the congregation to stay involved in the message.

At times the author's rhetorical style also resembles early Jewish interpretation techniques found in the Dead Sea Scrolls. In addition to biblical manuscripts, the Dead Sea Scrolls contain early forms of midrash, a method of biblical interpretation. The three-letter Hebrew root *d-r-sh* means "to investigate" or "examine"; therefore, midrash is the explanation of a biblical text. A foundational assumption of midrash is that the Bible is a unified whole, and midrash uses one biblical passage to explain or illuminate another. This method of biblical interpretation was developed further in the rabbinic period, most notably in the Mishnah and Talmud, after the temple was destroyed in 70 CE. The rabbis developed a variety of exegetical strategies. Like the Greek rhetoricians, the rabbis used a technique called *qal waḥōmer*, an argument similar to *synkrisis*, meaning "If one thing is true, how much truer is this next thing." The New Testament contains many examples of *qal waḥōmer* (e.g., "how much more" in Matt 7:11; Rom 11:12, 24). Another strategy, *gezerah shawah*, or "similar laws, similar verdicts," uses verbal analogy to interpret passages. An example of this is how Hebrews 7:1-3 interprets Psalm 110 in light of the encounter between Melchizedek and Abraham in Genesis 14.

Several experts have noted early examples of midrash in Hebrews (e.g., Attridge: 104; L. Johnson: 126). Daniel Boyarin, a scholar of Rabbinic

Judaism, actually calls Hebrews an early midrash because "the new points and ideas that it evokes are produced entirely through the speaking of the verses themselves and their recontextualization" (2016: 15). Hebrews, according to Boyarin, is full of biblical verses strung together to make new meaning, the basic purpose of midrash. Boyarin discusses the various midrashic techniques in Hebrews 3–4, where our author uses Psalm 95 and Genesis 1 to understand the meaning of "rest" and "today." Essentially, though, our homilist uses biblical verses to interpret biblical verses and thereby to create a new meaning. This is plain and simple midrash, according to Boyarin (2016: 23).

Our author uses more than biblical interpretative rhetorical techniques. Good rhetoric also keeps the audience engaged through clever use of words and good style. Sometimes these devices work in the original language but are difficult to translate. One example that does make the translation shift is anaphora, the repetition of keywords, like *by faith* (ch. 11) and *rest* (ch. 4). Another example, difficult to convey in translation, is alliteration, the repetition of initial sounds. That device is used at the beginning of Hebrews, in 1:1: *polymerōs kai polytropōs palai ho theos lalēsas tois patrasin en tois prophētais.* Several words here begin with *p*. However, the alliteration is lost in the English translation: *Long ago God spoke to our ancestors in many and various ways by the prophets.*

Another element of style that the homilist uses is something called *inclusio*, a literary term that describes how an author places the same, or similar, words at the beginning and ending of sections of the text. Our homilist makes good use of this literary device; many uses of *inclusio* divide the text into smaller subunits. In fact, an *inclusio* defines the middle section (Thompson 2008: 14–15):

4:14-16	10:19-23
Since, then, we have a great high priest who has passed through the heavens, Jesus, the Son of God, let us hold fast to our confession. For we do not have a high priest who is unable to sympathize with our weaknesses, but we have one who in every respect has been tested as we are, yet without sin. Let us therefore approach the throne of grace with boldness, so that we may receive mercy and find grace to help in time of need.	*Therefore, my friends, since we have confidence to enter the sanctuary by the blood of Jesus, by the new and living way that he opened for us through the curtain (that is, through his flesh), and since we have a great priest over the house of God, let us approach with a true heart in full assurance of faith, with our hearts sprinkled clean from an evil conscience and our bodies washed with pure water. Let us hold fast to the confession of our hope without wavering, for he who has promised is faithful.*

The two groups of verses do not match exactly, but the language and the themes are the same. And together, they create the section of the text about Jesus, the high priest.

Essays

Since this commentary focuses mainly on content, we have limited our discussion of style and language to points where it is crucial to the overall understanding of the text. For a detailed discussion on other uses of good style, consult Craig Koester's commentary (2001: 94–95).

One last example of good rhetoric is excellent prose writing. The prose in Hebrews is often rhythmic, avoids monotony, and includes variety wherever possible. Variety is present not only in vocabulary, but also in sentence structure. Some sentences are long and complex. Some are artfully designed and polished. Some are short, pithy, and pointed. This variety of language play—including metaphors, parallelism, puns, antitheses, and other artistic forms of speech—indicates an ample literary education. Hebrews contains many words that are either unique or are used infrequently in the rest of the New Testament and other Christian texts (L. Johnson: 8). The large proportion of these rare words, compared to other New Testament texts, is another indication of the high educational level of the author. The author also uses different moods, celebrative poetic passages, serious logical arguments and warnings, creative interpretation, and a style that alternates between exposition and exhortation.

In sum, Hebrews kept the original listening audience of the homily, as well as generations of readers, engaged by a variety of interpretational techniques, good writing, and well-chosen words.

THE ROLE AND USE OF THE JEWISH SCRIPTURES BY EARLY CHRISTIANS The initial affirmation that God was truly speaking through the Hebrew Scriptures was challenged early in the history of Christianity. Marcion (ca. 150 CE) insisted that the god of the old covenant was violent and wrathful, a different god from the one revealed in Jesus Christ. He discarded the Hebrew Scriptures and Jewish-Christian writings that depended on the Old Testament. He also edited some New Testament writings to purge their references to the Jewish god. He preferred the Gospel of Luke and the writings of Paul, both of which he edited to remove signs of their dependence on the Old Testament. There is no record of whether he saw or knew of the Letter to the Hebrews, but if he had, he presumably would have found Hebrews totally unacceptable.

The impulse to discard the Old Testament or downplay its importance continues in the church today. One manifestation of this tendency was the Jesus Only movement in the United States in the 1960s. Another more academic example in our century is found in German New Testament scholarship during World War II, when everything Jewish was denigrated and supposedly purged from German culture. Old Testament connections were ignored or denied, and "Christian" connections with historical pagan religions were embraced.

Many churches that claim the New Testament as their rule of faith and practice tend to neglect the role and force of the Old Testament in their teaching. Hebrews is a superb reminder that God is speaking through the Old Testament and that the message of God's faithfulness runs through all of Scripture, even when the medium of its expression takes a new form.

252 Essays

Because the author of Hebrews assumes not only the validity of the Jewish Scriptures, but also their revelatory nature, these Scriptures play a central role throughout the text. From the opening catena of texts in 1:5-14 and through the long list of the faithful cloud of witnesses in Hebrews 11, we are confronted with the voice of God in Scripture. Psalm 110 and Jeremiah 31 are foundational to the message. George Guthrie says it well:

> More than any other NT book, Hebrews, from beginning to end, *preaches* the OT. The author's explanations of the text serve ultimately to communicate a forceful message aimed at convincing the hearers/readers to respond by persevering [in] following Christ and standing with his church. [Its] Christology vies for a christocentric life. [Its] hortatory material has one aim: to present a resolute call to endurance and holy living. This is the task . . . in taking up the OT, . . . [carried] out with rhetorical power and artistry. (923, emph. in the original)

Let the preacher preach!

THE SEPTUAGINT IN HEBREWS The Septuagint is the Greek version of the Hebrew Bible; the beginning of the translation effort dates to the third century BCE in Egypt. Technically, the word Septuagint and its Roman numeral abbreviation, LXX (70), refer only to the Greek translation of the Pentateuch, the first five books of the Hebrew Scriptures. Other books were translated much later. The term Septuagint derives from a document, the Letter of Aristeas, which gives a story of how and why the translation efforts of the Pentateuch began. The letter itself is hard to date; it probably originated in the second century BCE, much later than the translation of the LXX.

It is challenging to distinguish between the straightforward documentary and the fantastic legend incorporated in the Letter of Aristeas. According to this account, King Ptolemy II (285–246 BCE) commissioned the librarian of the famous library in Alexandria, Egypt, to gather all known writings of the world. When the librarian told the king about Judean books of law, which had to be translated into Greek, the king commissioned seventy Jewish elders (other accounts say seventy-two) to translate it. Miraculously, even though they were all working separately (two on each portion, in later tradition), all produced the same translation (for the text, translation, and further discussion of the letter, see White and Keddie: 31–172).

The Septuagint is often similar to the Hebrew, or Masoretic Text, translated in our modern Bibles. However, from time to time, the texts differ: both Job and Jeremiah are about one-eighth *shorter* in the Septuagint than they are in the Hebrew; Daniel and Esther are much *longer* in Greek than in Hebrew; the chapters in Jeremiah are also in a different order in Greek than they are in Hebrew.

The large cache of biblical (Hebrew and Aramaic) manuscripts discovered among the Dead Sea Scrolls has confirmed that the translators of the

Essays

253

Septuagint had access to Hebrew manuscripts that predated those used for the Masoretic Text. The most important and most complete manuscripts of the Septuagint are from full Bibles produced by Christians in the fourth and fifth centuries CE, most notably Codex Sinaiticus, all of which can be viewed online.

Throughout this commentary we stress the importance of the Septuagint for the writers and compilers of the New Testament. Modern English Bibles obscure the variety of textual forms available to the followers of Jesus in the earliest centuries of the Common Era. For an accessible book-length discussion, see Timothy Law's *When God Spoke Greek: The Septuagint and the Making of the Christian Bible*. For a recent English translation of the LXX, see Albert Pietersma and Benjamin Wright.

The Septuagint was used extensively by ancient Jews living outside the land of Israel, in Egypt, Asia Minor, and other places around the Mediterranean. Paul, the gospel writers, the author of Hebrews, and other New Testament authors used this ancient translation. The sheer volume of the quotations in Hebrews is evidence that the author held these Scriptures in the highest regard. Depending on how the citations are counted, our homilist quotes between twenty-nine and forty specific scriptural sources and alludes to several others. The citations are not just passing references. For example, the quotation of Jeremiah 31:31-34 (38:31-34 LXX) is one of the longest quotations of biblical material in the New Testament. It is fair to say that without the Scriptures, Hebrews would not exist. The importance of the Scriptures in Hebrews cannot be overstated.

When quoting scriptural material, our author makes sole use of the Greek (Septuagint [LXX]) rather than the Hebrew text. Why is this important, and how does it inform our understanding of Hebrews and its earliest readers? The answer is twofold: by looking at which texts the author used and how the author used them, we can understand something about the author and the congregation and their relationship with the Scriptures. We can get a better understanding of the variety of texts and translations used in antiquity and how those texts and translations, along with the flow of the manuscripts that contained the texts, influenced the thinking of both writers and readers.

Our author did not have a Bible that could be opened and consulted at will. In fact, our author was not able to consult the Scriptures in our modern "codex," or book, form. Our author apparently had access to scrolls that needed to be unrolled every time a text was consulted. Scrolls, especially those of larger texts like Jeremiah, were bulky, difficult to transport and use, and apparently kept in the synagogue (cf. Luke 4:17; Acts 13:15). The convenient features of a codex—an index, page numbers, Eusebian canon tables developed in the fourth century, and chapter or verse numbers not developed until the early modern period—were not available to our author (or any other NT writer). Through a detailed analysis of the textual form of the biblical citations in Hebrews, Martin Karrer has suggested that our author probably had access to scrolls of Psalms, Jeremiah, Genesis, Exodus, and Deuteronomy. For other texts, the author probably

254   Essays

relied on memory, or possibly small collections of quotations. Surprisingly, despite the author's deep reliance on themes in Leviticus, especially chapter 16, the author of Hebrews never directly quotes from it (Karrer: 342–43). This suggests that the quotations we do find in Hebrews reveal the source material to which our author had access.

Almost certainly, our homilist did not know the Hebrew language. Even if our author had some facility with it, the only sources our author had available were those of the LXX. A simple example of this occurs in Hebrews 11:21, where our author quotes the LXX version of Genesis 47:31: *By faith Jacob, when dying, blessed each of the sons of Joseph, "bowing in worship over the top of his staff."* The Masoretic Text of this same passage in Genesis reads, "Then Israel [Jacob] bowed himself on the head of his bed" (Karrer: 338). Interestingly, "bed" and "staff" have the same three-letter root in Hebrew. The LXX translators chose staff instead of bed, whether by mistake or design. Our author does not attempt to "correct" a possible mistranslation. (As an aside, the word "staff/scepter" also appears in Psalm 110:2, a psalm our author uses extensively. Attridge discusses the possibility that our author understood, like some other early commentators, that the "LXX translation [of Gen 47:31] reflects a messianic interpretation of the OT text in the light of the 'staff' prophecy of Num 24:17 or the 'scepter' of Ps 110:2" [336n46]. Attridge himself disregards this notion as "fanciful" and instead claims that our author "understood that Jacob in his last hours did indeed 'worship'" God, but did so as "an expression of faith [(Heb) 13:15]" [336], not connected to any messianic hope expressed in Psalm 110. In other words, although the word "staff" appears in Genesis 47:31 and Psalm 110:2, our author did not make a clear interpretive connection between the two. In any case, our author clearly follows the Greek translation to speak about the faith of Jacob in chapter 11.)

Another example is Psalm 110. The LXX translation of the Hebrew for Psalm 110:1 is precise (*kyrios* for Adonai, both meaning "lord"). We would not be able to know which language our author was using from the quotation of this verse. But for the study of Hebrews, much more interesting is our author's unique use of 110:4, "You are a priest forever according to the order of Melchizedek," in Hebrews 7:17.

It is possible that the original Hebrew of Psalm 110:4 did not refer to the *person* Melchizedek. Perhaps the LXX translators, confused about the meaning of the Hebrew, transliterated the Hebrew word and assumed it was the name Melchizedek. No other New Testament author refers directly to Psalm 110:4, so we cannot compare how other authors interpreted the text. Our author was clearly using the Greek text of Psalm 110, traditionally regarded as a royal psalm and likely composed for a coronation (cf. Ps 2). The LXX translators may have overinterpreted the meaning of the compound Hebrew word "melchizedek." The three-letter Hebrew root *m-l-k* (king) in the first part of the name, when combined with its second part, the Hebrew *zedek* (rightful or righteousness), can be the name Melchizedek (especially if one is reading this alongside Gen 14). But it can also be translated "a rightful king by my edict" (NRSV mg.; cf. NJPS) or "a king of righteousness" (Philo, *Allegorical Interpretation*

Essays 255

3.79–82). Confusion about the meaning of the Hebrew led the Jewish Publication Society to include the name Melchizedek only in the margin of its translation of 110:4 (NJPS): "You are a priest forever, a rightful king by My decree."

In addition, the LXX phrase "according to the order" is not a clear translation of the Hebrew, which depends on the context. Levine and Brettler note that, in Psalm 110:4, the most likely meaning of the introductory Hebrew phrase is "because of" or "with regard to" (2020: 162–63). The word/concept *order* is not in the Hebrew text. By using it, the LXX translators are trying to smooth out and interpret a difficult Hebrew text.

Similar textual problems occur in Psalm 110:3 (MT), which Hebrews does not use, but which should give us pause regarding the accuracy of one translation over another. Translators of this verse have offered their educated guesses for a translation, but no one is certain what the translation should be (Levine and Brettler 2020: 159–60). What we can say with some certainty is that without the LXX translation, our author would probably not have connected the term "Melchizedek" of Psalm 110:4 to the story of Abraham and Melchizedek in Genesis 14.

A third example occurs when we examine our author's connection between Psalm 95 and Genesis 2:2 in developing the theological concept of rest. Without the LXX, this concept would not be present in Hebrews (Law: 112). Our pastor developed it by noticing that two passages, Psalm 95 and Genesis 2:2, share the Greek word *katapausis* (rest). Using a Jewish interpretational technique that explains one passage in light of another, our author builds the theological concept of rest. Our author—if using the Hebrew Masoretic Text, where the words for the concept of rest differ— would have been unable to create the connection between the texts, and the biblical basis for the concept would have been missing. Only by using the LXX was our homilist able to allow the Genesis text to inform the reading of Psalm 95.

Although much of the LXX and Masoretic Text share a close correspondence, this is not true for Jeremiah. The LXX version is about onesixth shorter than the Masoretic Text and is ordered differently from the Masoretic Text at various points. When we say that Hebrews 8:8-12 quotes Jeremiah 31:31-34, we are referring to the location in Masoretic Text. The same important passage occurs at 38:31-34 LXX. The Hebrew text of Jeremiah used for modern English Bibles is from a later edition than that used for the LXX translation to which our author had access. We know this because of the Dead Sea Scroll manuscripts of Jeremiah discovered at Qumran *[Jewish Literature in Antiquity, p. 238]*. From them, scholars have determined that the Hebrew text of Jeremiah used by the LXX translators is older than the Hebrew text of Jeremiah used for modern translations. At some point, the Hebrew text was expanded by later editors and scribes, whereas the text of the LXX manuscripts stayed roughly the same. Our author was certainly working with a Jeremiah text that differed from the one with which modern Bible readers are familiar.

In the following example, manuscript discoveries of Deuteronomy in the mid-twentieth century demonstrate that the LXX is older than the

256 Essays

Masoretic Text we are accustomed to reading in English translation. The LXX therefore witnesses to older versions of the Scriptures themselves. Look at the difference between the LXX and the Masoretic Text of Deuteronomy 32:43, which our author quotes in Hebrews 1:6 (*Let all God's angels worship him*). Here are English translations of the entire verse of Deuteronomy 32:43 in both the LXX and Masoretic Text:

Deuteronomy 32:43 according to the LXX in NETS (slightly modified by Bucher)	Deuteronomy 32:43 according to the MT in KJV	Deuteronomy 32:43 according to the MT and LXX in NRSV
Be glad, O heavens, with him, let all the sons of God fall down and worship him. Be glad, O nations, with his people, and let all the angels of God prevail for him. For he will avenge the blood of his sons and take revenge and repay the enemies with a sentence, And he will repay those who hate, and the Lord shall cleanse the land of his people.	Rejoice, O ye nations, with his people: For he will avenge the blood of his servants, And will render vengeance to his adversaries, And will be merciful unto his land, and to his people.	Praise, O heavens, his people, worship him, all you gods! For he will avenge the blood of his children, and take vengeance on his adversaries; he will repay those who hate him, and cleanse the land for his people.

The author of Hebrews does not quote the text word for word but combines the second and fourth lines of the LXX by saying *Let all God's angels worship him* to indicate that the relationship of the angels to the Son is one of service and worship.

English readers who use Bibles that translate Deuteronomy directly from the Masoretic Text could find Hebrews' use of the LXX confusing. In addition, different translations have different readings. In some older translations, such as the King James Version, we find the translation in the middle column of the chart.

The KJV translators worked with a Hebrew text that differs from the Greek text known to our author. The KJV reads, "Rejoice, O ye nations, with his people: For he will avenge the blood of his servants." Reading from the LXX, our author has "Worship him, all you gods/angels." We can see other similar differences when looking at the two translations side by side.

English versions depend on the work of archaeologists, textual critics, philologists, and translators! In the early seventeenth century, the KJV translators used a Hebrew text derived from a single manuscript of the Masoretic Text that is usually dated to around 1000 CE. This all changed when biblical manuscripts were discovered among the Dead Sea Scrolls at Qumran, one of which was a manuscript of Deuteronomy, probably

Essays

written in the first century CE, or maybe even earlier. They also noticed that the Hebrew of Deuteronomy was more similar to the LXX translation than it was to the later Masoretic Text! In other words, the LXX witnesses to an earlier Hebrew text that had been lost until the discovery of the Dead Sea Scrolls. Later, when the New Revised Standard Version was commissioned, the translators emended the Deuteronomy text to include new manuscript evidence from the Dead Sea Scrolls (corroborated by ancient Greek manuscripts). So the NRSV (and more recent NRSVue) incorporates the second line of text from the LXX and the Qumran scrolls. The resulting reading appears in the third column of the chart.

This is an excellent example of how the LXX can serve as a corrective for later copies of the ancient biblical text.

SUPERSESSIONIST AND ANTI-JEWISH INTERPRETATIONS OF HEBREWS The recent work of Pamela Eisenbaum (see esp. 2005) and Boyarin (2016) suggests that Hebrews was written at a moment when the author was attempting to work out a new way of living within first-century Judaism. This new pattern needed to be informed by the experience of Jesus and the absence of the sacrificial system set up in Leviticus and practiced until 70 CE at the temple in Jerusalem. All this was well before there was a "parting of the ways" between what became known as Judaism and what became known as Christianity (see also the Introduction, "Names, Categories, and Definitions"; and the essay *The Parting of the Ways, p. 243*).

The Hebrews text offers a "replacement theology" of sacrifice: the sacrificial system of Leviticus is replaced with a once-for-all system based on the sacrifice that Jesus made on the cross. The author of Hebrews uses the language and the sacrificial framework of Leviticus and employs Psalm 110 to assign to Jesus the priesthood according to the order of Melchizedek. For the author of Hebrews, this is the "new covenant" of Jeremiah 31, prophesied by the prophet shortly before or during the Babylonian exile. The new covenant replaces the animal sacrifices with the sacrifice of Jesus, who is now both the sacrificer (the priest) and the sacrifice. The text invites its readers to participate in this new system by following Jesus and living faithful, sacrificial lives themselves.

Neither Eisenbaum nor Boyarin was the first to suggest that our homilist was preaching from within first-century Judaism. C. Koester discusses two mid-twentieth-century German biblical scholars, Ernst Käsemann and Otto Michel, who placed Hebrews firmly within the "Hellenistic synagogue" (2016: 308) and were convinced that the text is not anti-Jewish at all. As important, they sought to find ways to have Hebrews speak to the difficult circumstances in Nazi Germany (1933–45). Both were members of the Confessing Church, a movement that opposed Nazi-sponsored attempts to unify all Protestant churches into a single government-controlled denomination. Michel, a former member of the Nazi Party who had come to understand the error of his ways, interpreted Hebrews as a "call for the church to hold firmly to the Word of God" (C. Koester 2016: 305). Käsemann, author of *The Wandering People of God*, a

258 Essays

study of Hebrews, drafted the book in a Gestapo prison. Echoing Michel's focus, he wrote this 1939 book for the "express purpose of speaking to the Confessing Church" so it could remain firm in its opposition to the Nazis (C. Koester 2016: 307).

Käsemann and Michel operated during a terrible time in history. They both attempted to resist prevalent assumptions about Christianity and Judaism, some of which we can see in James Moffatt and Alexander Balmain Bruce, who were active during a time when "the sense that both nature and religion were products of historical development" (C. Koester 2016: 301). The idea that religion naturally developed from the primitive to the more sophisticated allowed (mostly Christian) scholars of religion to create a narrative that relegated Judaism (along with every other pre-Christian religious tradition) to the "primitive" category and saw Christianity as the most developed and therefore perfect religion. This mindset influenced both Moffatt's and Bruce's work with Hebrews. Bruce's introduction provides some examples:

- Bruce claims that the author of Hebrews "regards Christianity as the *perfect*, and therefore the *final*, religion" (15, emph. in the original).

- Bruce states that the author of Hebrews considers Christianity "the religion of *free, unrestricted access to God*; the religion of a new, everlasting covenant, under which sin is completely extinguished, and can act no longer as a separating influence" (15, emph. in the original).

Our author of Hebrews does not use categories like "Christian" or "Jew." For Bruce to do so in explaining Hebrews is not only anachronistic but also misleading and, in this case, anti-Jewish. C. Koester concludes by remarking that each of the commentaries he studied "engages the book seriously, but that engagement is guided by a particular point of view" (2016: 312).

In this commentary we have tried to deal with the alleged supersessionist approach of the author by reading it within a context of what we see as deep connections with and appreciation for Judaism and its Scriptures. We state firmly that the text does *not* reject Judaism outright. Rather, it advocates for a new *covenant* that supersedes the old covenant *within* Judaism (see comments on ch. 8, esp. 8:13). We have also tried to avoid categories that those in the first century would probably not have used (such as "Christian"). Thus we have tried to avoid falling into an anti-Jewish interpretation by generalizing concepts, such as sacrifice, instead of dealing with the specifics of sacrifice within Hebrews. In doing so, we hope to have steered clear of formulating a supersessionist reading of the entire religion of Judaism, not just the facets under discussion in Hebrews.

But this approach is probably still too apologetic. Post-Holocaust Christian theology and biblical scholarship have attempted to be more self-critical and self-aware of the assumptions and worldview we bring to our readings, with varying degrees of success. We must remain faithful in our continued attempts to understand the Scriptures. Texts like Hebrews may produce discomfort, especially when we realize that the discomfort derives not just from our own unexamined assumptions, but also from the

Essays

text's own tendencies. Several scholars, both Christian and Jew, argue that despite its absolute dependence on and reverence for the Jewish Scriptures, and despite its utter lack of criticism of Judaism as a religion, Hebrews remains a supersessionist text (Williamson: 267–71; Levine and Brettler 2020: 171–77).

According to Hebrews, the sacrificial system set up in Leviticus is inferior. It has been replaced by the better, once-for-all sacrifice of Jesus and by Jesus. Jesus is the better high priest. He is sitting at God's right hand and lives forever. He is perfect. The mortal high priest is none of these things. Throughout the text, the author of Hebrews reminds the audience to continue their faithful living while holding these truths about the "new covenant." Levine and Brettler suggest that "Hebrews colonizes the Jewish tradition—taking from it all material it feels is usable and repackaging the tradition in a way its own adherents would not have recognized" (2020: 175). Eisenbaum, who has made excellent observations regarding the possible social-historical (Jewish) context of the author of Hebrews, states that Hebrews makes a supersessionist argument that cannot be neglected or smoothed over (see Eisenbaum 2017: 460–62).

Practicing Christians who claim exegetical integrity must acknowledge both the biases we bring to the text and the biases in the text itself. Clark Williamson urges those who read Hebrews as inherently supersessionist to "preach against [supersessionism] and instead preach the good news of God's justification of the ungodly, which if it is not true for Jews it is also not true for Christians" (275). Ekkehard Stegemann and Wolfgang Stegemann discuss the difficulty of making an argument based on the text's historical context when so little is known for certain about that context. For them, it is impossible to know whether the text is inherently anti-Jewish or whether interpreters bring that to the text. Stegemann and Stegemann admit that it is almost impossible to eliminate anti-Jewish interpretations of Hebrews. The words of the text signify meanings that cannot be free of anti-Jewish interpretations (367). Whether the same can be said for the original audience is impossible to know.

Over the centuries, Christian interpreters have used Hebrews (among other texts) to argue that Christianity replaces Judaism. For a detailed discussion on the history of supersessionist thought and practice in Christianity, see Scott Bader-Saye's *Church and Israel after Christendom: The Politics of Election* (1999). Too often, Christians have interpreted biblical texts through the lens of religious superiority without pausing to understand either how the text's historical background should affect its meaning or how a modern interpretation might affect other people. We often fail to bring new eyes and ears to a text we think we know. We fail to allow the text to speak to us. Instead, we find "proof" for our own assumptions in the text. Slowly, many Christians have begun to formulate alternate theological constructions that do not depend on Christianity being the "final" and "most perfect" form of religious thinking and practice. Christians are asking important questions about how to base a theology on Christlike principles of love and acceptance instead of triumphant conquest.

260 Essays

TEXTUAL VARIANTS The New Testament in English is the product of hundreds of years of scholarly attention to issues of translation. However, the task of interpretation begins with determining what the actual Greek text is. Over five thousand handwritten copies (manuscripts) contain portions of the collections of text we now call the New Testament. Some are small scraps of papyrus carrying only a verse or two; others are magnificent complete Bibles written on carefully prepared parchment. Since every manuscript had to be copied by hand, errors were bound to happen. Sometimes, scribes (the men and women who copied the texts) even changed the text knowingly. Both intentional changes (intended improvements) and unintentional changes (mistakes) produced what we call textual variants, different words in different manuscripts.

Generations of Christians, dating all the way back to Origen in the third century, have noticed these differences and commented on which manuscript was likely to be more reliable, more likely to contain the wording of the original author. Not until the Greek New Testament became a printed book (the first edition was edited by Erasmus of Rotterdam in 1516) was there a full-scale analysis of the variants. Erasmus had to decide which manuscript(s) to use. He had at his disposal manuscripts copied in the late medieval period. All of them were copied after 1000 CE. Since then, many other manuscripts ranging in date from the second to the fourth centuries have been discovered and have changed the text of the New Testament in significant ways.

The easiest example to see is the ending of the Gospel of Mark. The manuscripts that Erasmus used went all the way to Mark 16:20. However, we now have much earlier manuscripts whose text ends at Mark 16:8. You do not need to know Greek to be aware of this major textual variant. Modern English versions—especially study Bibles such as those published by Oxford University Press or HarperCollins—indicate this and other variants with the phrase "other ancient witnesses." These "witnesses" are ancient manuscripts.

Textual variants are one way for us to see people's active engagement with the biblical text. We have thousands of scribes, monks, librarians, and ordinary Christians—indeed a cloud of witnesses!—to thank for copying and preserving all these manuscripts and for passing on to us the rich manuscript history of the New Testament. For more on the practice of textual criticism, see Metzger's textual commentary.

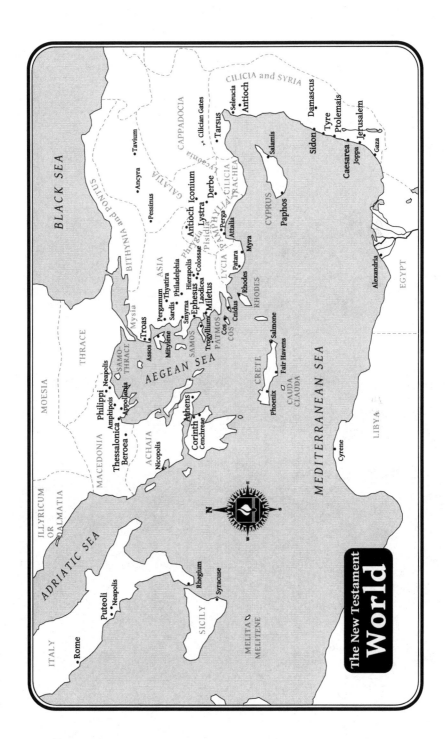

Bibliography

Commentaries

Attridge, Harold W.
    1989   *The Epistle to the Hebrews: A Commentary on the Epistle to the Hebrews.* Hermeneia. Philadelphia: Fortress.

Beavis, Mary Ann, and HyeRan Kim-Cragg
    2015   *Hebrews.* Wisdom Commentary. Collegeville, MN: Liturgical Press.

Bruce, Alexander Balmain
    1899   *The Epistle to the Hebrews: The First Apology for Christianity; An Exegetical Study.* New York: George Scribner's Sons.

Cockerill, Garreth Lee
    2012   *The Epistle to the Hebrews.* New International Commentary on the New Testament. Grand Rapids: Eerdmans.

DeSilva, David A.
    2000   *Perseverance in Gratitude: A Socio-Rhetorical Commentary on the Epistle "to the Hebrews."* Grand Rapids: Eerdmans.

Koester, Craig R.
    2001   *Hebrews: A New Translation with Introduction and Commentary.* Anchor Bible. New York: Doubleday.

Johnson, Luke Timothy
    2006   *Hebrews: A Commentary.* Louisville: Westminster John Knox.

Moffatt, James
    1924   *A Critical and Exegetical Commentary on the Epistle to the Hebrews.* International Critical Commentary. Edinburgh: T&T Clark.

Thompson, James W.
    2008   *Hebrews.* Grand Rapids: Baker Academic.

Witherington, Ben, III
    2007   *Letters and Homilies for Jewish Christians: A Socio-Rhetorical Commentary on Hebrews, James and Jude.* Downers Grove, IL: IVP Academic.

Bibliography 263

Primary Sources

Braght, Thieleman J. van
- 1837 *The Bloody Theatre, or Martyrs Mirror of the Defenceless Christians: Who Suffered and Were Put to Death for the Testimony of Jesus, Their Savior, from the Time of Christ until the Year A.D. 1660.* Dutch original, 1660. Translated into German. Corrected and translated into English by I. Daniel Rupp. Near Lampeter Square, Lancaster Co., PA: David Miller. See via Google Book or HathiTrust.

Bunyan, John
- 1987 *Grace Abounding to the Chief of Sinners.* Edited by W. R. Owens. London: Penguin Books.

Charlesworth, James, ed.
- 1983–85 *The Old Testament Pseudepigrapha.* 2 vols. Garden City, NY: Doubleday.

Clark, Gillian, trans.
- 2000 *Porphyry: On Abstinence from Killing Animals.* London: Bloomsbury.

Dirk Philips [son of Philip]
- 1966 *Enchiridion, or Handbook of Christian Doctrines.* Translated by A. B. Kolb. LaGrange, IN: Pathway Publishing.
- 1992 *The Writings of Dirk Philips, 1504-1568.* Translated by Cornelius J. Dyck, William E. Keeney, and Alvin J. Beachy. Scottdale, PA: Herald Press.

Elliott, J. K., ed.
- 1993 *The Apocryphal New Testament: A Collection of Apocryphal Christian Literature in an English Translation.* Oxford: Clarendon Press.

Koop, Karl, ed.
- 2006 *Confessions of Faith in the Anabaptist Tradition, 1725-1660.* Kitchener, ON: Pandora Press.

Menno Simons [son of Simon]
- 1956 *The Complete Writings of Menno Simons.* Translated by Leonard Verduin. Edited by John C. Wenger. Scottdale, PA: Herald Press.

Musurillo, Herbert, trans. and ed.
- 1972 *The Acts of the Christian Martyrs.* Oxford: Clarendon Press.

Vermès, Géza, trans. and ed.
- 1997 *The Complete Dead Sea Scrolls in English.* New York: Penguin.

White, L. Michael, and G. Anthony Keddie, trans.
- 2018 *Jewish Fictional Letters from Hellenistic Egypt: The Epistle of Aristeas and Related Literature.* Atlanta: SBL Press.

Yonge, C. D., trans.
- 1993 *The Works of Philo: Complete and Unabridged.* New updated ed. Peabody, MA: Hendrickson Pub.

Other Books and Articles

Aulén, Gustaf
- 1969 *Christus Victor.* New York: Macmillan. Swedish original, 1930. Translated by A. G. Hebert, 1931.

Bader-Saye, Scott
- 1999 *Church and Israel after Christendom: The Politics of Election.* Boulder, CO: Westview.

Bibliography

Becker, Adam H., and Annette Yoshiko Reed, eds.
2007   *The Ways That Never Parted: Jews and Christians in Late Antiquity and the Early Middle Ages.* Minneapolis: Fortress.

Berlin, Adele, and Marc Zvi Brettler, eds.
2004   *The Jewish Study Bible.* Jewish Publication Society TANAKH Translation. Oxford: Oxford University Press.

Borg, Marcus
1994   *Meeting Jesus Again for the First Time.* San Francisco: HarperSanFrancisco.

Boyarin, Daniel
2007   "Semantic Differences; or, 'Judaism'/'Christianity.'" In *The Ways That Never Parted: Jews and Christians in Late Antiquity and the Early Middle Ages,* edited by Adam H. Becker and Annette Yoshiko Reed, 65–85. Minneapolis: Fortress Press.

2015   *A Traveling Homeland: The Babylonian Talmud as Diaspora.* Philadelphia: University of Pennsylvania Press.

2016   "Midrash in Hebrews / Hebrews as Midrash." In *Hebrews in Context,* edited by Gabrella Gelardini and Harold W. Attridge, 15–30. Leiden: Brill.

Brock, Rita Nakashima, and Rebecca Ann Parker
2001   *Proverbs of Ashes: Violence, Redemptive Suffering, and the Search for What Saves Us.* Boston: Beacon.

Bruce, Alexander Balmain.
1899   *The Epistle to the Hebrews: The First Apology for Christianity. An Exegetical Study.* Edinburgh: T&T Clark.

Callahan, Allen Dwight
2006   *The Talking Book: African Americans and the Bible.* New Haven: Yale University Press.

Chilton, Bruce
1992   *The Temple of Jesus: His Sacrificial Program within a Cultural History of Sacrifice.* University Park: Pennsylvania State University Press.

Churches in the Believers Church Tradition
1992   *Hymnal: A Worship Book.* Scottdale, PA: Herald Press.

Cohen, Shaye J. D.
1996   "Ioudaios: 'Judaean' and 'Jew' in Susanna, First Maccabees, and Second Maccabees." In *Geschichte—Tradition—Reflexion: Festschrift für Martin Hengel zum 70. Geburtstag,* edited by Hubert Cancik, Hermann Lichtenberger, and Peter Schäfer, 1:211–20. Tübingen: Mohr Siebeck.

Donelson, Lewis
2011   "Hebrews as Pseudepigraphon: The History and Significance of the Pauline Attribution of Hebrews." *Horizons in Biblical Theology* 33 (2): 191–93.

Dunnill, John
1992   *Covenant and Sacrifice in the Letter to the Hebrews.* Cambridge: Cambridge University Press.

Dunning, Benjamin
2009   *Aliens and Sojourners: Self as Other in Early Christianity.* Philadelphia: University of Pennsylvania Press.

Easter, Matthew C.
2017   "Faith in the God Who Resurrects: The Theocentric Faith of Hebrews." *New Testament Studies* 63, no. 1 (January): 76–91.

Bibliography

Ehrman, Bart D.
2011 *The Orthodox Corruption of Scripture: The Effect of Early Christological Controversies on the Text of the New Testament.* New York: Oxford University Press.

Eisenbaum, Pamela
1999 "The Virtue of Suffering, the Necessity of Discipline, and the Pursuit of Perfection in Hebrews." In *Asceticism and the New Testament,* edited by Vincent Wimbush and Leif Vaage, 331–53. New York: Routledge.

2004 "Father and Son: The Christology of Hebrews in Patrilineal Perspective." In *A Feminist Companion to the Catholic Epistles and Hebrews,* edited by Amy-Jill Levine, 127–46. Cleveland: Pilgrim.

2005 "Locating Hebrews within the Literary Landscape of Christian Origins." In *Hebrews: Contemporary Methods, New Insights,* edited by Gabrella Gelardini, 213–37. Leiden: Brill.

2014 "Redescribing the Religion of Hebrews." In *"The One Who Sows Bountifully": Essays in Honor of Stanley K. Stowers,* edited by Caroline Johnson Hodge, Saul M. Olyan, Daniel Ullucci, and Emma Wasserman, 283–93. Providence: Brown Judaic Studies.

2016 "Ritual and Religion, Sacrifice and Supersession: A Utopian Reading of Hebrews." In *Hebrews in Context,* edited by Gabrella Gelardini and Harold W. Attridge, 343–56. Leiden: Brill.

2017 "Hebrews: Introduction and Annotations." In *The Jewish Annotated New Testament,* edited by Amy-Jill Levine and Marc Z. Brettler, 460–88. 2nd ed. New York: Oxford University Press. 1st ed. 2011, 406-26.

Filtvedt, Ole J.
2015a "Creation and Salvation in Hebrews." *Zeitschrift für die neutestamentliche Wissenschaft und die Kunde der älteren Kirche* 106 (2): 280–303.

2015b "Exploring the High Priesthood of Jesus in Early Christian Sources." *Zeitschrift für die neutestamentliche Wissenschaft und die Kunde der älteren Kirche* 106 (1): 96–114.

Gamble, Harry
1985 *The New Testament Canon: Its Making and Meaning.* Philadelphia: Fortress.

Gelardini, Gabriella, ed.
2005 *Hebrews: Contemporary Methods, New Insights.* Leiden: Brill.

Gelardini, Gabriella, and Harold Attridge, eds.
2016 *Hebrews in Context.* Leiden: Brill.

Girard, René
2011 *Sacrifice.* Translated by Matthew Pattillo and David Dawson. East Lansing: Michigan State University Press.

Goodman, Martin
2007 "Modeling the 'Parting of the Ways.'" In *The Ways That Never Parted: Jews and Christians in Late Antiquity and the Early Middle Ages,* edited by Adam Becker and Annette Yoshiko Reed, 119–29. Leiden: Brill.

Gorman, H.
2012 "Persuading through Pathos: Appeals to the Emotions in Hebrews." *Restoration Quarterly* 54 (2): 77–90.

Grabbe, Lester
    1995   *Priests, Prophets, Diviners, Sages: A Socio-Historical Study of Religious Specialists in Ancient Israel*. Valley Forge, PA: Trinity Press International.

Green, Joel B., and Mark D. Baker
    2000   *Recovering the Scandal of the Cross: Atonement in New Testament and Contemporary Contexts*. Downers Grove, IL: InterVarsity.

Guthrie, George
    2007   "Hebrews." In *Commentary on the New Testament Use of the Old Testament*, edited by G. K. Beale and D. A. Carson, 919–95. Grand Rapids: Baker Academic.

Hamerton-Kelly, Robert G.
    2015   "Survival and Salvation: A Girardian Reading of Christian Hope in Evolutionary Perspective." In *Can We Survive Our Origins? Readings in René Girard's Theory of Violence and the Sacred*, edited by Pierpaolo Antonello and Paul Gifford, 143–65. East Lansing: Michigan State University Press.

Harmon, S. R.
    2005   "Hebrews in Patristic Perspective." *Review & Expositor* 102 (2): 215–33.

Harnack, Adolph von
    1987   "Probability about the Address and Author of the Epistle to the Hebrews." Originally published as "Probabilia über die Addresse und den Verfasser des Hebraerbriefes." *Zeitschrift für die neutestamentliche Wissenschaft* 1 (1900): 16–41. Translated in *Women in American Protestant Religion, 1800-1930: A Thirty-Six Volume Reprint Collection Demonstrating the Breadth and Diversity of the Roles Played by Women in American Religion*, edited by Carolyn de Swarte Gifford, 392–415. New York: Garland.

Harris, James Rendel
    1908   *Side-Lights on New Testament Research: Seven Lectures Delivered in 1908, at Regent's Park College, London*. London: Kingsgate, James Clarke.

Hart, David Bentley, trans.
    2017   *The New Testament: A Translation*. New Haven: Yale University Press.

Hay, D. M.
    1973   *Glory at the Right Hand: Psalm 110 in Early Christianity*. Nashville: Abingdon.

Hays, Richard
    2009   "'Here We Have No Lasting City': New Covenantalism in Hebrews." In *The Epistle to the Hebrews and Christian Theology*, edited by Richard Bauckham, Daniel R. Driver, Trevor A. Hart, and Nathan MacDonald, 151–73. Grand Rapids: Eerdmans.

Heim, S. Mark
    2006   *Saved from Sacrifice: A Theology of the Cross*. Grand Rapids: Eerdmans.

Hershberger, Michele
    2019   *Why Did Jesus Die and What Difference Does It Make?* Harrisonburg, VA: Herald Press.

Himmelfarb, Martha
    2006   *A Kingdom of Priests: Ancestry and Merit in Ancient Judaism*. Philadelphia: University of Pennsylvania Press.

Bibliography

Hoppin, Ruth
 1997 *Priscilla's Letter: Finding the Author of the Epistle to the Hebrews.* San Francisco: Christian Universities Press; Fort Bragg, CA: Lost Coast.
 2004 "The Epistle to the Hebrews Is Priscilla's Letter." In *A Feminist Companion to the Catholic Epistles and Hebrews,* edited by Amy-Jill Levine, 147–70. Cleveland: Pilgrim.

Horton, F. L.
 1976 *The Melchizedek Tradition.* Cambridge: Cambridge University Press.

Isaacs, Marie E.
 1996 *Sacred Space: An Approach to the Theology of the Epistle to the Hebrews.* Sheffield: JSOT Press.

Jamieson, R. B.
 2017 "When and Where Did Jesus Offer Himself? A Taxonomy of Recent Scholarship on Hebrews." *Currents in Biblical Scholarship* 15, no. 3 (June): 338–68.

Johns, Loren L.
 2012 "Reading the Maccabean Literature by the Light of the Stake: Anabaptist Appropriations in the Reformation Period." *Mennonite Quarterly Review* 86, no. 2 (April): 151–73.

Johnson, Elizabeth A.
 1998 *Friends of God and Prophets: A Feminist Theological Reading of the Communion of Saints.* New York: Continuum.

Kaalund, Jennifer T.
 2019 *Reading Hebrews and 1 Peter with the African American Great Migration: Diaspora, Place, and Identity.* London: T&T Clark.

Karrer, Martin
 2006 "The Epistle of the Hebrews and the Septuagint." In *Septuagint Research: Issues and Challenges in the Study of Greek Scriptures,* edited by Wolfgang Kraus and R. Glenn Wooden, 335–54. Atlanta: Society of Biblical Literature.

Kim, Lloyd
 2006 *Polemic in the Book of Hebrews: Anti-Judaism, Anti-Semitism, Supersessionism?* Princeton Theological Monograph Series. Eugene, OR: Pickwick.

King, Martin Luther, Jr.
 1967 "The King Philosophy—Nonviolence 365." From *Where Do We Go From Here: Chaos or Community?* Boston: Beacon Press. https://thekingcenter.org/about-tkc/the-king-philosophy/.

Kinzer, Mark S.
 2005 *Post-Missionary Messianic Judaism: Redefining Christian Engagement with the Jewish People.* Grand Rapids: Brazos.

Kinzig, Wolfram
 1994 "*Kainē Diathēkē*: The Title of the New Testament in the Second and Third Centuries." *Journal of Theological Studies* 2/45, no. 2 (October): 519–44.

Kittel, Gerhard, and Geoffrey W. Bromiley, eds., Gerhard Friedrich, trans.
 1964–76 *Theological Dictionary of the New Testament* [*TDNT*]. 10 vols. Grand Rapids: Eerdmans.

Kittredge, Cynthia Briggs
 1994 "Hebrews." In *Searching the Scriptures,* vol. 2, *A Feminist Commentary,* edited by Elisabeth Schüssler Fiorenza, 428–52. New York: Crossroad.

Bibliography

Klawans, Jonathan
2006   *Purity, Sacrifice, and the Temple: Symbolism and Supersessionism in the Study of Ancient Judaism*. New York: Oxford.

Koester, Craig R.
2016   "'In Many and Varied Ways': Theological Interpretation of Hebrews in the Modern Period." In *Hebrews in Context*, edited by Gabriella Gelardini and Harold W. Attridge, 299–315. Leiden: Brill.

Koester, Helmut
1963   "'Outside the Camp': Hebrews 13:9." *Harvard Theological Review* 55:299–315.

Koltun-Fromm, Naomi
2010   *Hermeneutics of Holiness: Ancient Jewish and Christian Notions of Sexuality and Religious Community*. New York: Oxford.

Kraemer, Ross S.
1991   "Women's Authorship of Jewish and Christian Literature in the Greco-Roman Period." In *"Women Like This": New Perspectives on Jewish Women in the Greco-Roman World*, edited by Amy-Jill Levine, 221–42. Atlanta: Scholars Press.

2020   *The Mediterranean Diaspora in Late Antiquity: What Christianity Cost the Jews*. New York: Oxford University Press.

Kraft, Robert A.
1975   "The Multiform Jewish Heritage of Early Christianity." In *Christianity, Judaism and Other Greco-Roman Cults: Studies for Morton Smith at Sixty*, edited by Jacob Neusner, 174–99. Leiden: Brill.

2007   "The Weighing of the Parts: Pivots and Pitfalls in the Study of Early Judaisms and Their Early Christian Offspring." In *The Ways That Never Parted: Jews and Christians in Late Antiquity and the Early Middle Ages*, edited by Adam Becker and Annette Yoshiko Reed, 87–94. Leiden: Brill.

Law, Timothy
2013   *When God Spoke Greek: The Septuagint and the Making of the Christian Bible*. New York: Oxford University Press.

Lehne, Susanne
1990   *The New Covenant in Hebrews*. Sheffield: Sheffield Academic Press.

Levine, Amy-Jill, and Marc Zvi Brettler
2020   *The Bible with and without Jesus: How Jews and Christians Read the Same Stories Differently*. New York: HarperOne.

Levine, Amy-Jill, and Marc Zvi Brettler, eds.
2017   *The Jewish Annotated New Testament*. 2nd ed. Oxford: Oxford University Press.

Lieu, Judith
1994   "'The Parting of the Ways': Theological Construct or Historical Reality?" *Journal for the Study of the New Testament* 56:101–19.

Long, T. G.
1998   "Bold in the Presence of God: Atonement in Hebrews." *Interpretation* 52 (1): 53–69.

Mackie, Scott D.
2011   "Heavenly Sanctuary Mysticism in the Epistle to the Hebrews." *Journal of Theological Studies* 62 (1): 77–117.

Bibliography

McCruden, Kevin
  2002 "Christ's Perfection in Hebrews: Divine Beneficence as an Exegetical Key to Hebrews 2:10." *Biblical Research* 47:40–62.
  2013 "Elegant Blood of Jesus: The Neglected Theme of the Fidelity of Jesus in Hebrews 12:24." *Catholic Biblical Quarterly* 75, no. 3 (July): 504–20.

Metzger, Bruce M.
  1975 *A Textual Commentary on the Greek New Testament: A Companion Volume to the United Bible Societies' Greek New Testament (3d ed.).* Corrected ed. London: United Bible Societies.

Moffitt, David M.
  2011 *Atonement and the Logic of Resurrection.* Leiden: Brill.
  2014 "Perseverance, Purity, and Identity: Exploring Hebrews' Eschatological Worldview, Ethics, and In-Group Bias." In *Sensitivity Towards Outsiders: Exploring the Dynamic Relationship between Mission and Ethics in the New Testament and Early Christianity*, edited by Jacobus Kok, Tobias Nicklas, Dieter T. Roth, and Christopher M. Hays, 357–80. Tübingen: Mohr Siebeck.

Neusner, Jacob
  1991 *Studying Classical Judaism: A Primer.* Louisville: Westminster/John Knox.

Orlov, Andrei
  2000 "Melchizedek Legend of 2 (Slavonic) Enoch." *Journal for the Study of Judaism in the Persian, Hellenistic, and Roman Period* 31, no. 1 (January): 23–38.

Peterson, David
  1982 *Hebrews and Perfection: An Examination of the Concept of Perfection in the "Epistle to the Hebrews."* Cambridge: Cambridge University Press.

Pietersma, Albert, and Benjamin G. Wright, eds.
  2007 *A New English Translation of the Septuagint* [NETS] *and Other Greek Translations Traditionally Included under That Title.* New York: Oxford University Press. Reprinted, 2009; corrected, 2014, 2021. https://ccat.sas.upenn.edu/nets/edition.

Polen, Nehemia
  2009 "Leviticus and Hebrews . . . and Leviticus." In *The Epistle to the Hebrews and Christian Theology*, edited by Richard Bauckham, Daniel R. Driver, Trevor A. Hart, and Nathan MacDonald, 213–25. Grand Rapids: Eerdmans.

Porter, Stanley, and Jacqueline C. R. de Roo
  2003 *The Concept of the Covenant in the Second Temple Period.* Leiden: Brill.

Regev, Eyal
  2019 *The Temple in Early Christianity: Experiencing the Sacred.* New Haven: Yale University Press.

Rives, James B.
  2011 "The Theology of Animal Sacrifice in the Ancient Greek World." In *Ancient Mediterranean Sacrifice*, edited by Jennifer Wright Knust and Zsuzsanna Várhelyi, 187–202. New York: Oxford University Press.

Seely, David Rolph
  2011 "William Tyndale and the Language of At-one-ment." In *The King James Bible and the Restoration*, edited by Kent P. Jackson, 25–42. Provo, UT: Brigham Young University Press.

Bibliography

Stegemann, Ekkehard W., and Wolfgang Stegemann
2016 "Hebrews and the Discourse of Judeophobia." In *Hebrews in Context*, edited by Gabriella Gelardini and Harold W. Attridge, 357–69. Leiden: Brill.

Steyn, G. J.
2001 "'Jesus Sayings' in Hebrews." *Ephemerides Theologicae Lovanienses* 77 (4): 433–40.
2012 "The Ending of Hebrews Reconsidered." *Zeitschrift für die neutestamentliche Wissenschaft und die Kunde der älteren Kirche* 103, no. 2 (July): 235–53.

Stowers, Stanley K.
1995 "Greeks Who Sacrifice and Those Who Do Not: Toward an Anthropology of Greek Religion." In *The Social World of the First Christians: Essays in Honor of Wayne A. Meeks*, edited by L. Michael White and O. Larry Yarbrough, 293–333. Minneapolis: Fortress.

Svartvik, Jesper
2016 "Stumbling Block or Stepping Stone? On the Reception History of Hebrews 8:13." In *Hebrews in Context*, edited by Gabriella Gelardini and Harold W. Attridge, 316–42. Leiden: Brill.
2021 "The New Testament's Most Dangerous Book for Jews: Reading and Preaching Hebrews without Supersessionism." *Christian Century* 138, no. 19 (September 22): 34–36. https://www.christian-century.org/article/critical-essay/new-testament-s-most-dangerous-book-jews.

Thiessen, Matthew
2007 "Hebrews and the End of the Exodus." *Novum Testamentum* 49 (4): 353–69.

Thompson, James W.
2011a "Insider Ethics for Outsiders: Ethics for Aliens in Hebrews." *Restoration Quarterly* 53 (4): 207–20.
2011b "What Has Middle Platonism to Do with Hebrews?" In *Reading the Epistle to the Hebrews: A Resource for Students*, edited by Eric F. Mason and Kevin B. McCruden, 31–52. Atlanta: Society of Biblical Literature.

Tölölyan, Khachig
1996 "Rethinking Diaspora(s): Stateless Power in the Transnational Moment." *Diaspora: A Journal of Transnational Studies* 5:3–36.

Ullucci, Daniel
2011 "Contesting the Meaning of Animal Sacrifice." In *Ancient Mediterranean Sacrifice*, edited by Jennifer Wright Knust and Zsuzsanna Várhelyi, 57–74. New York: Oxford University Press.

Vandergriff, Kenneth A.
2017 "*Diathēkē Kainē:* New Covenant as Jewish Apocalypticism in Hebrews 8." *Catholic Biblical Quarterly* 79, no. 1 (January): 97–110.

van der Horst, Pieter W.
2004 "Jews and Christians in Antioch at the End of the Fourth Century." In *Christian-Jewish Relations through the Centuries*, edited by Stanley E. Porter and Brook W. R. Pearson, 228–38. New York: T&T Clark.

Vanhoye, A.
1989 *Structure and Message of the Epistle to the Hebrews*. Rome: Biblical Institute Press.

Bibliography

Weaver, J. Denny
 2001 *The Nonviolent Atonement*. Grand Rapids: Eerdmans.
Williamson, Clark M.
 2003 "Anti-Judaism in Hebrews?" *Interpretation* 57:266–79.
Wills, Lawrence
 1984 "The Form of the Sermon in Hellenistic Judaism and Early Christianity." *Harvard Theological Review* 77, no. 3/4 (July–October): 277–99.
Wink, Walter
 1984 *Naming the Powers: The Language of Power in the New Testament.* Philadelphia: Fortress.
 1986 *Unmasking the Powers: The Invisible Forces That Determine Human Existence.* Philadelphia: Fortress.
 1992 *Engaging the Powers: Discernment and Resistance in a World of Domination.* Minneapolis: Fortress.
 1999 *The Powers That Be.* New York: Doubleday.
Yoder, Perry B.
 2017 *Leviticus.* Believers Church Bible Commentary. Harrisonburg, VA: Herald Press.

Selected Resources

Bibles

Berlin, Adele, and Marc Zvi Brettler, eds. *The Jewish Study Bible.* Jewish Publication Society TANAKH Translation. Oxford: Oxford University Press, 2004. A translation from the Jewish Publication Society; the useful notes and essays in this Bible give insight into their meaning for Jews throughout the centuries.

Hart, David Bentley, trans. *The New Testament: A Translation.* New Haven: Yale University Press, 2017. With almost no commentary or notes, David Hart's translation of the New Testament is one of a kind. He aims for a literal translation that attempts to convey the tone and tenor of the original text. His translation exposes some of the strangeness of the ancient text and allows us to contemplate it in a new way.

Levine, Amy-Jill, and Marc Zvi Brettler, eds. *The Jewish Annotated New Testament.* 2nd ed. Oxford: Oxford University Press, 2017. Using the text of the NRSV, this Bible contains many excellent articles contextualizing the New Testament in its first-century Jewish background. Pamela Eisenbaum has contributed groundbreaking articles on Hebrews (see Eisenbaum under Other Books and Articles) and wrote the commentary for the Letter to the Hebrews (see Eisenbaum under Commentaries).

Pietersma, Albert, and Benjamin G. Wright, eds. *A New English Translation of the Septuagint* [NETS] *and Other Greek Translations Traditionally Included under That Title.* New York: Oxford University Press, 2007. Reprinted, 2009; corrected, 2014, 2021. Available at https://ccat.sas.upenn.edu/nets/edition/. As Pietersma and Wright explain, the LXX was meant to bring "the Greek reader to the Hebrew original" (xiv). Their new translation of the Greek aims to read like a translation, much like the LXX itself reads as a translation of the Hebrew.

Selected Resources

Commentaries

Attridge, Harold. *The Epistle to the Hebrews: A Commentary on the Epistle to the Hebrews.* Philadelphia: Fortress, 1989. Part of the Hermeneia series, Attridge's commentary is foundational for the study of Hebrews. Although it is now over thirty years old, the bibliography remains relevant. The commentary offers a comprehensive approach to the context and background of the text.

Eisenbaum, Pamela. "Hebrews: Introduction and Annotations." In *The Jewish Annotated New Testament*, edited by Amy-Jill Levine and Marc Z. Brettler, 460–88. 2nd ed. New York: Oxford University Press, 2017. 1st ed. 2011, 406-26.

Johnson, Luke Timothy. *Hebrews: A Commentary.* Louisville: Westminster John Knox Press, 2006. Johnson presents an erudite commentary that focuses on the translation of words and phrases in Hebrews. The sixty-page introduction is excellent, providing a detailed discussion of the historical context.

Thompson, James W. *Hebrews.* Grand Rapids: Baker Academic, 2008. Part of the Paideia commentaries, this approachable commentary includes historical background and explanation of terms and issues without being overwhelming. It is a good starting place for those less interested in the technicalities that Johnson and Attridge address.

Other Books and Articles

Bauckham, Richard, Daniel R. Driver, Trevor A. Hart, and Nathan MacDonald, eds. *The Epistle to the Hebrews and Christian Theology.* Grand Rapids: Eerdmans, 2009. See especially the section "The Problem of Hebrews' Supersessionism," with articles by Richard B. Hays, Oskar Skarsaune, Mark D. Nanos, Morna D. Hooker, and Nehemia Polen on 149–225, a thoughtful scholarly debate about supersessionism in Hebrews.

Eisenbaum, Pamela. "Locating Hebrews within the Literary Landscape of Christian Origins." In *Hebrews: Contemporary Methods, New Insights*, edited by Gabrella Gelardini, 213–37. Leiden: Brill, 2005.

———."Redescribing the Religion of Hebrews." In *"The One Who Sows Bountifully": Essays in Honor of Stanley K. Stowers.* Edited by Caroline Johnson Hodge, Saul M. Olyan, Daniel Ullucci, and Emma Wasserman, 283–93. Rhode Island: Brown Judaic Studies, 2014.

———."Ritual and Religion, Sacrifice and Supersession: A Utopian Reading of Hebrews." In *Hebrews in Context*, edited by Gabrella Gelardini and Harold W. Attridge, 343–56. Leiden: Brill, 2016.

These three articles form the backbone of Eisenbaum's groundbreaking work on Hebrews. Eisenbaum presents a convincing argument that Hebrews arose out of a period of unrest and displacement at a time when terms like "Christian" and "Jew" were not mutually exclusive. Therefore, the text does not represent a "Christian" perspective. Eisenbaum's perspective is summarized in her commentary on Hebrews in *The Jewish Annotated New Testament.*

Index of Ancient Sources

OLD TESTAMENT

Genesis–Deuteronomy
.... 118

Genesis
.... 130, 251
1 .... 48, 240, 248
1:1-3 182
1:26-28 69
2 92
2:2 .... 87–89, 253
3:17-18 117
4 184
4:1-16 182
4:10 184
5:22-24 184
5:24 .... 107, 182, 200
6 65
6–9 96–97
6:2 56
6:9–9:28 182
6:18 146
9 185
9:8-17 146
11–25 200
11:30 186
12:1-3 147

12:1-9 182
14 ...... 122–24, 129, 247
14:17-20 ... 123–24, 130
15 147
16 56
17:1-14 147
18 .... 56, 214
18:9-15 182
18:11-15 186
19 56
19:1-14 214
20:7 43
21:1-3 186
21:1-8 182
22 .... 56, 186
25 200
25–36 208
25:34 204–5
26:34-35 204–5
27:1-40 182
27:34 205
28:15 216
39–41 197
47:31 252
48 56
48:8-22 183
50:24-25 183

Exodus
.... 31, 218, 251
2:1-15 183
3 .... 113, 210
6:8 118
7:1 43
12:1–13:10 183
13:21 210
14–15 183
14:11-12 193
14:19 56
15:20 43
16:6-7 48
17 84–85
18 136
19 206
19–24 147
19:16 206
19:18 .... 207, 209
20:8-11 95
20:18-21 207
20:22–23:33 147
23:20 56
24:3-8 159
24:17 48
25 148
25–31 ..... 157, 163, 230

Index of Ancient Sources

25:9-40 142
25:16 163
25:22 .... 163, 231
25:40 .... 163, 243
28:30 131
29:1-35 108
29:9 242
29:12 159
29:38-42 128
32 193
33:7-11 163–64

Leviticus
.... 25, 31, 252
1–7 .... 128, 165
1–9 131
2:1–3:7 105
7–10 131
8–9 108
8–10 131
8:15 159
10:10-11 131
12 165
14 84
16 .... 108, 128, 131,
          166–67, 229–30
16:27 .... 216, 218
17–26 215
23:4-8 165
23:9-21 105
23:15-21 165
23:26-32 167
23:33-36 165
25:9 167

Numbers
2:7 57
3:5-10 131–32
5 131
5:12-15 95
5:12-31 133
12 84–85

12–14 92
12:1-8 83–84
14 84–85
16:9 141
18:20-32 124
19:2-3 216
24:17 252
25 193
28:3-8 128
29:7-11 167
32:11 127
35:25 108

Deuteronomy
.... 251, 253–54
4:21 207
4:23 207
4:24 .... 177, 207
6:4-5 62
9:5 118
9:19 206
10:8-9 132
11 117
13:13-18 176
16:1-8 165
16:9-12 165
16:13-15 165
16:16-17 164
17:2-7 176
17:8-13 131
18:15 43
28:25 235
31:7-8 216
32:35-36 175
32:43 .... 57, 59, 254–55

Joshua
1:5 216
2 200
2:1 188
2:1-21 .... 183, 188
6 .... 136, 183

6:15-25 188
7 136
22 176
24:2-3 118

Judges
4–8 183
4:4 43
6:11-14 214
11–16 183
13 56
13:2-25 214
14:6 183

Ruth
4 136

1 Samuel
.... 132, 183, 197
1 132
3:20 43
4:4 231
15:22-23 166

2 Samuel
.... 183, 196
7:14 57
8:17 108

1 Kings
.... 43
2:27 108
2:35 108
6–8 164
6:19 164
7:14 .... 58, 147
7:16 147
17:1-7 183
17:8-24 .... 189, 246
17:17-24 183
18:36-38 210
19 56

Index of Ancient Sources

19:3-9 183
19:13 183
19:19 183

2 Kings
.... 43, 197
2:1-12 107
2:25 183
4:18-37 ... 183, 189, 246
19:15 231
21:16 183

1 Chronicles
6:8-12 132
23-26 132

2 Chronicles
2-4 164
3:8 164
5 131
5:3-8 164
7 131
24:21 183
36:22-23 164

Ezra
.... 164

Nehemiah
.... 164
1:7-8 118
6:15-16 242
9:6-38 192
9:7-8 118

Esther
.... 250
4:11 .... 189, 246

Job
.... 237, 250
2:10-17 136

23:1-9 109
23:16-17 109
42:1-6 136

Psalms
.... 49, 251
2 ....58, 66, 101, 105–6,
252
2:7 .... 57, 58, 124
2:8 47
8 .... 46, 69, 70–72,
77–78
8:2 77
8:4-6 .... 70–72, 77
11:5 148
17:6 63
18:7 209
22 .... 74, 78
22:1-15 109
23 224
33:6 240
34:1-8 136
40 160
40:6-8 162
44:1 63
45:6-7 .... 57, 60
47:8 148
50:14-15 167
51:1-12 149
51:10 220
51:16-17 .... 167, 220
68:8 209
72:27 215
77:18 209
78:5-67 93
80:1 .... 224, 231
82:3-5 209
90:12-17 109
95 ....82, 84–86, 89, 92,
174, 248, 253
95:7-11 .... 84, 93
95:11 89

97:7 59
98 50
102:25-27 .... 57, 60
103:20-21 59
104 60
104:4 .... 57, 59
105–106 ..... 93, 192–93
105:2 192
110 .... 25–26, 44, 47,
60, 66, 77, 100–101,
105–6, 108, 129, 162–
63, 195–96, 222, 225,
247, 250, 252–53, 255
110:1 34, 41, 49, 57, 70,
77, 124, 190, 196
110:2 252
110:4 .... 122–27, 129,
196
114:4 209
114:7-8 209
118:6 216
135–136 193
137 208
137:2 31
146:2 235
148:2 59

Proverbs
.... 49, 237
2:2 62
3:11-12 203
8 .... 35, 237
8:22-26 48
8:22-31 46
8:27 45
12:5 203

Ecclesiastes
.... 237

Isaiah
.... 218

Index of Ancient Sources

1:3 63
1:11 167
1:11-13 220
1:16-17 166
1:17 220
2:12 174
5:1 215
5:4-8 215
6 210
6:1 148
6:1-8 209
6:3 48
6:9-10 62
8:17-18 74–75
13:10 209
13:13 209
26:11 177
26:20 180
34:4 209
35:3 204
37:16 231
40:5 48
40:11 224
42:5-8 147
49:2 92
50:5 62
52:7-10 50
53:4-5 78–79
53:12 134
55:10-11 92
57:3 215
66:15 177

Jeremiah
.... 250–51
3:6-10 215
5:21 62
7:21-23 166
13:27 215
20:9 210
25:11-12 164
29:10 164

31 .... 37, 155, 224, 250,
255
31:31 147
31:31-34 ... 25–26, 138–
39, 141, 143–46, 149,
163, 225, 251, 253
49:7-14 208

Ezekiel
.... 64
1 107
1–20 193
16:38 215
20 193
20:1-31 93
20:16 93
20:44 193
23:45 215
32:7-8 209
34:5 224
34:8 224
34:12 224
34:23 224
36–37 147
36:25 112
37:24 224
40–48 132

Daniel
.... 64, 218, 250
3 .... 183, 189, 197
6:19-23 .... 183, 189
7:9-10 107
7:13-14 196
7:16 56

Hosea
2 147
2:14-23 93
2:20 93
3:1 215
4:1-3 147

6:6 166
9:1 215

Joel
1:15 174
2:10 209

Amos
1–2 109
2:3-4 .... 180, 195
2:4 170
5:6-7 109
5:10-15 109
5:21-27 166
5:24 161
9:5-6 209

Obadiah
10-15 208

Micah
6:6-8 ...... 161, 166, 220,
217–18

Habakkuk
2:3-4 .... 180, 195

Zephaniah
1:18 177

Haggai
2:21 209

Zechariah
10:2 224
11:16 224

Malachi
2:6 207
2:21 207
3:3 210–11

Index of Ancient Sources

DEUTEROCANONICAL BOOKS
...64, 189, 197, 237–38, 246

Additions to Daniel
.... 237

Additions to Esther
.... 237

Baruch
.... 237

Epistle of Jeremiah
.... 237

1 Esdras
.... 237

2 Esdras
16:15-16................. 242

1 Maccabees
.... 132, 237
4:52-59.................... 194
6 197
10:18-22................. 108

2 Maccabees
.... 132, 237
5–10 183
6:18–7:42 .... 183, 194
7 194

3 Maccabees
.... 237

4 Maccabees
.... 79, 194, 237
6:10 195
7:13-15................... 242

17:11 195
17:21-22........... 79, 229

Judith
.... 189, 237, 246

Prayer of Manasseh
.... 237

Psalm 151
.... 237

Sirach
.... 237
16:18 209
24:1-12............. 45, 237
44:1–49:16 193–94
44:9 194
44:11-15................. 194
44:16 184
48:4-5..................... 246
48:12-13................. 246

Tobit
.... 237

Wisdom of Solomon
.... 49, 237
6–10 46
7:4 45
7:12 .... 45, 237
7:21 .... 45, 237
7:22-23.................... 92
7:24 35
8:4 237
9:1-2 240
9:4 45
10:1-21................... 194
10:9 194
10:15 194
18:15-16................. 92

PSEUDEPIGRAPHA
.... 33, 56, 64, 238

1 Enoch
.... 107, 184–85, 238
22:7 184

2 Enoch
.... 130, 184–85
69–73 130

Jubilees
.... 95

Letter of Aristeas
.... 250

Pseudo-Philo (Liber antiquitatum biblicarum)
.... 95

Testament of Abraham
13:2-3 184

DEAD SEA SCROLLS
.......33–34, 56, 64, 129, 147, 236, 239, 247, 250–51, 254–55
CD/Damascus Document 147–48
1QM/War Scroll.......... 129–30, 239–40
1QpHab 8.1-4 195
4QFlor (MidrEschat[a])
1.13 58
11QMelch/11Q13... 64, 129, 239–40

Index of Ancient Sources

ANCIENT JEWISH WRITERS

Philo

...33, 132, 187–88, 215, 238–41, 243–44, 246

Agriculture
112 195
119 195

Allegorical Interpretation
3.44–45 242–43
3.79–82 .... 130, 252
3.101–102 243

Contemplative Life
.... 238–39
4.36 95

Creation of the World
146 243

Embassy to Gaius
.... 238–39

Life of Moses
2.74 148
2.98 149
2.117 149

Posterity of Cain
.... 184

Sacrifices of Cain and Abel
.... 184

Special Laws
1.66 149

Worse
.... 184

Josephus

.... 132, 239

Against Apion
.... 239

Jewish Antiquities
.... 238–39
1.177–182 130
5.1.2 188

15.380–402 164

Jewish War
.... 239

The Life
.... 239

NEW TESTAMENT

Matthew

.... 94
1–2 136
1:5 188
1:20 64
1:26-28 70
3:6 112
3:7 133
3:16-17 233
3:17 58
5–7 .... 94, 220
5:13 63
5:17 126
5:22 211
7:11 247
7:28 94
9:18 112
11:1 94
11:15 62
11:28 95
12:8 95
13:9-17 62
13:53 94
14:34-35 63
16:1 133
16:6 133
16:11-12 133
16:28 72
17 113
17:5 58
18:12-13 224
19:1 94
19:13 112
20:28 231
21:14 165

21:16 77
21:23 165
21:33-45 63
21:43 63
22:23 133
22:41-46 196
22:42 233
22:44 34
23:35 184
24 177
24:23 177
24:29 209
25:14-30 63
25:29 63
25:40 208
26:1 94
26:20-29 167
26:28 148
26:64 .... 49, 196
27:25 151
27:27-54 74
27:46 78
27:51 32

Mark

.... 34
1:1 233
1:11 58
1:44 133
2:27 95
5:23 112
8:23 119
9:7 58
9:33 35
9:50 63
10:17-31 109
10:45 231
10:46-52 136
11:27 165
12:1-12 63
12:18 133
12:35 233

12:35-37 196
12:36 34
13:33 218
14:17-25 167
14:24 .... 78, 148
14:62 .... 49, 196
15:24-34 74
15:34 78
15:38 32
16:8 258
16:20 258

Luke

1:5 133
1:8 133
1:12 133
1:26 64
1:35 233
1:55 75
1:68 231
1:72 148
2:7 58
2:8-14 64
2:22-24 .... 165, 167
2:37 165
2:41-42 167
2:41-51 165
3:16 210
3:21-22 236
3:22 58
3:37 185
4:17 251
9:20 233
9:35 58
9:62 96–97
11:52 184
12:49 211
13:13 112
14:34-35 63
14:35 62
15:3-7 224
16 76

16:1-17 234
17:14 133
18:13 229–30
19:11-27 63
20:9-19 63
20:27 133
20:41-44 196
20:42 34
21:36 218
22 45
22:8 167
22:14-38 167
22:19 78
22:20 148
22:32 134
22:69 .... 49, 196
23:32-49 74
23:35 233
23:45 32
24:21 231

John

.....34–35, 94, 113, 231, 240–41
1 .... 45, 237
1:1 48
1:1-14 50
1:17 94
1:29 167
1:36 167
3:14-15 94
3:16 231
3:22-23 112
4:2 112
4:20-21 31
5:7 112
6:31-35 95
6:51 78
7:19-24 95
8:12 113
8:33 75
10:14 224

10:22 194
11 66
11:27 233
12:20-33 149
12:25 149
13:1 167
13:1-20 81
13:15 194
14:6 35
14:9 49
17 134
17:19 35
19:17 217
19:17-37 74
19:20 217
21 120

Acts

2:3 210
2:6 210
2:31-36 232
2:32-36 196
2:33-35 49
3:1 165
3:10 165
3:25 148
4:25-26 58
5:14 23
5:18-22 215
5:21 165
5:21-32 49
6:3 23
6:6 112
6:7 133
7 94
7:38 .... 65, 92
7:55-56 49
8:3 215
8:17 112
8:19 112
9:2 231
9:12 112

Index of Ancient Sources

9:13 .... 23, 115
9:32 115
9:41 115
10:22 143
10:45 23
11:25 241
11:26 .... 21, 23
12:4-7 215
13:3 112
13:13-41 27
13:15 251
13:16 34
13:26 34
13:33 58
14:2 94
16:13 31
16:17 35
16:24-27 215
18:24-28 244–45
18:26 35
19:23 35
21:26 167
21:26-30 165
22:4 35
24:14 231
26:10 115
26:28 23
28:8 112
28:16-17 215

Romans

.... 28, 244
1:7 115
1:16 23
1:17 195
3:21-26 231
3:25 229–30
4 118
4:1-25 75
4:13 118
5:1-7 117–18
5:6 78

5:8 .... 78, 231
5:10-11 230
6:1-4 231
6:5-8 233
6:10 128
8:18-39 231
8:29 59
8:31-39 234
8:33-34 134
8:34 .... 34, 49
11:12 247
11:13 22
11:17-24 64
11:24 247
12:10 214
12:13 214
15:14 35–36
16:7 245

1 Corinthians

.... 27–28, 35, 244
1:2 .... 23, 115
1:17 28
1:24 46
1:30 48
3:11-15 210
4:17 35
5:6-8 167
5:11 215
9:13 217
9:24-27 195
10 64
10:1-13 .... 94, 113
10:11 94
11:17-33 64
11:23-25 148
11:24 78
12:14-26 215
12:31 .... 35, 191
13:1 167
15:3 78
15:6 128

15:20-28 233
15:25 .... 49, 77
15:27 77
15:29 112

2 Corinthians

1:1 115
2:21 194–95
3:6 .... 35, 148
4:4 49
5:17 231
5:18-20 230
5:19 231
8:1–9:15 115
12:1-10 .... 65, 107

Galatians

1:4 78
1:12 28
2:2 195
2:19-29 231
3 118
3:7 75
3:11 195
3:15-18 118
3:17 148
3:28 23
5:7 195

Ephesians

1:1 115
1:20-22 77
2:6 49
2:16 230
5:3-5 215
5:26 112
6:17 92

Philippians

.... 35
1 35
1:1 115

282 Index of Ancient Sources

1:30 195
2 51
2:5 194
2:5-10 232
2:5-11 77
2:9-10 49
2:16 195
3:4-6 22
3:12-14 195

Colossians

.... 35
1:2 115
1:15 49
1:15-20 .... 45, 48
1:18 59
1:20 230
1:22 230
2:18 64
3:1 49
3:6-9 35
3:19 65
4:15 245
6:2 36
6:10 36

1 Thessalonians

4 43
4:9 214
5:4 174

2 Thessalonians

2:3 177

1 Timothy

.... 134
3:2 214
4:14 .... 112, 119
6:2 23
6:11 192

2 Timothy

1:6 113
3:1-5 177
3:5 177
4:7 195

Titus

1:8 214
2:14 231

Hebrews
(not indexed. *See* Contents)

James

.... 237
1:2-4 211
2:15 23
2:25 188
5:14 119
5:14-15 112

1 Peter

1:7 211
1:12-25 35
1:18-19 167
1:19 .... 34, 229
1:22 214
1:23-25 92
2:9 135
2:11 35
2:11-12 192
2:21 .... 35, 194–95
2:22 34
2:25 224
3:18 .... 34, 128
3:22 49
4:9 214
4:16 23
5:4 224

2 Peter

1:7 214
2:5 185

1 John

1:7 .... 167, 229
2:1-2 234
2:2 229–30
2:18 177
2:24 177
4:1 65
4:10 229–30

Jude

14-15 185

Revelation

.... 43, 237
1:5 59
1:8 190
1:16 92
2–3 65
2:12 92
3:21 49
5:6-10 167
6:9 95
6:11 95
6:12 209–10
6:16 209–10
7:1 65
7:9-12 95
7:11 65
8 65
10 65
12:5 58
13:8 167
14:3-4 231
17–18 65
19:11-16 92
19:15 58
20:14 211

Index of Ancient Sources

RABBINIC WORKS
Genesis Rabbah
1:1 45

Mishnah
.... 37, 247

Talmud
.... 247

Targum Pseudo-Jonathan
2.1 188

EARLY CHRISTIAN WRITINGS
Apocryphal acts (genre)
.... 196

Augustine of Hippo
.... 244

Bede
.... 150

1 Clement
.... 30, 32
40–41 134

Didache
.... 112

Eusebius
.... 244, 251
History of the Church
6.24.11–14 28

Ignatius
To the Philadelphians
9.1 234

Irenaeus
Against Heresies
.... 153

Jerome
.... 230, 237, 244

John Chrysostom
Discourses against Judaizing Christians
.... 242

Marcion
.... 152, 249

Origen
..........28, 244, 247, 258

Polycarp
To the Philippians
14.3 234

Tertullian
.... 244
Against Marcion
.... 153

GRECO-ROMAN LITERATURE
Aristotle
Metaphysics
4.16.1021b 242

Cicero
.... 215

Epictetus
.... 215

Plato
Laws
4.716e–717a 161

Pliny the Elder
.... 239

Porphyry
Abstinence from Killing Animals
2.34 161

The Authors

Debra J. Bucher is Head of Collections and Discovery at Vassar College Libraries. She has also taught first-year writing seminars on the history of the Bible as book, and most recently a course on race and racism in the historical collections at Vassar. She grew up in the Church of the Brethren and received a PhD from the University of Pennsylvania in 2009. She also enjoys gardening, baking, singing, and taking long walks in the Hudson Valley with her husband Mark Colvson.

Estella Boggs Horning is a retired professor of biblical studies at Bethany Theological Seminary and Northern Baptist Theological Seminary. She is also an ordained minister in the Church of the Brethren and served as a missionary in Ecuador for fifteen years and in Nigeria for four years. She received her PhD in religious and theological studies from Northwestern University and Garrett Evangelical Theological Seminary. She currently lives in Lombard, Illinois.